"With clear insights and e   )ook
teaches how to develop self-   med
into a more peaceful state of ...."

> —Kristin Neff, PhD, author of *Self-Compassion* and associate
> professor of human development and culture at the University of
> Texas at Austin

"In *The Compassionate-Mind Guide to Managing Your Anger*, Russell L. Kolts provides us with a novel approach to managing anger: compassionate mind training. Pointing out that we may not have a choice about how our brains react to provocation, Kolts skillfully shows that we do have a choice of how we respond. By calling upon our ability to experience compassion and empathy for others, he provides a number of helpful techniques that can turn anger around."

> —Robert L. Leahy, PhD, director of the American Institute for
> Cognitive Therapy and clinical professor of psychology at Weill-
> Cornell University Medical College

"This intriguing book will bring a sigh of relief to anyone struggling with anger. It's not your fault that you experience anger, yet there is a lot you can do about it. Why do we get angry? What happens within us when we're angry? Why is it so sticky? Russell L. Kolts gently escorts the reader to a deep, comprehensive understanding of anger and offers revolutionary new strategies for taming this common affliction. There is much here to inspire and illuminate both professional and non-professional audiences."

> —Christopher K. Germer, PhD, clinical instructor at Harvard
> Medical School and author of *The Mindful Path to Self-Compassion*

"Cultivating compassion for ourselves and others can bring balance and harmony to our lives in a way we never dreamed of. Russell L. Kolts tells us how to do this with the gentleness, humor, and patience of someone who practices his own advice and, from first-hand experience, knows it works."

> —Thubten Chodron, Buddhist teacher and author of *Working with
> Anger*

THE COMPASSIONATE-MIND GUIDE TO

MANAGING YOUR ANGER

using compassion-focused therapy to calm
your rage and heal your relationships

RUSSELL L. KOLTS, PhD

New Harbinger Publications, Inc.

Publisher's Note

Distributed in Canada by Raincoast Books

Copyright © 2012 by Russell L. Kolts
New Harbinger Publications, Inc.
5674 Shattuck Avenue
Oakland, CA 94609
www.newharbinger.com

FSC
www.fsc.org
MIX
Paper from
responsible sources
FSC® C011935

Acquired by Tesilya Hanauer; Cover design by Amy Shoup;
Edited by Carole Honeychurch; Text design by Tracy Carlson;
Cover photo by Ron Watts / GettyImages

Library of Congress Cataloging-in-Publication Data

Kolts, Russell L.
  The compassionate-mind guide to managing your anger : using compassion-focused therapy to calm your rage and heal your relationships / Russell L. Kolts ; foreword by Paul Gilbert.
      p. cm.
  Includes bibliographical references.
  ISBN 978-1-60882-037-5 (pbk. : alk. paper)
  1. Anger. 2. Compassion. 3. Mindfulness-based cognitive therapy. I. Title.
  BF575.A5K66 2012
  152.4'7--dc23
                                        2012008369

Printed in the United States of America

14 13 12   10 9 8 7 6 5 4 3 2 1   First printing

This book is dedicated to the men of Airway Heights Corrections Center, who dare to cultivate compassion behind bars.

And to Lisa Koch and Dylan Kolts. My heart lives with you.

Contents

7

8

9

10

Foreword

We have always understood that compassion is very important for our well-being. If you are stressed or upset, it's always better to have kind, helpful, and supportive people around you rather than critical, rejecting, or disinterested folk. However, it's not only this common sense that tells us about the value of kindness and compassion. Recent advances in scientific study of compassion and kindness have greatly advanced our understanding of how compassionate qualities of the mind really do influence our brains, bodies, and social relationships, as well as affect our health and well-being. Yet, despite this common sense, ancient wisdom, and modern knowledge, we live in an age that can make compassion for ourselves and for others difficult. Ours is the world of seeking the competitive edge, of achievement and desire, of comparison to others who may be doing better, of dissatisfaction, of self-disappointment, and of self-criticism. Research has now revealed that such environments actually make us unhappy and that mental ill-health is on the increase, especially in younger people. As Dr. Russell Kolts helps us to understand, frustration, irritability, and anger are very common symptoms of the environments we're living in today. Be it irritation with long lines, overly complex gadgets we can't work out how to use, traffic jams, whining children, or what we see as incompetent politicians—the list of things that wind us up seems endless.

If feeling angry or irritable and stressed is not enough, we can act on these emotions and then justify our actions: "They had it coming to them; they shouldn't have done X or Y." And, of course, we label the people we're angry with as "dumb," "stupid," "a pain," or "thoughtless and unfeeling." There can also be subtle messages in society that anger is about being macho—a "no-nonsense" person. In fact, that kind of attitude can lie behind serious violence, in which people feel they have a need to save face, get their own back, and not be humiliated or disrespected. In some sectors of society, the fear of humiliation is so profound that explosive anger and violence are part of everyday life.

In fact, it can be easy to confuse aggressiveness with assertiveness, and when we do so, we can cause much hurt and upset to others. As Dr. Kolts points out, anger is a volatile, impulsive, and not very clever emotion. If we just go with its flow, we can regret acting on it in the days, weeks, or years to come. Anger also has a habit of being quite "sticky," in the sense that we tend to ruminate about the things that made us angry—we go over and over them in our minds. We don't stop to think what that process might be doing to our heads and bodies. For some people, feelings of anger can be quite frightening, so they seek to suppress these emotions in order to avoid conflict. Others can become self-critical and judge themselves for becoming angry or irritable and for not being nice or lovable people. So, we're critical of ourselves and think that by being angry with ourselves, we will stop being angry! Indeed, our society has a habit of blaming and shaming if we seem to be struggling with our emotions.

So why are we so susceptible to frustration and anger, and why are they seemingly on the increase in modern-day society? Dr. Kolts uses his wealth of knowledge and experience to guide our understanding and to help us recognize that, actually, many of our emotions are the result of a very long evolutionary history. The emotions we experience today were really designed to deal with immediate threats in the jungles and savannas of our ancestors' environment and aren't so well-adapted for the modern world. Nor do our emotions do so well when our angry minds use our new brains' capacity for thinking and rumination, locking us into anger. Humans are the only animals that have the capacity to sit under a tree ruminating about how angry they are because of some event or other, planning vengeance or just keeping themselves in an angry state. We can even be angry about what we feel—angry about feeling anxious, angry because we feel depressed, angry because we feel tired all the time, angry because we're just exhausted. So the way we think about and ruminate about the stresses in our lives can really do a number on us. Understanding this and being able to stand back from our emotions allow us to see that our vulnerability to anger is not our fault at all. After all, we didn't design our brains with their capacity for emotions like anxiety and anger. Nor did we design our capacity for complex thinking, which can actually make our experience of anger and frustration all the more intense. And we didn't choose our backgrounds or our genes, both of which can make us more susceptible to anger. This is a very important message in compassionate-mind training and compassion-focused therapy, because compassion begins with developing a deep understanding of just how tricky our brains are and a recognition that their functions may be stuck in past ways of operating. These two realizations may seem strange at first. But once we recognize how difficult our emotions can be, we can stand back from them and feel compassion for the difficulties we experience.

So, given that our brains have been designed by evolution and shaped by the environments we grew up and live in (none of which we choose), what can we do to help ourselves when we become angry? First, we can learn to pay attention to how our minds work, and become mindful and observant of the feelings associated with anger. In this helpful book, Dr. Kolts shows how people have learned to be very sensitive to the situations that can trigger our anger, such as frustrations and minor criticisms.

If we are to face anger and to really work with it, then the relationship we have with ourselves is very important. If we are critical and harsh with ourselves, then our inner worlds are not comfortable places to inhabit. Feeling ashamed and being self-critical, self-condemning, or self-loathing can undermine our confidence, making us feel worse. People who generally feel confident and like themselves are much less prone to anger than those who feel unsure about themselves, are easily victimized by others, and are vulnerable to rejection.

In addition, of course, anger isn't just directed outward; it can be directed inward, toward ourselves, and this really does cause difficulties. Sadly, many people today are self-critical, and when things go wrong or they make mistakes, rather than try to be helpful and supportive of themselves, they react by becoming frustrated and angry with themselves. This is not a good way to deal with anger because, as Dr. Kolts outlines, we are actually adding more fuel to the fire of our threat system. In contrast, self-compassion is a way of being with ourselves and all of our emotions (uncomfortable as they may be) without self-condemnation. Instead, we learn to experience them with support and encouragement. Research shows that the more compassionate we are toward ourselves, the happier we are and the more resilient we become when faced with difficult events in our lives. In addition, we are better able to reach out to others for help and feel more compassionate toward other people as well.

Compassion can sometimes be viewed as being a bit "soft" or "weak"; as if it means letting your guard down or not trying hard enough. These notions are a major mistake because, on the contrary, compassion requires the strength to be open to and tolerate our painful feelings, to face up to our own problematic emotions and difficulties. Sometimes it's anger that hides us from more painful things and it is compassion that gives us the courage to face them. Compassion does not mean turning away from emotional difficulties or discomfort, or trying to get rid of them. It is not a soft option. Rather, compassion provides us with the courage, honesty, and commitment to learn to cope with the difficulties we face, and alleviates our anger and other difficulties. It enables us to do things for ourselves that help us to flourish (however, not as a demand or requirement). Compassion enables us to live our lives more fully and contentedly.

In this book, Dr. Kolts brings to bear his many years of experience as a clinical psychologist, long-time meditator, and psychotherapist working in Washington state with people experiencing a variety of different emotional difficulties. He has a special interest in working with people in prison for anger-related behaviors. He also brings his experience of using compassion-focused therapy in the treatment of anger. In this book he outlines a model of compassion that seeks to stimulate and build your confidence so that you can engage with your anger. You will learn how to develop a supportive friendship with yourself that helps you when times are difficult. Dr. Kolts guides you to develop compassionate motivations, compassionate attention, compassionate feelings, compassionate thinking, and compassionate behavior. You will learn about the potential power of developing compassionate imagery, focusing on creating a compassionate sense of yourself, and drawing on your own inner wisdom and benevolent qualities. These are the qualities you are most likely to feel when you're feeling calm or are showing concern for others. Learning breathing techniques that help you slow down and engage with these qualities can be very helpful when frustration, anger, and rage wash through you like a storm. Using different compassionate images, you will discover that your compassion focus can be visual or aural (for example, imagining a compassionate voice speaking to you when you need it), and it can be especially useful in enabling you to get in touch with your internal compassionate feelings and desires at times of distress.

The approach that Dr. Kolts takes is called a compassionate-mind approach because, when we engage compassion, it can influence our attention, thoughts, feelings, and behavior—all the functions of the mind. The compassionate-mind approach outlined by Dr. Kolts draws on many other well-developed approaches, including those of Eastern traditions such as Buddhism. In addition, compassionate-mind approaches—especially those that form part of compassion-focused therapy—are rooted in a scientific understanding of how our minds work. Undoubtedly, over the years our understanding of the science will change and improve. One thing that doesn't change, however, is the fact that kindness, warmth, and understanding go a long way toward helping us. In these pages you will find these qualities in abundance, so you, too, can learn to be understanding, supportive, and kind, but also engaging and courageous when working with your anger.

Many suffer silently and secretly with a whole range of anger and frustration problems. Some people are ashamed of these emotions or angry about feeling them; others can be fearful that anger and frustration will get the upper hand. Sadly, shame stops many of us from reaching out for help. But by opening our hearts to compassion, we can take the first steps toward dealing with our difficulties in new ways. My compassionate wishes go with you on your journey.

—Paul Gilbert, PhD, FBPsS, OBE
August 2011

Acknowledgments

I feel grateful to many people who contributed to my development as a person and psychologist, and who, in this way, contributed to the book you now hold. Among the most important teachers and mentors in my life have been Debra Keil (Riddle), Tom Lombardo, Sandy Brown, David Thomas, John McQuaid, and Gail Hicks. These mentors, through direction and example, gave me exactly what I needed, exactly when I needed it. Special thanks also go to the many colleagues I've had the pleasure of collaborating with in the past, including Phil Watkins and Arif Khan. I'd also like to thank my wonderful colleagues at Eastern Washington University, who have created the perfect environment for me to grow personally and professionally, and the numerous students who have worked so hard as members of my research team over the years, with particular thanks to Aryn Ziehnert.

My journey in working to apply compassion in my clinical work is a direct result of the instruction and inspiration of several Buddhist teachers, most notably Lama Inge Sandvoss of Padma Ling in Spokane and His Holiness the Dalai Lama. I have also benefited greatly from the work of Thubten Chodron, Pema Chodron, and Jack Kornfield.

It's also important to acknowledge the many people involved in compassion movements around the world. Specifically in the inland northwestern United States, I want to acknowledge the inspiring work of all at Sravasti Abbey, the Spokane Friends of Compassion group, and the Eastern

Washington University Compassionate Interfaith Society. Thanks also to Crystal Contreras, my cotherapist in our prison anger-management groups; Lou Sowers; and all in the Washington State Department of Corrections who have helped to make this work possible.

I have tremendous gratitude for Professor Paul Gilbert, who developed compassion-focused therapy and taught me to use it. Paul is a great scientist and teacher, a masterful clinician, and an inspirational friend. His work is cited frequently in this book, and his influence and ideas are present throughout. It would make for an impossibly cumbersome text to credit him as he deserves, because he would be cited multiple times on nearly every page. My colleague and dear friend Dennis Tirch has provided invaluable feedback and inspiration as I've written, and I've also been shaped by my interactions with the CFT community, in particular Michelle Cree, Chris Irons, Deborah Lee, and Ian Lowens. In crafting this work, I have stood on the shoulders of giants. If you derive any benefit from reading this book, please direct your gratitude to them. All errors are my own.

Great thanks are also due to Fritha Saunders, my editor at Constable and Robinson. I can't imagine having a better guide as I write my first book. I am also very grateful to Kelly Falconer, my copyeditor, whose edits greatly improved the quality of the text. Thanks also to all at New Harbinger who helped make the U.S. version of the book a reality, including Tesilya Hanauer, Lo Merino, Julie Bennett, Tracy Carlson, Jesse Burson, Michele Waters, Carole Honeychurch, and Amy Shoup.

This book would not be possible if not for the many clients I have had the honor of working with over the years. The strength and courage you have shown in our work together has been an inspiration. Special thanks go to the men participating in the Compassion-Focused Therapy for Anger groups at Airway Heights Correctional Center outside Spokane, Washington. Your successful efforts to cultivate compassion in the hardest of circumstances inspired this book.

My never-ending gratitude goes out to my wife, Lisa Koch; my son, Dylan Kolts; my grandmother, Shirley Kolts; my parents, John and Mary Kolts; my siblings, Jason and Michelle Kolts; my extended family; and my second family: Don, Sandy, Robert, and Emily Koch, and Karen and Robert Winchell. All of you helped teach me how to work hard, love harder, and understand the things in life that are truly most important.

Finally, I want to thank you, the reader, for making the choice to work compassionately with your anger. I hope this book serves you well.

Introduction

This book presents a new model for thinking about and working with anger. It is based upon an approach developed by Professor Paul Gilbert, a noted British psychologist. Dr Gilbert's compassionate-mind approach is based upon several important ideas, one of which is that in order to work effectively with these minds of ours, we need to understand something about how they work. Compassion-focused therapy (CFT), the therapy model that flows from this approach, provides us with powerful strategies for working with difficult emotions like anger and for developing ourselves in ways that can help us have happier, healthier lives.

We'll discuss compassion a great deal in this book, but at its core is the recognition that we all want to be happy and to avoid suffering. This recognition, combined with sensitivity to the occurrence of suffering and a motivation to help alleviate it in ourselves and in others, provides the basis of a compassionate way of being in the world. Compassion has long been at the heart of various spiritual traditions, most notably Buddhism. However, it has historically held a much less formal position in the world of psychology than we might expect, given that mental health professionals spend most of their time helping patients work with suffering.

Many people involved in the mental health professions are beginning to understand that compassion can play a role in helping us to work with difficult emotions. Furthermore, research emerging from collaborative efforts between Western psychologists and Buddhist monastics reveals that compassion can also potentially help to strengthen parts of the brain that are important for emotion regulation. Specific therapies are emerging that apply the cultivation of compassion for ourselves and others in helping people to cope with life's difficulties.[1]

This book uses CFT to help you cope with anger, which is based in our brains' response to real or imagined threats and to our early learning experiences. My aim is to help you learn how to stop feeling ashamed of your difficult emotional experiences and to instead take responsibility for them. Together, we'll help you find ways to work with these emotions and learn strategies to help you cope with your anger. We'll look at many practices that can help you transform your relationship to your emotions, to your life experiences, and to other people. You will learn to be kinder to yourself and to others and to work with your anger to prevent it from getting in the way of how you would like your life to be.

Compassion-focused therapy draws upon compassion-focused practices that have been used for thousands of years, but it also benefits from a scientific understanding of the way the mind works. It draws upon evolutionary psychology, which considers the way our brains function given our evolutionary history (how we are in relation to how we got this way) and helps us make sense of some of the more frustrating aspects of our emotions and behavior. CFT also benefits from what is called *affective neuroscience*, which helps us understand our emotional experiences in relation to what is happening in our brains. In combining these understandings, the Compassionate-Mind model (upon which CFT is based) makes a case for compassion that is both unique and powerful: not only is the cultivation of compassion good for us, as the Dalai Lama suggests; it is also the only response that makes sense when we observe the difficult fit between the way our brains have evolved to deal with certain threats and the way we live now, in a world that presents us with very different sorts of threats.

In the first three chapters of this book, we'll take a close look at anger through the lens of compassion focused therapy. We will begin to understand it as the product of emotion-regulation systems that have evolved over millions of years, and we'll explore how these ancient systems can interact with our abilities to think and fantasize to trap us in cycles of anger and hostility. We will also explore other emotion-regulation systems that can help us to balance our anger with other emotions and gain control over the way we think and feel. Later, I'll introduce the concepts of compassion and the compassionate self, and a variety of exercises for working with your anger to cultivate a calm, confident, wise, and compassionate mind.

Some of the practices and approaches used in this book are unique to CFT, and some of them may be recognizable to you already. For example, assertiveness training and techniques for changing how we think are drawn from cognitive behavioral therapy (CBT). The idea behind CFT is not to reinvent the wheel. Rather, it seeks to provide us with a way of transforming ourselves that is compatible with powerful and established methods of change, while also adding something new—a compassionate understanding of how our minds work. My goal in this book is to help you develop your compassionate self so that you can cope with life's challenges in a way that allows you to manage your anger instead of being controlled by it.

My introduction to this subject came about through my efforts to work with my own anger. Over the years, I've had the opportunity to teach a variety of university courses in psychology, and there are a few points that I try to sneak into any class that I teach. Many of my students have told me they intend to be parents one day, and I frequently reply, "If you want to be a good parent, become the person you want your child to be. Cultivate in yourself the characteristics you want them to end up having." If you want your child to be kind, learn to treat others with kindness. If you want your child to cope well with difficult circumstances, learn to be able to face them yourself. The idea is that children learn how to cope with life by interacting with and observing those who are close to them. How we behave toward and around our children has much more influence on their character than if we only tell them about how they should or should not behave. When my own son was born, I began to notice that I behaved in ways that I wouldn't want to pass on to him, and most of the time this behavior involved being irritable and angry. In learning to work with my own anger, I encountered Buddhism and its practices of compassion, many of them thousands of years old. I began to practice them myself, and when I experienced their power to transform my own life for the better, I knew I had to find a way to integrate them into my work as a psychologist. This led me to Professor Paul Gilbert's compassion-focused therapy. As I've said, my approach to this work is influenced greatly both by traditional Western psychology and by my personal experience with Buddhist mind-training techniques. But don't worry—my goal in writing this book is not to convert anyone to Buddhism. I don't even call myself a Buddhist, and as you read, you'll find that this book is definitely not religious in tone. However, I think it's important to acknowledge the influence of Buddhism. It has shown me the power of cultivating compassion in our lives and has given us many powerful ways to change the ways we think, work with difficult emotions, and respond to challenging situations—strategies that have greatly impacted this book.

With this in mind, I'd like to conclude by referring once more to my Buddhist teachers. One of the things I noticed when I first started attending Buddhist teachings was the emphasis on motivation, which helps us reflect on why we are engaging in this activity at this time. What is our purpose for doing this, whatever "this" is? My teachers suggested that the outcome of an activity is very much related to the motivation we have while doing the activity, and that motivation is something that we can choose and develop.

I'd like to borrow from these teachers, then, and ask you to do your first exercise of the book: take a moment to reflect on your current experience of life in this present moment. Notice the environment you find yourself in. What do you see? Hear? Feel? What's the temperature like? Is it warm or cool?

Now be aware of your body. What does it feel like? Is it relaxed or tense? Are you sitting or lying down? How does it feel to be doing that? Comfortable? Uncomfortable?

Now extend your awareness to your emotions. How are you feeling right now? Interested? Excited? Irritated? Bored? What thoughts are you having?

Finally, consider your motivation for reading this book. Why did you pick it up, open it, and start reading? Was it curiosity? Have you struggled with anger and are perhaps looking for something that could help? Maybe someone gave this book to you and asked you to read it. Maybe you're reading it because you know someone else who struggles with anger—a friend, family member, or, if you are a mental health professional, a client or patient—and you're hoping to learn how to help them.

Consider your motivation and see if you can work with it. See if you can approach this activity—reading this book and doing the exercises it contains—with the motivation to be better able to understand yourself and others, and to be able to help yourself. Imagine doing this so that you can learn to cope more effectively with the difficult emotions that you will experience during your life, so that you can exist in the world in a way that is kind and helpful both to yourself and to everyone you encounter.

This is a perfect way to start.

1

Anger: Introduction and Overview

As I prepared to begin writing, I sat down and switched on the television, aiming to find an interesting story about anger. I was looking for an example that would grab your attention and hold it fast—giving you the feeling that you really want to read this book. I didn't think it would be difficult to find an example of anger on television (or on the Internet) that most readers could relate to, and sure enough, finding an example of anger wasn't a problem at all.

The problem was choosing which example to use. I wondered: should I write about the previously beloved celebrity caught on tape screaming racist abuse at someone who isn't even a member of that race? The star athlete placed on suspension for hitting a player on another team? The talk-show guests who colorfully insult one another's equally colorful outfits or lifestyles? I mean, I thought those boots were a bit gaudy myself, but *really*... Ultimately, feeling a bit overwhelmed by all these examples of mismanaged anger, I decided to try to use them *all*.

Sometimes it seems as if anger is all around us. We flip on the nightly news to hear stories of domestic violence, violent crime, feuding celebrities and politicians, road rage, and countless groups angrily protesting nearly everything imaginable. The "letters to the editor" section of the newspaper reveals more anger, with diatribes and hostile written attacks on politicians, public figures, and other letter writers. My local weekly entertainment paper even features a "Jeers" section, designed to give us a chance to publicly stick it to people who've ticked us off—in fifty words or less! Our political parties have noted the power of anger and fear, and sometimes it seems as if they purposefully stir these emotions in us as they angrily attack one another in an endless election and debate cycle, perhaps hoping to channel our outrage into votes for their causes and candidates. Examples of anger were amazingly easy to find.

TYPES OF ANGER

Anger takes many forms as it plays out in our lives. There is the frustration we feel when we're thwarted and our goals are blocked—when we work hard and yet things just don't turn out the way we want them to. Anger can hide just under the surface when we are feeling irritable, ready to respond to the smallest frustration. There is the impulsive anger we feel when we lash out. It can be so quick and powerful that it almost leaps from us with a life of its own. There's self-righteous anger, which emerges when we're faced with injustice or feel that we have been wronged or unfairly criticized. Anger can also come from a sense of powerlessness, from feeling unheard, when all we want is for someone to notice and listen to us. There are different names for the various types of anger, terms like "frustration," "irritation," and "outrage," but these experiences are all reflections of the same systems in our brain—systems aimed at helping us respond to threats—and they're all part of the same family of emotions.

Those of us who are easily frustrated may be having a wonderful day until we don't get what we want or something gets in our way, and then we have a burst of discontent. These various outbursts and feelings relate to something called "frustration tolerance." This tolerance can be pretty low for some people and, as a result, can cause problems. Our ability to tolerate frustration can be especially low when we are under time pressure or have too many things to do, a significant feature of many modern workplaces. It's interesting that, even though we know how frustrated it can make us feel, we often put such time pressures on ourselves and take on too many things.

If our anger takes the form of irritability, it can function more as a mood or an ongoing state of mind, particularly when we're stressed or depressed. We can find ourselves going through the day with our anger primed and ready to go, simmering just beneath the surface. These are the days when we find ourselves snapping at our family and friends or responding sharply rather than with kindness when our children ask us to play.

When it becomes even more entrenched, anger can seem to become a part of our personality itself, taking the form of hostility. Those of us who have deeply entrenched hostility can go through life as if it were a fight. We judge situations and other people in negative and overly critical ways, and have difficulty trusting and considering the feelings of others as they pursue their goals.

Anger can have different levels (with irritation and frustration at one end of the spectrum and rage at the other), can come on slowly or rapidly (building and bubbling versus lashing out), and can last for different lengths of time (chronic irritability and hostility versus short bursts of frustration or rage). We also differ from one another in how we express our anger and whether or not we express it at all. We may think of anger in terms of embarrassing examples of "under-controlled" behavior—the inappropriate e-mail, the snappish comment, the object thrown across the room. However, many of us also experience anger that is "over-controlled." This style manifests when we don't express our anger but spend hours seething about "how horrible she was to me," rehearsing arguments and fantasizing about that knockout statement that would "really put him in his place," or saying nasty things about others behind their backs. On the other hand, some people may believe that even feeling anger is unacceptable, and they can be very frightened by their angry thoughts, desires, and fantasies. People like this may approach life very passively, avoiding any disagreement or conflict even when it creates problems in their own lives.[1]

Like it or not, anger is a part of life, and entire systems in our brains are devoted to it. It's helpful to learn how to work with anger because, unmanaged, it can have negative impacts on both our mental and physical health. Poorly managed anger can damage relationships with our partners, children, friends, and colleagues. It can wear us down over time and has been linked to reduced immune-system functioning, hypertension, risk of stroke, and even coronary heart disease.[2] Over-controlled anger has been associated with depression and anxiety. In my acknowledgments, I mentioned the CFT groups I work with at a local prison. Members of these groups begin their therapy by briefly introducing themselves and sharing their motivation for learning how to deal with their anger. At least half the members of one of my recent groups indicated that the crimes they had committed were related to anger and the ways they had acted as a result of it.

Thankfully, our anger doesn't usually lead to such dramatic consequences as being sent to prison, but it can still have a huge impact upon our ability to have happy lives. For example, think about the problems you've had in your relationships with others. How many of these difficulties involved anger? Often, these conflicts or problems may be rooted in how we experience anger and our ability to express it (or lack thereof). The truth is that we all experience anger in our lives, and we all live in a world that is affected by it. In this book, we'll explore ways of understanding and working with anger to help us have better relationships, build happier lives, and contribute to a more peaceful world.

A CLOSER LOOK: STEVE'S STORY

Let's take a look at Steve, one of my patients who found himself struggling with the consequences of his anger. As he spoke, Steve's face reddened, and his words took on a harsh, forced quality as he described the encounter that might have cost him his job. He couldn't recall exactly what his colleague had said to him, but he knew that he'd been treated disrespectfully, and he wasn't going to put up with it. His anger had emerged automatically, so quickly that it might have frightened him if he hadn't been so caught up in it. Like so many times before, he began to yell, and threats were flying from his lips. Fists clenched, Steve didn't attack the man, but he'd wanted to; only the fear of jail kept him from doing so.

His colleague left, seeming both cowed and shocked at Steve's reaction, and Steve continued to seethe. His hands shook as he spoke: "No one treats me with respect. Not the people I work with, not my boss, nobody. To hell with them! I should have taught that jerk a lesson."

Steve had lost a number of jobs due to encounters just like this. His relationship with his wife and children was strained, and he could tell that they avoided him and walked on eggshells so that they wouldn't set him off. He had never struck his wife, but he experienced a range of emotions as he recalled the fear that sometimes filled her eyes as he was overwhelmed by anger. During these interactions, he sometimes felt strong and powerful;

but in his recollections, this quickly gave way to feelings of shame, sadness, and a sense of hopelessness. In truth, Steve rarely thought about his angry explosions at all. He tended to push them out of his mind as soon as they were over, much as he had learned to push out the memories of his time in Iraq and the beatings his father had given him and his mother when Steve was a child.

Although he avoided thinking about his angry explosions after they were over, he felt almost constantly agitated. He thought other people were "irritating, rude, lazy, and irresponsible," that other drivers were "idiots who shouldn't be allowed on the road." Steve felt that his wife and children took him for granted, failing to appreciate the life he'd given them with years of hard work at jobs he hated. When angry, Steve often thought about people who had harmed him or treated him disrespectfully, and about the parts of his life that hadn't worked out the way he'd wanted them to.

Steve felt betrayed and frustrated by his reactions. He struggled to get to sleep at night, and when he did sleep, he gnashed his teeth so forcefully that his jaw ached when he woke. His stomach was constantly upset and he'd been diagnosed with ulcers, which he tried to treat with the pocketful of antacids he carried with him wherever he went. His body hurt all of the time—his head, his back, his jaw. And he'd also recently had a heart attack, which had led a physician to recommend therapy so that he could work on his "stress." This is how he found his way to me.

As much anger as he directed toward others, Steve judged no one more harshly than he judged himself. In his more thoughtful moments, he admitted to the overwhelming feeling that he was a failed husband, father, worker, and man. Many of his fights with his wife happened after she criticized his parenting—not that he was too harsh with the children, but that he often didn't discipline them at all—criticism that he knew was at least somewhat true. Steve felt helpless. Didn't she see that he stood back from parenting because he was terrified to treat his children the way his father had treated him? Couldn't she see that he loved them, and that he wanted to spare them the lessons he regretted learning from his own father? Steve was terrified of his own anger and the loss of control that came with it. He felt he was losing his family and didn't know how to stop it. He hated himself for it.

Steve's story is similar to that of many of us who struggle with anger. To some of us, his life may seem extreme. On the other hand, those who have lost marriages, families, or even their freedom due to under-controlled anger may note his level of restraint. Like Steve, many of us may feel trapped by our anger and want to do something about it, but also feel disheartened because our best efforts haven't been successful.

WHAT DO WE MEAN BY "ANGER"?

One of the challenges of psychology is that even though many of the things we study may seem very familiar to us (such as love, self-esteem, and yes, anger), they can be somewhat slippery to define. Let's spend some time making clear exactly what we mean by "anger."

Anger is thought to be one of a few basic emotions,[3] along with other emotions like fear, disgust, happiness, and sadness. This means that it has been observed in people across time and various cultures. Angry facial expressions are understood everywhere, even in the animal world. The experience of anger can also be related to what we call *secondary emotions*, which reflect self-consciousness and include emotions such as shame,[4] pride, and embarrassment.

When we think of an emotion, we may quickly think of how we feel when we experience that emotion. The feeling of anger includes lots of experiences, including physical sensations, motivations, and ways of thinking. Anger and other emotions *organize the mind* in specific ways and affect our experience of life. This is consistent with how anger and other emotions play out in our brains—there isn't a specific place in the brain where anger is found. Rather, the parts of the brain that influence when we will become angry interact with many other areas of the brain and body,[5] which, together, produce an angry state of mind or brain pattern. In the Compassionate-Mind model, we often use the "spider diagram" (figure 1.1) to help explain how states of mind like anger can affect us.[6] This diagram shows how anger can change how we relate to ourselves, to other people, and to the world around us.

When we look at how anger organizes our minds, we can begin to understand that what we call "anger" is actually a progression that takes place in our brains, kind of like a line of dominoes falling across the table on their own once the first has been pushed over. By the time we even know that we're angry, our brains have already toppled that first domino, recognizing the situation as something worth paying attention to and labeling it as undesirable or threatening. The toppling of that first domino reflects the brain's activation of our threat-response system.

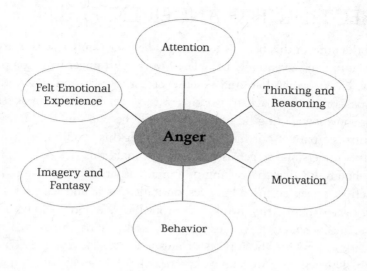

Figure 1.1: How Anger Organizes the Mind

Specific parts of the brain, like the *amygdala* (pronounced "ah-MIG-duh-lah"), determine when we will become angry. These parts are the primary players in what is known as the *threat system*, which I mentioned earlier and will discuss further in chapter 2. For now, it's enough to know that the job of the threat system is to detect threats and to quickly select responses to them. As we will see, this system has evolved so that it is activated *rapidly*, because defenses that come on too slowly may be too late. These parts of our brains are efficient, and often we're not even aware of what's happening as they activate us to respond to a real or perceived threat. The dominoes have begun to fall before we are aware that anything is happening. So, by the time we wake up to our experience, we've landed right in the middle of a very angry spot—and we've missed much of the build up. This is why it can feel as if anger emerges almost automatically.

It's important for us to understand that the way this happens is *not our fault*; it is simply the way our brains work. This brings up a key message that we will return to many times: handling anger is not just a matter of will-power or personal discipline. If you have difficulty controlling your anger, it does *not* mean that you don't want to change badly enough or that there's something wrong with you. Let's look a bit more closely now at the experience of anger.

DISSECTING THE ANGER EXPERIENCE

One of the aims of this book is to help you become familiar with the nature of your anger and eventually be able to work with anger in a compassionate way, based on wisdom and a sense of confidence and inner strength. A compassionate approach to working with anger is not about soothing it away or somehow getting rid of it. That would be impossible, because anger is an intrinsic part of our human design. With this in mind, we will learn instead to understand anger as part of what makes us tick—but not like a ticking bomb. It's like the ticking of a grandfather clock. A compassionate approach to anger means taking responsibility for it and learning to work with it, rather than letting it take over your life. We don't help ourselves by ignoring anger, hoping it will just go away, or by doing things that make it worse. So, let's revisit the aspects of anger depicted in the previous spider diagram. This will help us get a good sense of the different factors that make up anger, factors that can interact to organize our minds in ways that can trap us in a cycle of angry feelings, thoughts, and behaviors that are neither productive nor compassionate.

HOW WE FEEL IT: ANGER IN THE BODY

First, anger is something that we *feel*. Our bodies are sensitive to potential threats, and as I mentioned previously, there are parts of the brain (such as the amygdala) that work to quickly recognize these threats and activate our response to them. These parts exchange messages with many other areas of our brains and bodies.

You are probably somewhat familiar with this process—just think about how your body feels when you get really angry. This is the feeling of your body preparing you to fight—your nervous system is activated and chemicals such as noradrenaline are released into your bloodstream. Your heart starts racing, your breathing rate increases, and your blood pressure goes up as you become physically aroused. There are other bodily changes observable from the outside as well, as your muscles tense up, your jaws tighten, and your eyes open to a stare.

Now try an exercise to help you connect with how anger plays out in your body.

Exercise 1.1: Anger in the Body

Try to remember a time when you were angry, then focus on it. Consider the way you experience it in your body. What does your anger feel like?

- What physical sensations were present when you were angry?

- How do you know that you were angry? What sensations let you know that anger was what you were feeling?

When angry, some people experience a feeling of tightness in their stomachs or chests, or find it more difficult to breathe. Others report feeling pain at the back of the neck or of anger bringing on a headache. There is commonly a feeling of things "speeding up" and of wanting to move in a more animated way.

In my own life and in my work with clients, I've observed that many of us tend to ignore the ways that emotions play out in our bodies unless they are actually painful. It's important to understand that the arousal that builds in our bodies provides fuel that can drive our anger. As we learn to recognize and work with angry arousal in our bodies, we can begin to stop being caught up by it and can work to take control of it.

All this arousal isn't an accident, by the way. As we will explore in more detail in chapter 2, anger is an emotion that evolved to help us deal with setbacks, with things that thwart us from pursuing what we want, and with a range of threats to our survival. Anger prepares us to engage—to force a change—and it does this by getting our bodies ready for *action*. This process can bring on an emotional experience that feels powerful, strong, and energized. This, in turn, can make it hard for us to commit to reducing our anger, because we may often enjoy feeling like that. Later in the book, we'll talk about how to understand and work with these feelings so that you can stay motivated to work more effectively with your anger.

ATTENTION: THE SPOTLIGHT OF THE MIND

One of the brain's primary jobs is to filter through the amazing amount of sensory information we receive throughout every day, and then to alert and focus our attention on the information that is important for our survival. To an extent, we have control over what we pay attention to, but our brains are wired to focus very efficiently and powerfully when they perceive a real or imagined threat. When this happens, our brains narrow our attention, bringing our focus to threat-related information coming in from our senses as well as thoughts and memories of other, possibly similar, experiences. In these times, it can be difficult to refocus our attention away from the perceived threat. Think of a time you were embarrassed, for example, and how easy it was to become completely trapped in that experience. Experiences of threatening situations have the power to overshadow our other experiences—our brains prioritize them over other things that are going on.

This involuntary narrowing of our attention can be a powerful experience—I know this firsthand. When I was doing my internship at the University of California, San Diego, in the late 1990s, a few other interns and I would take advantage of how close we were to the ocean, heading straight to the beach to go bodyboarding as soon as the workday was done. These afternoons are some of my most pleasant memories of that time: the warm water of the Pacific, the smell of the ocean, the joyous rush of riding a wave in to the shore, and the beauty of watching the sun set over the water.

However, one day we were paddling our way back out as the sun was just beginning to set and was shining directly into our eyes. We couldn't see very well, but we were able to make out the shape of a fin coming out of the water about fifteen feet away from our small group. Instantly, everything else faded from our awareness—the beautiful sunset, the warm water, the fun of the day—it all disappeared, like a wisp of smoke, with a single, panic-inducing thought: *Shark!* My narrowed focus of attention and my body's almost instantaneous readiness to flee reflected the rapid activation of my threat system.

Now, even after years of meditation designed to help me direct my attention, I have rarely been able to experience such single-minded focus as when I looked out at that shadowy fin. Luckily, that day the experience only lasted a moment. As the fin moved out of the direct sunlight, we could see that it was curved and that there were four others with it. Terror was replaced with joy as we realized that this was no shark but rather a small pod of dolphins. With the threat gone, my focus relaxed as well, and after a few minutes I was again able to enjoy my surroundings and to consider the carne asada burrito I planned to have for dinner at the taco shop just down the road.

When our threat system quickly narrows our attention, our thoughts follow. This is one of the reasons we can feel trapped by our anger, why we may make decisions that don't seem to make sense when we examine them later. We tend to lose perspective when our threat system takes over. It becomes difficult to think flexibly and to gather information that isn't directly related to the perceived threat.

Sometimes anger also biases our attention. Most threats we perceive aren't as potentially life-threatening as a massive great white shark (okay, so it was a few playful dolphins—but in my mind, that was one huge shark!). We're more often faced with not getting what we want, or with fears of being embarrassed or of being seen negatively by others. In these cases, the overall focus of our attention can still be fairly broad, but we only tend to notice certain *parts* of what's going on—the parts that fit with and fuel our angry mood.

My own examples of this are easy to come by. For instance, I can recall leaving my laptop at home one morning and having to turn around, drive back to get it, and then rush back again to my university. I was concerned that I'd be late to my Statistics class, and that my eager but caffeine-addicted students wouldn't hang around long before they filed out of the classroom and headed to one of the many coffee shops nearby. As I rushed to campus, my mind began to fill with thoughts of all the material I needed to cover before the next exam, and I then began to worry that I wouldn't be able to get through it all.

As you might imagine, this left me feeling frustrated and angry. When I had to stop at a long red light, what was my attention drawn to? The song on the radio (that I really liked), or the person in front of me taking her own sweet time getting moving once the light turned green? And as I pulled in to the university grounds looking for a place to park, what did I notice—the many cars that were parked considerately, or the one car that was parked so that it took up two spaces instead of one? As I hurriedly walked to the classroom, did I observe the refreshing smell of the morning air, the sounds of the birds in the trees? Or was my attention drawn to the coffee stain on my shirt, which I thought would cause me to look not only late but unprofessional as well? Considering your own past, have you experienced something similar?

When our minds begin to organize around the experience of anger, our attention is drawn to the negatives—even the one small, irritating thing in the middle of a sea of positive experiences. Our angry selves can interact with twenty helpful people during the morning without even noticing; but if one person treats us rudely, we can focus on it for hours! We pick out the parts of our experience we don't like, which fuel our angry mood, and we attend to them while ignoring almost everything else (at least the good stuff).

Exercise 1.2: Anger and Attention

Recall a recent situation when you became angry.

- Where was your attention focused? What did you pay attention to?

- Consider the quality of your attention. Was it broad and open, or narrow and blinkered?

- Were there aspects of the situation that you weren't aware of? Things you didn't notice?

Anger and other threat-related emotions shape our attention to focus on information that reinforces the feeling of being threatened, so we tend to overlook information that is inconsistent with this state of mind. In this state, your brain is biased toward being angry. You don't choose this process, and it certainly isn't your fault; it's just the way your brain works.

In fact, the brain works this way on purpose: for our own survival, to protect those we care about, and to help us defend our status or our belongings. If there is a real threat to our survival, we *want* our awareness to be single-mindedly focused and preoccupied with it, noticing aspects of the situation that give us information about the threat so that we can respond in the best possible way. If we're standing on the tracks of a speeding train, we want our attention focused on that train, not distracted by the pretty wildflowers a few feet away.

The trouble is that we have more "late for class" experiences than we have "shark" experiences. Think of recent situations when you became very angry. What was the focus of your anger? What triggered it? Was it a physical threat, or was it something else? Many of the threats we face in modern life have little to do with our physical safety and more to do with our jobs, social status, self-image, or relationships. We may also use anger as an emotional defense against painful feelings such as loss, embarrassment, or shame. If that weren't enough, our brains are also capable of *creating their own* "threats" in the form of thoughts, imagery, and fantasies.

THINGS WE TELL OURSELVES: THOUGHTS, REASONING, AND RUMINATION

When angry, we tend to have lots of what psychologists call *automatic thoughts*: thoughts that seem to automatically pop into the mind and that are often related to things we don't like. We also tend to take things very personally when we become angry: *This shouldn't ·have happened! This shouldn't happen to me! They shouldn't do this! They are taking advantage of me! Why did this have to go wrong now?!*

Angry thoughts are often linked to feeling threatened. For example, if you're in a new relationship and your partner doesn't phone you at the time you'd agreed, you may automatically think, *He doesn't care enough to call me.* Such thoughts are often linked to deeper concerns, frequently based in our pasts. *He doesn't care enough to call me* may be linked to a deeper issue such as self-worth and, in turn, to various difficult memories from childhood. This thought also reflects an angry reaction to a perceived threat to the relationship. The interesting thing is that these automatic thoughts can often be wrong, fueled by our hyperactive threat-detection system rather than by the reality of the situation.

One of my favorite examples comes from the Venerable Thubten Chodron, a Tibetan Buddhist nun who is abbess at Sravasti Abbey in the northwestern United States. She is also a prolific author and teacher.[7] A number of years ago, I attended a talk she gave on working with anger. Early on, she asked the audience about road rage—a topic that, in the United States at least, had recently been in the news. Chodron asked, "Is there anyone here who becomes really angry when someone cuts you off on the freeway?"

Immediately, about two-thirds of the audience raised their hands. She then asked us to consider the thoughts we have when this happens, and a number of people shared theirs. They usually involved negative thoughts about the other driver—that he or she is outrageously stupid, of poor character, or purposefully endangering the lives of other drivers for personal fun and entertainment. *That jerk! What an idiot! Doesn't she have eyes? He's trying to run me off the road! I'd like to lob a bologna sandwich at her head!*

Venerable Chodron did something next that I now realize was designed to promote a sense of compassion and connectedness with other drivers: she asked how many of *us* had ever cut off another driver. At this point, almost all of us sheepishly lowered our gazes and slowly raised our hands into the air (it was apparently an extraordinarily truthful bunch). She then asked us to give reasons for our "reckless" behavior. No one shouted, "Because I'm a jerk who cares nothing for the lives of others!"

Instead, there were murmurings of, "It was an accident," "I was about to miss my exit," and "I didn't see her." The irritated tone in the room evaporated, replaced with kindness and compassion for others as we mentally placed ourselves in the position of other drivers. We then considered the many potential reasons for their behavior that *didn't* involve being stupid, nasty, or selfish. We connected with the compassionate understanding that sometimes it's difficult to get around on the freeway, and that sometimes we *all* do things that inconvenience others, purposefully or not.

Such compassion can be a powerful antidote to anger, and research has shown that having sympathy for a person who insults you (for example) reduces brain activity linked to anger.[8] We can begin to manage our anger by realizing the things we share in common, such as cutting one another off when we're driving. Angry and compassionate states of mind are both associated with motivations: anger to hurt, compassion to help. Compassion helps us gain a perspective that motivates us to slow down and give that other car room to pull in front of us, rather than moving up to block its path.

Rumination

As you may have observed, anger can seem to take control of our thoughts. Have you ever tried to do a complicated task at work, study for an exam, watch a television program, or read a book when you were really angry? It's difficult to do because your mind tends to be drawn back to the focus of your anger. Try as you might, your brain keeps thinking about that insulting comment, playing out the situation over and over in your mind, visualizing it again and again. We can spend hours ruminating about what the other person said, about what we wish we had said, and rehearsing what we'll say the next time.

When we are angry, our minds tend to stay stuck on the perceived threat—the situation that made us angry. We pick the situation apart, analyzing every aspect of it. We ruminate, thinking about it over and over again. We magnify and generalize it, so that the only aspects of the person or situation that exist to us are the ones that make us angry. We may feel as if the other person exists for the sole purpose of pissing us off, or that our whole job (or relationship or life) is crap. In many cases, anger is related to having thoughts and feelings of being disliked, isolated, taken advantage of, and not being valued by others. As you'll learn, the compassionate approach to working with anger helps to counter this by helping us to feel connected with others, to feel valued and supported—feelings that help reduce our anger.

Reasoning

Being in an angry state of mind doesn't just impact the content of our thoughts; it also impacts the *way we reason and interpret information* in our environment. Our attention is already focused on the more threatening aspects of our lives, and once we notice these things, what do you think we do with them? When angry, as we do at other times, we make evaluations about what happened and try to blame or make attributions about what we discover: *Who did it? Why did they do it? What is going on here? How should I respond?*

The answers we come up with are often strongly biased by and toward our anger. As we saw in the road rage example, it shapes our thoughts about others—when we're feeling threatened, anger makes it *personal*. In the grip of anger, we tend to demonize others and hold them responsible for our discomfort. We tend to judge their actions harshly and make the worst possible assumptions about their motivations, assuming that they are trying to intentionally harm or inconvenience us. We feel disconnected from others, isolated from them. In these situations, the ways we evaluate the situation and others' contributions to it can be both defensive and aggressive in nature. That person isn't just moving slowly in the grocery aisles; he is intentionally trying to inconvenience *me* and ruin my day. That comment a colleague made in the staff meeting wasn't constructive criticism; it was an *attack*. The point here is that when we're angry, we not only tend to form negative opinions of the other people in the situation and their motives, but we often do so in error. We may even direct our harsh criticism and judgments at ourselves: *I can't believe I did that! I'm so stupid! I can't do anything right!*

There are other problems with how we reason when we're angry. Research has revealed that, compared to other threat emotions like sadness or anxiety, anger is linked with a feeling of *certainty*.[9] When we're angry, we tend to feel very certain of the thoughts that we're having, even if those thoughts are unrelated to what we're angry about, and even if they are dead wrong. In fact, we may even be more likely to be wrong when we're angry. Research shows that the certainty of anger is linked with processing information more superficially[10]—we think less carefully when making our judgments and rely more on stereotypes.[11]

Under these conditions, it's very easy to make bad decisions, the kind that can potentially harm relationships and make our lives more difficult—decisions like insulting a partner or embarrassing a colleague. Take a minute to consider: do you recall any really terrible decisions (or at least ones you regret) made under the sway of powerful emotions like anger? I sure can. If you can't, you likely have either a very poor memory or have good emotion-regulation skills, which can give us the ability to resist making major decisions when we are caught in the grip of strong emotions.

Exercise 1.3: Angry Thinking

Consider your thoughts and reasoning when you are angry.

- What are your thoughts focused on? What are you thinking about?

- Do any memories come to mind when you're angry? What kinds of memories?

- Consider what happens to your thinking when you are angry. Do you ruminate? Do your thoughts seem to come quickly? Are they easy or difficult to control?

- Consider how your thoughts interact with your anger. Do they fuel it or calm it?

PLAYING IT OUT IN OUR MINDS: IMAGERY AND FANTASY

Our brains have an amazing ability to imagine and fantasize—to picture something in our minds, such as a scene that plays out like a little film. The ability to do so, however, varies somewhat from person to person. Some people, like my wife, Lisa, can bring up visual or mental images at will.

When we were in graduate school together, she told me that while taking an exam she could scan the pages of her notes in her mind to find the answer. I'm more auditory, so while my visual imagery isn't as good as hers, I can name just about any popular song from the 1970s to the 1990s and can play it to myself as if my mind were a jukebox. We can use our imaginations to practice everything from assertiveness skills to running through guitar scales—it works!

The reason it works is that by going through a situation in our imaginations, we are lighting up many of the same cells in the brain (called *neurons*) that are activated when we *are actually in* the situation. Parts of your brain, such as your emotional centers (including anger), respond powerfully to imagery and fantasy, and the content of your imagination is, in turn, shaped by your mood. This is great news if you're reminiscing or savoring a positive experience, but it doesn't work so well when your threat system has taken over and starts to direct your imagination and fantasies. As with rumination, we tend to imagine the situation that angered us, playing it over and over again in our minds. We may visualize variations of the situation, or fantasize about all the angry ways we could have responded or things we could do in the future to really "stick it to them." These fantasies and imagery serve to keep our anger burning hot. It's a vicious cycle: when we're angry, we tend to experience anger-related fantasy and imagery; then these angry images and fantasies fuel our emotional response, keeping us angry. This is just the way our brains and bodies work—they can't always tell the difference between the external world and the world we create in our minds.

Our use of imagery affects our bodies and emotions all the time. You don't have to believe me though; check it out for yourself. The next time you're hungry, imagine a plate of your favorite food. How does it look? How does it smell? Taste? Then, shift your attention to your body's reaction. Are you salivating? As sexual beings, we regularly use imagery and fantasy to become aroused and keep ourselves "in the mood." The images and fantasies stimulate our pituitary glands to release the hormones associated with sex and arousal.

Here's another little mental experiment—have some fun with it. Start by bringing to mind different memories of your life that are linked with feeling certain ways, and see what happens (I'd recommend using happy memories!). I'll do it, too, as I write. First, I'm imagining attending a football game with my college friends, and a comfortable smile spreads across my face. Next, I'm picturing my son being born, and I feel a surge of love as I imagine him nestling against my wife. Then, I imagine myself at my grand-father's funeral, and tears well up in my eyes. And just as we have physical and emotional reactions to these happy and sad memories, so, too, can we have reactions to angry scenes as they play out in the mind's eye. I'll refrain from doing that one; it's been an emotional paragraph for me. How has it played out for you, as you've remembered certain things?

The good news is that you can learn to use the power of your imagination and fantasies to create *compassionate* states of mind to help you feel safe, confident, and connected with others—and to help you manage your emotions more effectively. You can use these powers to practice skills that will diffuse conflict rather than promote it. In this book, you'll learn to take control of your brain's ability to create thoughts and imagery, and to use these thoughts and images to gain control over your state of mind.

Exercise 1.4: Anger and Imagery

Consider the kinds of things you imagine and the fantasies you have when you're angry.

- What sort of fantasies and imagery do you have when you are angry? What are they like?

Consider the effects of your thoughts, imagery, and fantasies upon your mood.

- Do they fuel your anger or calm it?

- Do they make it easier to deal with the situation or more difficult?

DRIVEN TO ACT: THE POWER OF MOTIVATION

One of the main functions of our emotions—love, anger, fear, joy, desire, sadness, and attraction (to name just a few)—is to motivate our behavior. Emotions like anger, particularly those involving lots of arousal, carry with them a strong *motivation to act*: to couple, to flee, to fight, to seek out things we want or need. These motivations are a defining part of what it means to be angry. In the body, anger can seem a lot like fear: your heart races, your breath quickens, your blood pressure increases, your muscles tense. However, the motivations associated with anger are different from the motivations associated with fear. With fear, you're motivated to flee, to escape, to get away from the source of threat. In contrast, anger tends to motivate you to go *toward* the thing that angered you.[12] You are driven to attack and insult, to undermine, conquer, and dominate.

This motivation isn't just an intellectual desire, like, "After thinking about this, I've decided that I'd really like to knock your block off." Instead, it can be felt more as an urge, like the sensation of having an itch that you really, really want to scratch. It's important to acknowledge this sensation as you learn to use compassion to help deal with your anger. It is also important to understand that, when we are angry, we don't often *choose* to have an aggressive motivation; often, it's just something we *feel*. Our responsibility is to figure out how to handle it and to avoid engaging in behavior that lands us in trouble or harms other people. As we've discussed, when we are in the midst of an angry threat response, our bodies are activated for action and our minds experience a motivation to fight off whatever we feel threatened by. Our motivation is to defend ourselves, to retaliate, perhaps even to punish the other person so that he will never, ever consider crossing us again. And with a motivation like this, it's easy to see how our anger can cause problems in our lives, particularly in our relationships with others.

To work well with anger, you need ways to work with your motivation so that you can broaden your focus and connect with a desire to be more helpful to yourself and other people. As you'll learn in the next chapter, the brain is wired to respond to threat; however, it's also wired to respond to caring and to provide care. These motivations will help you activate your brain's compassionate responses and enable you to deal with difficult situations without getting lost in anger.

Exercise 1.5: Anger and Motivation

Consider your motivation when you are angry. What do you want to do?

- What does your angry self feel like saying?

- What does your angry self feel like doing?

THINGS WE DO: ANGRY BEHAVIOR

Toward the beginning of this chapter, we saw how anger-driven behaviors can emerge when our threat systems are in control. These range from trying to conceal and ignore our anger to actually committing violence. We act out anger in many different ways, ways that are unique to us and that are related to a number of factors. As you'll read in chapter 3, these factors include temperament, early relationships with our caregivers (including our observations of their behavior when they were angry), social roles, coping resources, and the myriad other situations that make up our lives.

Of the many ways that we act on our anger, aggression is perhaps the most obviously problematic, particularly as it affects our relationships with others. There are contexts (for example, at home or at work) in which we can get away with acting our anger out aggressively, and other contexts in which there would be dire consequences for doing so. For this reason, those of us who learned to act out our anger in aggressive ways may end up taking it out on the people who mean the most to us, because with them we can get away with it. You may find yourself acting most harshly toward those who are weaker or whose relationships with you make it unlikely that they will harm you in return—toward your employees, partners, or children rather than toward the boss who yelled at you unfairly or the police officer who wrote you a ticket.

Aggression isn't the only angry behavior that can create distance between you and those you love. Instead of lashing out, you can pull in: denying affection, stewing in resentment, giving constant signs of disapproval. Ignoring or withholding love from our children can be as harmful as hitting them, although in different ways. Quiet, constant criticism can destroy a spouse's self-esteem. It's scary to think about what can happen when our anger and threat systems are ruling the day.

As you read this, you may find yourself cringing a bit in remembrance of the times you've harmed and been harmed in these ways. I am. *Pay attention* to the hurt you feel when you recall these sorts of memories, because this feeling can help you sympathize with others and fuel your compassionate resolve to treat them better—because you know what that pain feels like.

All too often, we cover up that pain and the vulnerable feelings that go along with it by giving in to anger, which can feel powerful in comparison. But make no mistake: doing this is an avoidance strategy that allows us to only temporarily escape difficult feelings. The problem is that this temporary numbing of our pain is a high-cost, short-term strategy. Although you may feel a bit less vulnerable now, using anger to escape from other emotions sets you up to have more problems down the road. Compassion challenges you to be stronger than that and helps you to use your pain as a way to better understand and identify with others.

It can be tough when we become aware of how our anger has harmed our relationships. Many of the clients I've worked with have painfully admitted that they have behaved the most harshly toward those they cared most about—toward those who loved them enough to stick around even in the face of such treatment or who didn't have the resources to escape. This realization is common, and it's one reason that people finally decide to learn to work with their anger more productively.

Exercise 1.6: Anger and Behavior

Consider your behavior when you've been angry. What did you do?

- What actions did you engage in?

- Did those actions reflect the person you want to be?

- If you have children, do those actions reflect the sort of person you'd like them to become?

Consider the consequences that your angry behaviors have had on your life.

- How has your life been impacted by your angry actions?

- How have your relationships been impacted by your anger?

I would argue that it *should* be a painful thing to become aware that we are harming or scaring those we care about, that sometimes we make things worse instead of better. These realizations are crucial (and tricky), because how we respond to them makes all the difference. If we respond to them by shaming ourselves—convincing ourselves that we are *bad* people—that just makes things worse, and we are setting the stage for yet another retreat into anger. The key is to commit ourselves to doing things better: to use our guilt and regret as fuel for our motivation to work with anger in positive ways and then to actually take the steps needed to become better parents, spouses, and colleagues. You're taking one of those steps right now.

Fortunately, there are many positive ways to respond to difficult, anger-producing situations. You can learn to recognize when you're angry and work with your emotions directly by slowing your body down and observing your thoughts. You can speak assertively and directly with the other people involved in the situation, respecting both them and yourself. You can even learn to observe this situation as an example of a pattern that comes up again and again in the course of your life, and extend compassion to yourself and to others, even as you deal with it. You can recognize that we are all human beings who simply wish to have happy lives, and that there are powerful tools and traditions to help us do this. The fact that you are reading this book tells me that this is the road you've chosen to take, and I'm going to do my very best to help you along the way. Your family, your life, and your future are worthy of this effort.

CONCLUSION

In this chapter, we've explored the different forms that anger can take and the powerful way that anger organizes our minds as our evolved brains work to protect us from threats. It's important to recognize that this process—the fact that you experience anger—is not your fault. But regardless, you must still take responsibility for it, lest your anger continue to create great difficulties for you and the people around you. You can help yourself in this effort by becoming more familiar with your threat system and how it operates in response to anger, and by learning ways to work with this powerful emotion. That's how we'll be spending the rest of this book.

2

The Compassionate-Mind Approach to Understanding Anger

In CFT, we recognize that anger is an emotion that evolved to help us survive. It has alerted us to things we need to attend to or change, and motivated us to defend ourselves when we're in danger. However, we've also seen that out-of-control anger can create real problems in our lives and relationships. You can never get rid of your anger, any more than you can get rid of your nose (actually, getting rid of your nose would be much easier, if more painful). However, you can learn to *understand* your anger—why your brain makes it so easy for you to experience it, how it feels in your body, and how it can take control of your thoughts and behavior. You can learn about the specific things that trigger your anger and work with your reactions to these triggers. In this book there's a lot of focus on learning how to step back from your anger and take a compassionate approach to managing it. You may not be able to always choose whether you *experience* anger, but you *can* learn to choose what you do with it.

You'll be doing a lot of work in this book to develop your "compassionate self." It may seem strange to suggest that when we begin to deal with anger (which so often involves acting harshly or harmfully toward others), the first place we need to learn to direct our compassion is *toward ourselves*. However, once we understand where our anger comes from and why it can be so difficult to manage, we may find that relating to ourselves and our anger with compassion makes a good deal of sense.

FINDING OURSELVES HERE

In the first chapter I used the example I'd learned from Thubten Chodron, a Tibetan Buddhist nun. You'll recall that she prompted the audience to explore how we felt when someone else cut us off in traffic, and then how we behaved and felt when we cut someone else off. This exercise prompted us to shift our perspectives and put ourselves into the shoes of the people we might otherwise have criticized. This is an example of *empathy*, a key part of compassion that allows us to understand situations from other people's point of view—a perspective that isn't driven by our experience of feeling threatened. By learning to step back from your emotions and think about yourself and others in kind, friendly, and understanding ways, you can free yourself from threat-driven emotions like anger, see things more clearly, and gain more control over your life.

One of the most important ideas in compassion focused therapy is the recognition that we all just find ourselves here, part of the flow of life that has emerged on this planet over millions of years. We're all in it together, as they say. You and I, like every other being on this planet, did not choose to be here. We arrived here, at this particular time in history, in these particular forms, with these particular brains, experiencing a whole range of motivations, desires, and feelings. We all find ourselves here, born into situations we had no control over, with bodies and minds that we didn't design or choose, surrounded by people whose company and characteristics we didn't select. We didn't choose our coloring or any of our physical features—our tendencies to be tall or short, thin or round, whether our teeth would be straight or crooked, our hearts resilient or flawed. And we didn't choose our brains or design how they work.

Many of us are painfully aware of this, at least occasionally. Who wouldn't choose to alter something about themselves if given the choice? I'm quite happy with my height and twenty-twenty vision, for example, but I wouldn't mind having a nicely chiseled jawline, and my meager typing and guitar-playing abilities would benefit from replacing my short, sausage-shaped fingers with long, slender ones.

There are things about our brains that we might wish to change if we could. From one perspective, they are miraculously complex systems that are capable of doing truly amazing things. They allow us to remember, learn, plan, and negotiate the nuances of complicated social relationships. They allow us to weigh options and consequences, such as whether or not to have coffee with dessert, knowing that the caffeine may keep us up late. However, a human brain is also something of an evolutionary patchwork quilt—a stitched-together, complex, and varied system of structures and functions, some of which date back almost to the beginnings of life itself. Our brains have evolved with a host of extremely powerful emotions that are capable of harnessing our thoughts and attention, often without our awareness. Further, the *way* these emotions play out in us often seems suited to earlier times in the human story. They prepare us to fight, flee, or lie down in submission when we'd be better served by pausing and taking a moment to become more mindful and perhaps to analyze, consider, or negotiate. So, while our brains often serve us well, they also function in ways that we probably wouldn't have chosen or designed—ways we might change, given the choice.

Just as we don't get to choose the way we look or the way our brains function, we also don't get to choose the situations we're born into, and these situations shape what our lives will look like. Our early environments play a large role in determining how we will interact with the world around us, and they shape our abilities to work with difficult emotions like anger. We all emerge into the world with brains that contain preset systems that are ready to be activated by how life treats us. Certain experiences in our lives can literally "turn on" certain genes and modify the way our brains work. This is one reason why early attachments are so important, as we will explore in chapter 3. When talking with my colleagues about how we are shaped by the situations we're born into, I often hear such things as, "If I'd been born into a drug cartel, chances are that I would now be a drug dealer, or possibly in prison, dead, or a murderer." It's easy to mentally divide the world into "good people" and "bad people," but those distinctions aren't real. When we look more closely, we see the stories behind these people's lives (and our own), and the labels begin to fall away. We find that so many of the people we may have looked down on were born into violent, hostile, abusive, or neglectful situations—situations that can shape our personalities, and even our brains, in ways that set us up to have great difficulties in life.

If we can connect with a compassionate perspective, we see that if we had been born into the circumstances of those who irritate us, we could easily be acting as they do. Our behaviors might have been similar, for better or for worse. It's easy to judge others (and ourselves), but we often don't see or credit the strength of character that actually may have prevented things from turning out so much worse than they have. Had I been born into a neglectful environment, it's likely that the current version of me—the psychology professor sitting here writing this book—almost certainly would not exist. These reflections are important, because they help us recognize that we didn't *choose* the way our brains work or how they have been shaped and conditioned by our lives. This realization also helps us to recognize the challenges we face in life. These may include acknowledging that, although it isn't our fault that we have these tricky brains, we can claim responsibility for our lives and learn to train our minds in compassionate ways that are focused on our own well-being and that of others. Likewise, we can work to have more understanding and empathy for those who were born into situations that were much more difficult than our own, and for everyone else as well.

OLD BRAINS AND NEW BRAINS

When we study the human brain, we see that we share many basic drives and motivations with organisms (like reptiles) that appeared long before we did in the evolutionary chain.[1] The lives of reptiles aren't nearly as complicated as yours and mine. They're generally interested in the "four Fs": fighting, fleeing, feeding, and...reproduction. You may find that some of these concerns occasionally enter your mind as well. From an evolutionary perspective, as new species emerge into the flow of life, their brains aren't completely new; rather, they contain new abilities that make them unique *and* many of the structures and characteristics that had been present in previous forms of life. In rough terms, you could say that we each have an "old brain," which is still generally focused on the "four Fs" and is responsible for our basic desires and emotions. This old brain is linked up to a new brain, which is the part that makes us uniquely human—capable of fantastical and creative thinking, imagination, rumination, planning, and so on.

In CFT, we think it's important to recognize that this link between old brain and new brain is very tricky. Think about many of the strong passions you have had in your life, such as falling in love, having a relationship with your children, developing friends and alliances, having a good sexual relationship, seeking acceptance and avoiding rejection, getting angry and having conflicts, getting anxious when there is danger around, and feeling joy when things are going well for you. We can actually observe these behaviors and experiences in many other animal species. You will see them enacted by the family cat and dog, and by the chimpanzees at the local zoo. This is just the way it works; these drives, motivations, and emotions are basic parts of our psychological makeup. Think about the plots of most movies we watch. They involve love, sex, violence, sacrifice, betrayal, and so on. These are the themes that guide the flow of life.

Our old brains are in charge of these more basic processes and emotions—those that help us take care of the things we need to do to survive and reproduce. Old-brain structures keep our hearts beating and our lungs breathing, and they regulate our sleeping, eating, and reproductive cycles. Other old-brain structures help us interact with our environment in ways that help us survive into the future and pass along our genes. They motivate us to seek out the things we need and are responsible for our natural tendencies to be attracted to suitable mates, to care for our young, and to respond emotionally when aspects of our environment threaten us.

These old-brain tendencies evolved over millions of years and can be seen in countless species of animals. For example, if we look at reptiles and amphibians, we can see examples of aggression, fear, and attraction (mating), but we also see that these species don't nurture their young. However, when mammals emerged about 120 million or so years ago, something really important emerged with them: a *psychology of caring* for one another. Mammals—and this category includes rodents, cats, dogs, monkeys, dolphins, and eventually humans—nurtured and cared for one another. This psychology of caring is the basis of the compassionate mind. You may have observed this process in action with your family pet, watching the mother carefully nursing, grooming, and comforting her young.

This nurturing behavior isn't accidental—it is *necessary* for the survival of baby mammals, which produce far fewer young than do species such as reptiles, amphibians, and fish. Unlike these species, mammalian young are nearly helpless at birth. The relatively few mammal offspring need to be protected from dangers, fed, and comforted when distressed by having close contact with the mother. They need to be cared for. Like the babies of other mammals, human babies certainly need to be cared for and will die very quickly if they aren't. As we will see later, this caring relationship also has profound effects on how our infant minds develop. On several occasions, I've heard the Dalai Lama mention this innate capacity for nurturing as evidence that we are "wired" for compassion. As babies, we are designed to seek out and obtain care (this is why babies are so cute and good at drawing our attention).

In addition to these old-brain functions, we also have the ability to consider, fantasize, plan, contemplate, reflect, and *assign meaning* to events occurring in our lives. These abilities are unique to us and to our "new brains," particularly the *frontal cortex*—the soft, wrinkly outer covering of the brain located toward the front of the head. This new brain is the reason that we are the dominant species on the planet: it enables us to develop technology, build huge and complex societies, and have deeply nuanced relationships. We have amazing brains!

Unfortunately, problems arise from the combination of the old brain's focus on the four Fs (particularly its strong focus on detecting threats) and our new-brain abilities to create meaning, ruminate, and develop complex mental fantasies. As you saw in chapter 1, when you're angry, these new-brain abilities can be harnessed by your threat system. Then, your thoughts, reasoning, and fantasies all work to *keep you angry*. Our amazing brains also allow our anger to be manifested in uniquely destructive ways—through the development and use of weapons like swords, guns, and nuclear bombs. Our inventive new brains can combine with the desires and motives of the old brain to produce rather tragic consequences.

Let's look a bit more closely now at how our brains work, so that we can learn to use them to heal rather than harm.

A MODEL OF EMOTION

Our brains are made up of cells called neurons, and we have *lots* of them— billions and billions. These cells are linked together by a breathtaking number of connections, called *synapses*. Everything we experience (every thought we have; everything we do; everything we see, hear, feel, smell) is reflected by a corresponding pattern of activity in the brain. What this means is that every time you think of something—say, an orange—cells in the brain "light up" and allow you to "see" this object in your mind, to understand its shape and color, to imagine its smell, the way it feels and tastes. Other cells light up that allow you to recall whether or not you like oranges. And still other cells allow you to bring up other memories and feelings, such as visiting an orange grove with your beloved grandfather during a childhood holiday, and perhaps even the warm feeling of being cared for at that time.

Just as the word "orange" can activate certain cells in the brain, so, too, can anger and compassion; each lights up different brain pathways associated with different emotional experiences, bodily reactions, patterns of attention, and ways of thinking and behaving. We don't usually think about all these things when we talk about emotions; we just say "anger." But as we've seen, our emotional experiences organize our minds in a number of different ways and turn on different light switches in our brains. Emotions, such as anger, aren't just about how we feel.

THE THREE CIRCLES

In CFT, the complex world of human emotion is organized into three emotion-regulation systems that help us with three types of situations:[2]

- Systems that help us detect and respond to threats and challenges.

- Systems that help us be interested in seeking and obtaining resources, that help us detect and respond to opportunities, and that reward us for doing so.

- Systems that help us settle into a state of calm, restfulness, and openness when we aren't faced with threats, challenges, or urgent desires—when we're satisfied. We'll see that this emotion-regulation system is closely related to experiences of affection and what we call "affiliation"—experiences that soothe us and reduce the activity of our threat systems.

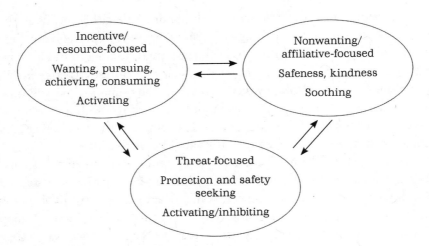

Figure 2.1: Three Types of Emotion-Regulation Systems
Reprinted from *The Compassionate Mind* by Paul Gilbert (London: Constable and Robinson, 2009).

The "three circles" model in figure 2.1 was derived from a long line of research showing that positive and negative emotions are processed differently in the brain and affect different systems in our bodies. You'll recognize the threat system, which is involved in activating our fight-or-flight response. It can also prevent us from doing either, leading us to submit or freeze.

In the Compassionate-Mind model, we understand that there is a further distinction: that there are *different types of positive emotions*. We focus in particular on the differences between emotions that involve excitement and energy, and those linked with feeling safe, calm, and contented. By distinguishing between these two types of positive emotions, we can begin to understand how compassion can help us deal with difficult experiences.[3] The reality of how our emotions work is complicated, and our model of emotions is a simplified one; there are many different models that attempt to explain how our emotions work. We use this one because it helps us understand where our emotions come from, the relationships between our different emotion-regulation systems, and the ways that they can organize our minds.

THE THREAT AND SELF-PROTECTION SYSTEM

Let's examine these systems in more detail, beginning with the threat and self-protection system, which we'll shorten to "threat system" for convenience.

The experience of threat is partly linked to our motives and goals, and it has evolved to organize our minds around protecting ourselves. This system is activated when the brain perceives a potential threat or danger to us or to those we care about. (I say "the brain" rather than "we," because sometimes the brain can perceive and react to something as a threat even if we have no conscious awareness that this has happened.)

When the brain perceives a threat, it sets in motion a cascade of reactions (the dominoes we saw in chapter 1) designed to help us respond rapidly in the face of danger and avoid potential danger in the future. We experience bodily reactions and bursts of emotion, prompting us to *act* in response to the real or imagined threat. Common threat-related emotions include anger, fear, anxiety, and disgust, and each of these is associated with an urge to act. As I've pointed out, in the case of anger, we feel the need to attack; with fear, the desire to flee; with disgust, the desire to avoid contact with whatever it is that happens to be grossing us out. If we think of things that commonly disgust us—signs (sights and smells) of decay and contamination or things that could cause us to be ill or sick—they tend to be things that could threaten our survival. This is also played out in the way we experience disgust in response to foods that have previously made us sick. For example, if you ate some scrumptious shrimp at dinner but were up all night vomiting because you caught a virus, it's not likely that you'll order shrimp again soon. In the future, the mere sight or smell of shrimp may even turn your stomach. This is an example of a type of learning called *classical conditioning*, which is a way we acquire emotional responses to things and which we'll discuss further in chapter 3.

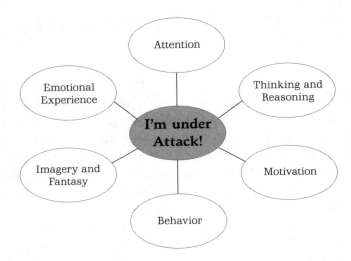

Figure 2.2: How the Threat System Organizes the Mind

So one way the threat system organizes the mind is by helping us to very powerfully and efficiently learn associations between different things (for example, connecting the way the food tastes and smells with the experience of being sick). The threat system doesn't just affect how we feel, it affects what we learn and how quickly and easily we learn it. As the shrimp example demonstrates, learning to associate threat emotions (like disgust) with situations (like food) occurs unconsciously—*it can even occur when we intellectually know very well that these things don't go together.* For example, when your roommate was sick and throwing up for two days before you ever ate the shrimp: you know your being sick likely has nothing to do with the food that you ate, but tell that to your stomach the next time you smell shrimp! Threat-related emotions like anger can feel powerful and uncontrollable because learning them often *is* uncontrollable, and so is recalling them. Your brain recalls these associations without your choice or awareness: the next time you see or smell shrimp, you feel sick, even if it had been one of your favorite foods and you desperately want to enjoy it again—even though you know that it probably wasn't responsible for making you sick.

Each of the three emotion-regulation systems is linked with physical experiences. The threat system, in particular, involves the release of stress hormones (such as *cortisol*) into the bloodstream. The various threat-related emotions play out in our bodies in very different ways. Take a moment to consider again how you've felt, physically, when you've been angry. In the short term, you may tend to experience heightened arousal, the classic "fight" response, with an increase in your heart rate and your breathing. This response prepares you for action. However, if you're in this response mode for a longer period—for days, weeks, or months—this heightened arousal gives way to other physical sensations such as muscle tension, stomach upset, and headaches. Why? Because anger stimulates the release of stress hormones *even after the situation that angered us is over.*[4]

The emotion-regulation system also involves our attention, and this is particularly true with threat-related emotions like anger, which operate on a principle of "better safe than sorry." As you read in chapter 1, threat emotions like anger focus and narrow our attention, thoughts, and mental imagery on the source of the threat. When feeling threatened, we tend not to notice or attend to other things (such as alternative explanations for the situation), because we're so focused on the source of the perceived danger and on reacting to it in an attempt to protect ourselves.

I imagine our threat systems to be like airport security agents who examine each potential threat, perhaps by giving the threat an X-ray scan or a rather intimate pat-down (do you get a cigarette after that one?). But usually it's best not to joke with airline security—they're all business, all about keeping us safe with no distractions—and the threat system works in a similar way. It's designed to override positive emotions. If you're having a wonderful lunch and the restaurant catches fire, you'd better forget about lunch and get out of there ASAP (in an orderly fashion, of course). The threat response can make us forget all about the positive things in our lives, keeping our attention on the danger (real or imagined) and locked in on those threat-related emotions.

Exercise 2.1: Examining the Threat Response

Try to remember a time when your threat system was in charge—when you felt that you were being attacked or undermined, or that your progress was blocked.

- What emotions were you experiencing? How did you feel? What physical sensations did you have?

- Consider your attention. What did you pay attention to? Where was your focus?

- What were you thinking about? How did your thoughts relate to your emotional experience?

- What sort of imagery or fantasy were you picturing in your mind?

- What was your motivation like? What did you want to do?

- What sort of behavior did you engage in?

If we want to succeed in dealing with anger, it's important that we learn to recognize when our threat systems have been activated. As we've seen, this system is good at hijacking the mind, leading to the domino effect of experiences explored in chapter 1. The dominoes fall as you find yourself feeling angry; your attention narrows to focus on the threat; thoughts race through your head; you play the situation over and over in your mind; you're motivated to attack. With all of this going on, things can get out of hand pretty quickly if you aren't aware of what's happening. The key is to recognize this process as it begins and interrupt it before it takes over.

THE DRIVE AND RESOURCE ACQUISITION SYSTEM

As noted previously, we have two very different types of positive emotion-regulation systems. Western society tends to emphasize only one of these systems, teaching us that in order to be happy, we must be "achieving" and "doing." The emotion-regulation system that reflects this is called the *drive and resource acquisition system*, which I'll sometimes shorten to "drive system" for ease of discussion.

The drive and resource acquisition system evolved to help us seek and obtain resources, things we need to survive and prosper. As such, it serves two purposes: to motivate us to pursue desired objects and goals, and to reward us once we've obtained them. If the overriding message from the threat system is "Protect yourself!" then for the drive system, the messages are "Go get it!" (before you get it) and "This is great!" (after you get it). The drive system motivates and organizes our efforts to obtain things such as food, sex, recognition, and various other things we associate with happiness and comfort. This system can keep us working toward our goals and is associated with emotions like excitement, desire, and pleasure.

Figure 2.3: How the Drive and Resource Acquisition System Organizes the Mind

Like the threat system, the drive system organizes the mind in specific ways. It motivates us and focuses our attention on obtaining the object or experience we desire. This system activates and energizes us, causing our thoughts to return again and again to the object of our pursuits. Think about how you behave during a competition, the way an athlete or a chess player behaves and focuses her attention during a match, or the frenzy of shoppers at a preholiday sale. Recall the first time you fell in love. How often did you find your thoughts returning to that other person? And, later, when we have obtained the goal, won the competition, or received the recognition we crave, we tend to experience excitement or a rush of pleasure.

Like the threat system, the drive and resource acquisition system involves various chemicals in the brain. One of these chemicals is a neurotransmitter called *dopamine* (a primary chemical messenger in the brain), which is associated with experiences of pleasure, drive, and energy. We can experience a flush of dopamine when we fall in love, have sex, ace a test, or win an award at work. The emotions produced by dopamine are powerful in their ability to harness our drives. Imagine winning the lottery and immediately having an extra $200 million or so. When you found out that you'd won, it's likely that you would have a rush of dopamine in the brain and would experience a surge of energy. You might have a hard time sleeping and be ert to thoughts racing through your mind as you think about everything you could do with the money. People who take cocaine and amphetamines are, in essence, trying to simulate this feeling—to give themselves a rush of energy, drive, and excitement. There are, of course, lots of problems with using drugs to stimulate the brain in this way, including the nasty come-down (which leaves you feeling worse than you did before you started) and the fact that these drugs are highly addictive.

Exercise 2.2: Examining the Drive and Resource Acquisition System

Try to remember a time when your drive and resource acquisition system was in charge. Think about an instance when you were really excited about doing something, such as pursuing a goal, or when you'd just succeeded at some-thing important to you.

- What emotions were you experiencing? How did you feel? What physical sensations did you have?

- Consider your attention. What did you pay attention to? What were you focused on?

- What were you thinking about? How did your thoughts relate to your emotional experience?

- What sort of imagery or fantasy were you picturing in your mind?

- What was your motivation like? What did you want to do?

- What sort of behavior did you engage in?

Just as the threat system organizes your mind around perceived threats, the drive and resource acquisition system organizes your mind so that it directs you toward your goals—directing your emotions, attention, thoughts, fantasies, motivations, and behavior toward whatever it is that you're pur-suing. We can also observe interactions between the drive system and the threat system: if we're being blocked from our goal, when we're "on the hunt" and something gets in our way or prevents us from getting the object of desire. When this happens, the lines can blur, because our drive and threat systems are activated at the same time. Competitors who are striving after the same goal that we seek can be seen as threats, such as those shoppers lining up for the rush of a Christmas sale, racing through stores toward the items they seek, even fighting over the last item on the shelf. Sadly, this can also lead to dangerously aggressive behavior. For example, in 2008, a temporary worker at a Wal-Mart store in New York was trampled to death by holiday shoppers frantically pushing to get in.[5] The language we sometimes use reflects the interaction between the threat and drive systems, reflected in statements like, "You have to *fight* to get what you want!"

So if you're pursuing something you want but are blocked from obtaining it; your drives are thwarted or blocked, and this can lead to frustration, which then can become anger. In fact, anger is intimately linked with the drive system. Although it's true that we can feel sad or anxious if the path to a goal is blocked, anger tends to be the more usual threat-system response to such obstacles. This makes sense when we consider that anger is an emotion that encourages us to "approach"—to move forward and do what is necessary to remove blocks, to overcome potential threats to our happiness or the achievement of our goals.

In Buddhist psychology, grasping at or clinging is seen as a main source of human suffering—we experience many negative emotions when we really want something but can't have it, or when we have it and lose it and can't bear to let it go. In CFT, when we're dealing with difficulties, we often ask, "What is the threat behind this emotion?" As we've seen, the threats that are associated with anger often involve being stopped or thwarted: something preventing us from getting what we want, threatening to take away what we have, or preventing us from being in control. In the case of shame-related anger, we experience a threat to how we see ourselves, to our sense of personal identity, or to how we want others to think of us. In summary, anger is often related to the threat of things *not being the way we want them to be* and to our habit of continuing to grasp at our preferred view of reality, regardless of how things actually are.

If you think about how we all go about the world, pursuing the things we want, with brains designed to experience frustration and anger when things don't go our way—well, it's easy to see how conflicts can arise. A compassionate perspective can give us the power to stand back, observe, and understand this process, and as a result to begin to take control of it and to avoid having big conflicts over small things. We can learn to step out of the cycle of anger by realizing that we all just want to be happy, that no one wants to suffer, and that all of our grasping, fighting, and angry behaviors are simply what happens when our old brains and our new brains conflict in the effort to help us survive and prosper. With this understanding comes a choice: do you just want to go on like this? Or would you rather use your knowledge of how your brain works to find ways of balancing your emotion-regulation systems so that you can build better relationships and a better life? If you like that second option, keep reading, because we have one more emotion-regulation system to discuss.

THE SOOTHING AND SAFENESS SYSTEM

Luckily, we have a system that can help calm down the threat and drive systems. We'll call this third system the "safeness" system, and we'll now look at the ways this system makes us feel, the types of behaviors it's linked to, and the brain systems and chemicals that it involves.

With a few exceptions (sadness, for example), the threat and drive systems tend to organize the mind in active and focused ways that involve strong desires to either deal with a threat or to pursue a goal. In comparison to these two other two systems, the safeness system organizes us more in a "settling in" sort of way and is sometimes referred to as the "contentment system." It is associated with emotional experiences like contentment, peace, serenity, and feelings of being safe and connected to others. While the threat and drive systems often involve different kinds of *striving* and are largely about changing the current state of things, the soothing system involves an experience of *being*—of being grounded, being safe, and being comfortable in the present moment. Instead of the urgency we experience when the threat and drive systems are in charge, the safeness system promotes a slow and settled experience (without being boring). Next to the "Protect yourself!" of the threat system and the "Go get it!" of the drive system, the central message of the soothing system is "It's okay. You're safe."

We can understand the way the soothing system works by observing animals, such as my dog, Sadie, who lies peacefully in the warmth of the sun shining in through our porch window when she's content and feels safe. Like Sadie, when other animals are not threatened and are satisfied, when they don't need to achieve or acquire things, they enter into states of contentment and peaceful well-being. Humans can too, and studies show us that when we (both humans and animals) are in this state of contentment, our bodies behave differently.[6, 7] When our safeness system is activated, the stress-related activity in the nervous system decreases, and we calm down and feel more at peace.

The safeness system is strongly rooted in the process of *attachment*, our experiences of being accepted and valued, and of nurturing, which pertains to both being cared for and caring for others. This is a major difference between the safeness system and the threat and drive systems, in which relationships are secondary to protection and pursuits. In the case of the threat system, our interactions with others tend to involve overcoming, avoiding, or pacifying those who are in our way. In the drive and resource acquisition system, the relationship aspect may take the form of sexual desire or of competing together or against each other in pursuit of goals. In contrast, warm relationships with others are at the *very center* of the safeness system, which has evolved as a response to our nurturing interactions with others and is involved in the giving and receiving of kindness and love, and in feeling valued and cared for.

Think of experiences when you felt completely safe, accepted, and cared for (if you can't recall an experience like that, try to imagine what it might be like). A good example of these interactions can be evoked by the image of a loving mother holding or nursing her infant child or an older couple holding hands. Soothing interactions involve experiences of warmth and trust, and lead to a sense of being safe and connected with one another. Like the threat and drive systems, the safeness system is sensitive to cues from the environment. Specifically, it responds to messages that we are valued, accepted, and cared for.

Imagine that you're at a new job, just finishing up your first week, and that you're a bit anxious because you still don't know exactly what to do. You're wondering if you have the ability to meet expectations. Imagine that your new boss calls you into his office, and notice how your body might feel in this circumstance. In this situation, your threat system might be on edge, and your pursuit system as well—it's important that you succeed at this job, and you want to do it well. Imagine that you sit down in your boss's office and that he smiles kindly and warmly, saying, "I just wanted to tell you that we're very happy to have you here. It's a lot to learn at once, and you are doing very well. We have to work as a team here, and you're fitting right in—everyone enjoys working with you. We're happy to have you here." Wow.

Imagine what it feels like to hear this from him, to know that you are liked, accepted, and valued. Your safeness system would likely respond to these positive messages, in part by working to reduce your arousal. This, in turn, would help to balance out the activity coming from your threat system, and you'd no longer feel as anxious.

It would be great if we had that kind of affirmation more often, wouldn't it? We benefit from these sorts of interactions, and we can provide them to others. It doesn't have to be as over the top as that example, either. Soothing interactions can take many forms. A smile, a kind word, a pat on the back, or a friendly squeeze to the shoulder can all communicate, "You're safe with me," "I accept you," "I like you." The idea of *warmth* seems to be particularly important here. Warm interactions are soothing and signal interest, kindness, caring, liking, affection, and trust.[8] These interactions—particularly with those we love and trust—can stimulate our safeness systems and help us feel less threatened.

CALMING DOWN THE THREAT SYSTEM

The ability of our safeness systems to calm our threat response is demonstrated nicely by a study published in 2006 by James Coan, Hillary Schaefer, and Richard Davidson.[9] In this study, sixteen married women were faced with the threat of a mild electric shock. Using functional magnetic resonance imaging (fMRI), which allows you to look at what parts of the brain activate during specific situations, researchers were able to examine what was going on in the women's brains as they anticipated being shocked—clearly a situation designed to stimulate their threat systems. During this procedure, the women had varying levels of a specific form of social contact: touch. Some of the time, the women's husbands held their hands. At other times, a stranger held their hands, and at yet other times, the women were alone.

When they looked at what was going on in these women's brains during the experiment, the researchers observed that the parts of the brain associated with emotional and behavioral responses to threat were much less active when the women were holding hands with their husbands. The experience of having physical contact with their husbands during the experiment actually *reduced their brains' response to threat*. The researchers also found that the better the marriage, the greater the reduction in threat response. Physical contact did reduce the response to threat when the women were holding hands with strangers, but the reduction was less than when they'd been holding hands with their husbands. This demonstrates the power of the safeness system and its links to our experiences of attachment and feelings of connectedness with others. It is an example of how the safeness system can help reduce our experience of threat and help balance our emotional responses.

Just as in the other systems, there are specific chemicals in the body that are associated with the safeness system. You may have heard of *opiates*—drugs that are abused because they can make us feel a sense of well-being and happiness. Well, the chemicals in our bodies that we call *endorphins* are examples of natural opiates that help soothe us with a sense of peacefulness and connectedness.

This soothing effect of the endorphins is no accident. You may remember the amygdala, which I introduced in chapter 1 as a core part of the threat system, rapidly identifying threats and activating us in response to perceived sources of danger. Well, the amygdala is sensitive to the effects of chemicals such as endorphins. These chemicals inhibit the activity of the amygdala and help us feel calmer, safer, and less focused on threats.

Over the course of evolution, this safeness system has become intimately linked with the process of attachment. So, for example, babies often become peaceful when they are at the breast or lying gently in their mothers' arms: feelings of *closeness* create feelings of *safeness*. Later, children who are distressed will return to a parent, often the mother, who may cuddle them, kiss them, or stroke their backs. This contact helps to soothe and calm the child. Such affection and affectionate relationships are linked to the release of chemicals such as the endorphins and the hormone *oxytocin*, which is involved with nurturing behavior and with the inhibition of stress, irritability, and aggressiveness.[10] While oxytocin has typically been associated with physical contact, new research shows that this isn't the only way to experience the benefits of this hormone. In fact, the release of oxytocin and the sense of comfort and safeness it gives can occur in response to a number of activities, including being comforted verbally (even over the phone![11]) and mental imagery, which you'll be using later in the book to help you deal with your anger.

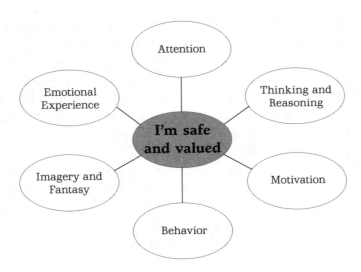

Figure 2.4: How the Safeness System Organizes the Mind

In summary, when we're neither threatened nor actively focused on pursuing a goal, we can experience a sense of being safe, comfortable, and content. You can experience yourself as lovable and worthy of kindness and respect. Your attention broadens, and you can become aware of all the good things that you'd overlooked when you felt threatened. When you're at peace and are comfortable, your mind can relax and begin to think flexibly and broadly: to contemplate, consider options, and think more creatively. This can help you discover new, more effective ways of handling difficult situations, rather than being bound to the habits dictated by the threat system. This is called *response flexibility*, and growing scientific evidence indicates that the nurturing, attachment interactions that are at the core of the safeness system may actually activate and promote growth in brain areas that help us to have this flexibility.[12]

Considering all this, we can see the safeness system as a balancing influence in relation to the threat and drive systems. We can learn to stimulate our soothing systems in order to slow ourselves down and consider situations more broadly: "Am I really in danger, or are there alternative explanations I haven't considered?" This broader perspective allows us to consider whether we really *need* that thing we're pursuing and if it's really true that we can't be happy without it. This system can help calm the storm of anger. It can give us the freedom to consider not just the threat or desire of the moment, but also larger questions: "What sort of person do I want to be, and how do

I go about becoming my best self?" "What can I do to take good care of the people I love?" "How can I create the conditions in my life that will lead to these things?"

Exercise 2.3: Examining the Safeness Response

Try to remember a time when you felt safe and completely comfortable. If you can't recall a time like that, close your eyes for a moment and imagine what it would feel like to be completely at ease, content, and safe.

- What emotions were you experiencing? How did it feel? What were your physical sensations?

- Consider your attention. What did you pay attention to? What did you focus on? Was your focus broad or narrow?

- What were you thinking about? How did your thoughts relate to your emotional experience?

- What sort of imagery or fantasy did you see in your mind?

- What was your motivation like? What did you want to do?

- What sort of behavior did you engage in?

Contrasting the Threat and Safeness Responses

When we are under the influence of the threat system (for example, caught up in anger):

- We experience threatening emotions like anger and fear.

- Our thoughts and attention are focused on sources of potential threats.

- We have bodily sensations of arousal and tension, and when anger lingers, we can experience pain, stomach upset, headaches, and sleep disruption.

- We see few options—our attention narrows, and we may feel trapped or stuck on a track that we can't get off of.

- We have a hard time seeking aid from others, because we're on the defensive and may feel isolated.

When we are balanced and our safeness system is active:

- We still experience negative emotions but are not overwhelmed by them.

- We have a better, broader perspective and a sense of confidence about being able to work with our threat and drive systems.

- We can experience physical relaxation and are able to work with our bodies to release tension.

- We can think flexibly, seeing many options. We can consider different ways of working with difficult situations and decide which is best.

- We feel connected with others and can access them for help or support.

CONCLUSION

When we consider our emotions in terms of these three emotion-regulation systems—the three circles—we can begin to understand anger from a broader perspective. If we consider how these emotion-regulation systems evolved, we can begin to understand why our emotions work the way they do. The threat system works to protect us, so that we can survive in the face of danger. The drive and resource acquisition system activates and rewards us for pursuing resources, mates, and social status, and keeps us working so that we can obtain what we need and fulfil our goals. Finally, the safeness system shapes us to form close, nurturing relationships with our loved ones, helps us to relax when threats are gone and the work is done, and works to balance the effects of the other two systems.

Our problems with threat-related emotions like anger occur when the systems become unbalanced. In chapter 3, we'll look at how this can happen and explore why some of us have difficulties with anger while other people don't seem to. We'll explore the ways that we can differ from one another that can impact our experience of anger. Understanding these differences can help us let go of the shaming and blaming that often go with anger, freeing ourselves up to deal with our anger more effectively—and with compassion.

3

When Things Become Unbalanced

In the preceding chapter we explored the "three circles": the threat and self-protection system, the drive and resource acquisition system, and the safeness system. We saw how these three emotion-regulation systems serve different purposes and interact with one another to shape our experience of life and how our emotional health depends on the balance between them. In this chapter, we'll look at a number of ways that the three circles can become unbalanced, leading to problems with anger and difficulties in finding more effective and positive ways of feeling, thinking, and behaving.

EVOLVED BRAINS IN THE MODERN WORLD

As we have seen, our threat system has a "better safe than sorry" default setting that works to protect us and organizes our brains around defending ourselves. The drive and resource acquisition system motivates us to obtain the things we need to survive and prosper: to pursue mates, reproduce, and acquire, accumulate, and defend our resources. In comparison, the safeness system may seem to serve an important but often neglected role.

CHASING IMBALANCE

Research shows that we may be creating imbalances in our emotion systems through the way we choose to go about our lives. Over time, rates of depression and anxiety have increased in young people, and one explanation for this shift seems to be that we are neglecting time to relax and engage in meaningful relationships with others in favor of pursuing status and wealth.[1] Keep in mind that our feelings of safeness are commonly conveyed and received when we experience connectedness with other people—when we share and receive feelings of warmth and feel accepted and valued. Jean Twenge and W. Keith Campbell wrote about this in *The Narcissism Epidemic: Living in the Age of Enlightenment*, arguing that changes in mental health and well-being are linked with reductions in community values and an increase in competitive, self-focused pursuits.[2] It's easy to get caught up in chasing after more money, status, and material possessions, and there are myriad cultural messages telling us that this is the way to be happy—what Australian epidemiologist (someone who studies patterns of disease and health in populations of people) Richard Eckersley calls "cultural fraud."[3] By believing in these cultural messages and emphasizing achievement over connectedness with those around us, we may be setting ourselves up for just the sort of imbalances that can drive our anger problems.

One of the difficulties with the drive and resource acquisition system is that it can be easily frustrated, which can send us right back into the threat system. We can feel constantly under pressure to acquire and defend our social position or to protect ourselves from criticism or rejection. It's easy to be worried about losing our jobs or about things going wrong for us, particularly in troubling economic times. When our threat system or drive system is running all the time, the safeness system, based on building and experiencing good relationships with others, may not have much input into the regulation of our emotions. Additionally, our culture has developed in such a way that our threat and drive systems are activated by many experiences that have little to do with our survival[4]: we are constantly being presented with potential sources of threat and advertisements that are specifically designed to stimulate our desires. However, most of the threats we face in modern life don't physically endanger us. Many of us have also learned to crave things that contribute little to our survival or happiness (a fact my wife likes to remind me of when I'm eager to buy yet another electric guitar). Many of our problems arise from having brains and bodies that seem designed to deal with the world faced by our Neolithic ancestors. They seem poorly adapted for life in the modern world, now filled with a much greater variety of potential "threats"—threats that our old-brain threat systems are ill-equipped to handle.

WHY ME?

So far, we've explored where our anger comes from and how our threat and drive systems can lead us to have difficulties with it. We may find ourselves wondering why some of us have such difficulty managing our anger while others don't seem to. It makes sense to wonder: *If it's not my fault because all our brains are constructed to turn on the light switch of anger under certain conditions, why do some people struggle with anger while other people don't?* Let's explore some potential answers to this question.

Temperament and Our Early Interactions

We have explored how we have no choice or influence over many of the factors that affect our emotional development and our abilities to regulate our emotions. For example, you have no say over the characteristics you're born with, such as your temperament. If you've spent any time with babies, you'll know they can differ greatly in terms of how happy or irritable they tend to be: some babies seem contented almost all of the time; others appear irritable, fussy, and exhausting to be around.

Your temperament is colored by your genetic makeup, which influences how you experience the world and how you interact with it. While the scientific discussion of temperament is far from settled, it's clear that we differ from one another in many different ways that appear shortly after we are born. Examples of differences include the ways our brains and bodies work (our hormonal activity, heart rate, electrical activity in the brain), our activity level (how active we tend to be), our level of self-control (how patient or impulsive we tend to be), our ability to concentrate and focus, our sensitivity and adaptability to changes in our environment, and the ways we experience happiness and emotional distress, to name just a few.[5]

Since babies have a difficult time *telling* us exactly how they feel, much of what we know about them comes from observing their behavior. Some babies get worked up over the slightest temperature change or frustration over dropping a toy out of reach; other babies can seem fairly placid by comparison. Some babies cry and fuss all the time, while others seem calm and collected. Some seem impossible to comfort, while others snuggle in and go right to sleep. Some are picky eaters, while others happily gobble down anything placed in their mouths.

These traits immediately begin to shape the environments in which we are raised. Imagine two babies, one fitting the "fussy" descriptions above and the other fitting the "good-tempered" descriptions. Consider how the behavior of these babies, acting out their given temperaments, impacts the world around them. Which baby would be more likely to receive the most coddling and nurturing, the loving contact that will stimulate their safeness systems and help them learn that the world is a safe place and that their needs will be met? Which would be more likely to be treated harshly, to have adults raise their voices to them, set them down abruptly, ignore them, or otherwise activate and shape their threat systems to become even more sensitive? Even during the earliest moments in our lives, one set of factors that we have no control over (our genetic makeup and related temperament) interacts with other factors that we have no control over (how our care-takers react to us) to shape the experiences of our lives, and even the ways that our infant brains develop.

Exercise 3.1: Exploring Individual Differences

Consider your own temperament and personality. Remembering that you don't choose many aspects of how you respond to the world, consider the following questions:

- Are you easygoing or easily frustrated? What feelings emerge in you when things don't go your way?

- Do you like it when there are many things going on at once, or are you easily overwhelmed, preferring quiet time to yourself?

- Do you like being around lots of people? Or do you prefer being with just a few close friends?

- Do you like to try out new experiences (for example, new dishes at a restaurant), or do you prefer to stick with what you're familiar with?

- Would you say that you tend to be set in your way of thinking, or are you flexible, thinking "outside the box"?

- Do you like surprises, or do you prefer things to be stable and predictable?

These are just a few of the many ways that we tend to differ. By being familiar with your own characteristics, tendencies, and preferences, you can be more aware of your comfort zones and of situations that may tend to trigger your threat systems (and your anger).

The *playing field is not level.* Some of us are born with certain temperaments that are more likely to have difficulty handling emotions like anger, so we have fewer opportunities to acquire the skills and insights for handling them. This doesn't excuse us from needing to manage our emotions, by the way; it just means we'll probably need to put more purposeful effort into doing so (for example, by reading this book). This is because we may not have had as many opportunities as others to come by these skills naturally or to acquire them by observing others. Our ability to regulate our emotions largely develops through our relationships with others, in particular our caretakers. This second factor, our relationships with our caretakers, merits its own section.

Attachment and Emotion Regulation

Your early relationships are incredibly important in shaping your ability to regulate emotions such as anger.[6] Research shows that the relationships we have with our primary caregivers have huge effects on our development, particularly very early in our lives. These interactions stimulate our brains when we are still only babies, when our young brains are growing and developing at a phenomenally quick rate. An oft-repeated phrase in neuroscience circles is "cells that fire together, wire together." When we're stimulated in various ways (for example, being held and stroked by our mothers), the cells in our brains fire together in particular patterns and form connections that are strengthened every time the pattern is activated. What this means is that *the more often a particular pattern of brain cells is activated, the easier it is for that pattern to be activated in the future.* The pattern becomes more "worn in," sort of like a path in the woods that we have walked on over and over. Our experiences, in combination with our genetic tendencies, create paths of least resistance in our brains, shaping our future reactions and perceptions of the world. In babies, this effect is magnified by the fact that the basic organization of their brains is still being shaped—the interconnections between cells in a baby's brain are growing rapidly in response to stimulation coming in from the outside world. This stimulation (for example, from being nurtured) impacts the development of key structures of the brain itself. One area of the brain that is influenced by the affection and caring we receive as infants is the frontal cortex, which is where we regulate the powerful emotions that arise from our old brains. It also influences our ability to experience empathy—to understand our own emotions and the emotions of others.[7, 8]

For now, let's imagine what is happening in a baby's brain when her mother is playing with her, perhaps making kind or funny facial expressions that cause the baby to smile back or giggle. This baby's brain is buzzing with the activity of positive emotion, and pathways are lighting up that reflect this experience and feelings of connectedness with her mother. Next, let's imagine that the baby is distressed and that her mother picks her up, strokes her gently, and speaks softly to her—the baby begins to calm down. By comforting and soothing her, the mother stimulates the child's safeness system, which begins to turn down the volume of her threat response. Over time, the child will begin to form soothing mental representations of herself and her mother as she is being cared for. She'll also create representations of help being available when she needs it. Both of these forms of representation will be available to call upon when she needs to soothe *herself.* Research increasingly shows that our brains are shaped and changed by the ways that our parents care for and soothe us—or by the ways that they don't.[9]

Let's consider another scenario. Imagine a depressed or irritable mother who has a great deal of stress in her life and very little support. Imagine that she doesn't have much energy or interest in stimulating joyful interactions between herself and her baby, perhaps because she's exhausted after working several double shifts to support their small family. Instead, she just wants a moment of peace. When this mother hears her baby's cry, she feels overwhelmed and responds with frustration and irritation. We can imagine that when her baby is distressed, instead of comforting him, this mother might leave him alone or pick him up roughly. How might this baby's brain be stimulated in ways that are very different from the brain of the baby girl we discussed previously, and what was she gaining that he might miss out on? While she learned that comfort would be there when she needed it, he learned that his cries would be ignored or met with harshness. While she learned that she could call upon others to help soothe her when she's upset, he learned that no such help would be available. Her brain was stimulated by the action of another person appropriately responding to her emotional experience. He gained no such appropriate response and may have felt punished for displaying his emotions at all. If we imagine the stories of these children's lives playing out over hundreds or thousands of similar interactions, we can see how their brains and their emotional development could be shaped in very different ways—ways for which each child is entirely blameless.

The purpose of observing these differences in care and responsiveness isn't to blame or credit caregivers, who have also been shaped by their own experiences and environments. We can understand the stress the second mother faces—that it might make it almost impossible to give her son the nurturing he needs and that, in fact, she needs such nurturing herself. We can imagine how the differences in these parents' own backgrounds shaped their ability to connect with their children. Evidence shows that our own attachment histories (and how we make sense of them in our minds) can profoundly affect our ability to form nurturing, secure attachments with our own children.[10]

Secure-attachment relationships involve caretakers who give us warm, loving, safe, and predictable environments and who engage us in ways that mirror our own emotional responses. This sort of environment gives our developing brains exactly what they need and sets the stage for us to be able to handle difficult emotions in the future. Alternatively, when our early relationships involve caretakers who are disconnected, overreactive, underreactive, inconsistent or scary, it can affect the developing brain's capacity to help us regulate our emotions, potentially impairing our ability to form healthy connections with others and to nurture our own children. Such an environment can tune our threat systems so that they are almost always on, and it can feel as if we are alone and vulnerable in a scary world, with no reliable source of safety or help. There are a number of excellent books devoted to this subject, and I have listed some of them in the appendix.

Next, there are some questions designed to help you explore your own relationship history. Doing this may help you begin to understand yourself better and understand a bit about the development of your anger; however, it may also stir up painful feelings. If you find that the exercise is too difficult right now, feel free to skip it and return to it later, after we've covered some skills for working with difficult emotions. Sometimes, when we start digging into our pasts, we uncover painful memories that can cause us great distress. If this is the case for you, I'd like to encourage you to get support and perhaps to even think about talking with a therapist. We all need help sometimes, and knowing when to get it is an important part of working with our emotions.

Exercise 3.2: Exploring Attachment

Consider your memories of your early relationships with your caretakers. How might they have shaped your experience of life?

- Whom did you feel close to while you were growing up?

- What did you do when you were upset? Whom could you turn to?

- Did your parents or caretakers help you to feel safe? Were they able to help you calm down when you were upset?

- Do you recall your parents or caretakers getting angry? What was it like when they were angry? How did you feel at those times?

- Did you have a consistent group of caretakers? Did the same people care for you throughout your childhood, or were there changes in terms of the people who cared for you?

- How do you think that your experiences with your parents or caretakers may have affected your adult personality?

- If you plan on having children, how would you describe the sort of relationship you'd like to have with them?

IF YOU DIDN'T GET WHAT YOU NEEDED

As we've seen, anger is a threat response that has evolved to protect us and that can take control when we feel as if we are in danger. To examine and uncover the story behind your anger might be difficult and painful because you may have grown up in environments where you rarely felt safe. You may even have been abused or traumatized. You may have had caretakers who weren't able to handle their own anger, or who couldn't respond to you in ways that would help you feel safe, cared for, and valued. You may have learned to use anger as a response to difficulty because that was how your caretakers related to you. Likewise, you may have learned to push others away in an effort to feel safe because there were no other options available and no one else there to protect you emotionally. You needed a way to protect yourself, and you found one: anger. You may feel a lot of shame about different parts of your life, and you may find yourself using anger to cover up this feeling of shame.

This realization can be heartbreaking. But if you can allow yourself to experience the pain of the heartbreak, you may be able to see your anger as a cry for help from the vulnerable part of you that desperately needs to feel safe, secure, and valued. You're going to learn how to help yourself feel safe, to soothe your threat system, and to replace your angry, knee-jerk responses to threat with compassionate responses that will help you to protect yourself, have good relationships, and lead a happy life. This is hard work, and I want you to know that my heart goes out to you. I respect the courage you're showing in doing this and the effort it involves. You are worthy of this effort. You are worthy of compassion.

LEARNING TO BE ANGRY

Now let's look at three different types of learning.

Classical Conditioning

The human brain is a learning machine. As we go through our lives, our brains are constantly linking different things together so that we learn to associate different feelings with different situations, different behavior with different perceptions we have. When you hear chirping from above, you know it's a bird. When you look out the window and see snow or rain, you know to grab a jacket on your way out the door. Our brains are forming these sorts of connections *all the time*; it's the way they make sense of the world so that we can function more efficiently in our lives. It's also the way our emotional lives work.

We are very good at learning to associate particular sounds, sights, smells, and feelings with *emotional* reactions. For example, a dog isn't born afraid of rolled-up newspapers. But if it's been hit with one a few times, it rapidly learns to fear them. Many things naturally provoke responses in us. Seeing or smelling food we enjoy causes us to salivate. Seeing attractive people can cause us to feel aroused. We naturally experience fear of, and anxiety about, things that can harm us or threaten our social standing. And we naturally experience anger when we're faced with having our progress blocked, when we're challenged or perceive that we're being attacked. When these experiences are paired with people, places, and situations, our brains link them together. When this happens, those previously neutral people, places, and situations can acquire the power to provoke reactions in us— arousal, anxiety, anger, and so on. This process is called *classical conditioning*, and when it involves our threat system, it is a very efficient and powerful form of learning.

With classical conditioning, our brains connect innocent aspects of our experience—a song (even if it's merely playing in the background), a phrase, or an internal experience—with the emotions we feel at the time (terror, anger, heartbreak). Then, the next time we come in contact with the song, phrase, or experience, those same emotions come rushing forth. More often than not, this type of learning isn't conscious: we aren't aware that we're learning associations between things. But whether we're aware of them or not, these connections are constantly being stored in our brains, shaping the way we understand the world, and ready to be activated by our future experience. If the same story gets written into the brain many times, it can be pretty hard to erase it or to change it's meaning.

This form of emotional learning can create real difficulties in our relationships. For example, imagine that you are in a relationship that is undergoing conflict and unsettling interactions—there will be periods of difficulty in any long-term human relationship. The problem comes when the two people involved have lots of negative interactions and very few positive ones. We can think of it as a scale, with positive interactions on one side and negative interactions on the other. When the relationship scale is consistently tipped in the negative direction, over time we *learn to associate the other person with the negative emotions we feel during our conflicts.* So, if you have lots of angry interactions with your partner or with your child, your brain learns to associate that person with the experience of anger. It's as if your old brain (in particular, the amygdala) puts a big sign on that other person's forehead that says, "Threat!" What's more, we're generally not aware that this is happening or that it's already happened. So when you next see that person, even if it's on an otherwise good day without any reasons to have conflict with him, you can find yourself becoming angry.

Imagine that you have a thirteen-year-old son who has been acting out at school and has become belligerent when you've tried to deal with the situation—repeatedly. You've had lots of conflict with him recently, and he's begun to avoid you (as adolescents sometimes do avoid us), so you haven't interacted with him outside of the arguments. Imagine next that he comes home one day, walks in the door, and says, "(Mom or Dad), I need to talk with you about something." Now, he could be about to talk with you about anything, but how do you feel? What thoughts spring to mind? For many of us, it would be easy to react automatically with anger, anticipating *yet another* problem and perhaps sharply saying something like, "What is it *now?*" You can imagine that the interaction would go downhill from there.

So, when you've had lots of negative interactions with another person and very few positive ones, it can train your brain in a certain way—putting into motion a cycle that sets you up for more difficulties. You learn to associate that person with the angry conflicts, so that when you see him (or some other aspect of your experience that you've come to associate with conflict), your amygdala begins to activate your body's threat response. Then, you start to *feel* angry, even when there's nothing to be angry about. And as your new brain observes what is happening in your body, it looks for ways to explain what's going on. You start *looking for* reasons that will justify your anger—and when you've been having conflict with another person, you can usually find those reasons. The result? Yet another conflict, manufactured out of thin air, which serves to strengthen the connection your brain has learned between the other person and your anger. Over time, your son can become "that kid who's always causing problems" in your mind (even as you become "the overbearing parent who's always mad at me" in his mind). It can be a hard cycle to break.

This is how our brains work. When we are in a relationship with someone, she *will* learn to associate us with certain emotions, just as we will learn to do with her. The only question is, what emotions will she associate us with? As a parent, partner, friend, or colleague, do you want to stimulate the other person's threat system, or would you rather she learn to associate you with feelings of safeness, acceptance, and kindness? Which do you think gives you more power to affect that person's life in positive ways? Which do you think will bring about the sort of relationship that is more likely to stimulate your own safeness system?

Modeling and Observational Learning

There are other types of learning that can occur without our being aware of it. If we grow up in a situation where we see anger in action (for example, with a parent who yells, screams, or becomes aggressive), we may learn to respond in similar ways. Many of us intuitively know this, as we observe ourselves acting out the same irritating behaviors our parents used to do (the very things that drove us crazy when we were growing up!). This is called *modeling, observational learning,* or *social learning.*[11]

We learn by observing others, and this is particularly true when we're observing our caretakers, whom we look to as we attempt to discover how to interact with the world. If our caretakers displayed lots of impulsive anger, became easily frustrated, or were quick to become verbally or physically aggressive—well, it's easy for us to learn these behaviors too (and then to pass them on to our own children). We can learn to respond with anger simply by observing others doing so—we don't even have to be involved in the situation.

This is a common experience for people who have difficulties with anger. Time and time again, I've listened to clients describe their parents' anger: yelling, screaming, hitting, and throwing things. In the next breath, these same clients would look down to the ground as they described doing the same things themselves. If you're a parent, this can lead to a new problem: feeling anxious about losing control and teaching your own children the angry behaviors that you wish you'd never learned from your own parents. In one of our anger management groups, the majority of men reported that the most common criticism they'd received from their partners about their parenting wasn't about their anger or harshness—it was about their *unwill-ingness* to discipline their children. Every single one of them said that they had fears of disciplining their kids because they were afraid of teaching them the wrong lessons. One man even said that he had decided to never have children: "I know I'd just screw them up."

In fact, this concern was the basis of my desire to work with my own anger. I wanted to become the sort of person I hoped my child would grow up to be—to use the power of modeling to teach my son things that would help him as he makes his way through life rather than hinder him. We didn't get to choose the lessons our parents taught us, but we *do* have a choice about what we teach our own children (and everyone else we come into contact with in our lives, as we all learn through our interactions with one another). This is a good reason to take responsibility for your anger; just as you weren't able to choose who your caretakers were, your children usually won't get to choose their caretakers, either.

Learning Anger through Consequences: Reinforcement and Punishment

Another reason that we may learn problematic anger behaviors is that sometimes, in the short run, they work. If you sock the bully in the nose, sometimes he leaves you alone. If you scream at your fussy child, she sometimes becomes quiet. If you are aggressive toward critical colleagues, they'll sometimes back off. As children, we may find ourselves being praised for lashing out by parents who have problems with anger themselves ("Oh, he's all boy!"; "You're just like your mother!"). When we do something that seems to work, even if it's just in the short term (and despite the problems in the long term), we will naturally tend to repeat the strategy. This is how reinforcement works—behaviors that are followed by a reward will tend to be repeated.

On the other hand, if your expression of anger is met with negative consequences, you may learn to fear becoming angry. Behavioral psychologist C. B. Ferster noted that if children are consistently punished for being angry, they will learn to *suppress* angry behaviors rather than learn to express anger in appropriate ways.[12] In these cases, the child can learn to associate the internal experience of anger (and the urge to act on it) with the expectation of punishment and anxiety about being punished. Over time, feelings of anger may automatically trigger anxiety and various behaviors the child develops to cover up her anger (like fingernail-chewing or just shutting down). When we're caught in a cycle like this, we can end up being passive, easily overwhelmed, and unable to behave assertively and stick up for ourselves when we need to.[13]

Whether we learn to cope by acting out our anger or by locking it away, over time these responses can become habitual, especially if they are the only coping strategies we have. It's like the old saying, "If all you have is a hammer, then everything looks like a nail." We keep trying to use that hammer because it feels like it should work. But in the long term, these habitual strategies can keep us from learning to deal with our feelings. We don't choose to use ineffective strategies; it's simply that we're using the only ones we know. We cling to them because, sometimes, they seem to work. But it's time now to learn new strategies that work better.

Exercise 3.3: Exploring Anger and Learning

Consider what you learned about anger from interacting with your caretakers and from your own experience as you were growing up.

- What did you learn about anger from your caretakers?

- What did you learn about *when* you should become angry?

- How did you learn to behave when you are angry? How do you interact with others when you are angry?

- How do you feel after your anger subsides? What do you do when the situation is over?

- How has your anger worked well for you in the past? How did it benefit you?

- How has your anger not worked for you? What negative consequences have you faced because of it?

We can begin to see how problems can arise from difficult relationship experiences with our caretakers combined with a learning history that shapes us to feel anger easily and to express it in unhelpful ways. Wade was one of the participants in our very first compassion-focused anger-management group at the prison. He described his home life as being characterized by the "beating of the day," which was doled out for any reason or for no reason at all. He grew up watching his father beat his mother and his siblings, and Wade was often beaten himself. He was haunted and shamed by the fact that he had been helpless to stop it. As you might suspect, Wade didn't learn how to regulate his emotions, and his threat system was poised on a hair trigger. As he grew up, he began to fly off the handle at the slightest provocation, violently attacking others just as he had experienced his father doing so many times. To Wade, aggression sprang forth automatically—it didn't even feel as if he had a choice.

Wade's anger ruled his life, and his prison convictions had all been for violent offenses. At first he was reluctant to change, as his reputation for violence meant that people left him alone. In this way his aggressive anger seemed to work for him, at least in the prison environment. Wade ultimately came to our group because he hoped to have a better life, to be a better father. He didn't want to spend the rest of his life in prison, and he didn't want to teach those lessons to his children. I remember Wade in the first session, looking at me as if he thought I was crazy as I talked about compassion as a way to work with anger. Now, Wade talks about compassion as a strength and has made great changes in the way he is seen by others, in the way he sees himself, and in the ways he handles his anger. We'll learn a bit more about Wade's story later in the book.

IMPLICIT MEMORY AND THE CONSTRUCTION OF "REALITY"

The automatic way that Wade's anger seemed to take control of him isn't uncommon. Once all of the learning has taken place, the way it is stored in our brains helps to shape the way we perceive and interact with the world. This learning is largely stored as "implicit" memory. Next I'll briefly define that term and it's opposite: "explicit" memory.

First, let's look at *explicit* memory, which refers to memories of facts, events, and ourselves. Also called "narrative" memory, recalling explicit memories is something we're aware of doing, and we can recount what it is that we've remembered. When you say, "I remember _____," whatever comes after the word "remember" is an example of explicit memory. You can remember it and describe it, and you are aware that what you're dealing with is a memory.

Implicit memory is a bit more difficult to describe. It involves a range of experiences and associations that are stored in the brain, by the brain, so that we can make sense of the world. Implicit memory includes things like the emotional reactions and bodily responses that we learn (and which we discussed a bit in the section on classical conditioning). When we sense the same smell as the food we got sick on two weeks ago and then feel a bit nauseated, that's implicit memory. When we play a chord we've practiced on guitar or piano and our fingers go straight to all the right places, that's implicit memory. When we see the person we argued with yesterday walk by in the hall and our stomachs tense up, that's implicit memory. All of the examples we used in the classical conditioning section play out in terms of implicit memory.

Unlike explicit memory, which we use when we intentionally remember something, with implicit memory there is no sensation that we are recalling anything—intentionally or not. It's like when you ride a bike: you don't have the sense that you're *remembering* how to ride (although that's just what our muscles are doing); you just have the experience of riding. When you get on the bike, the parts of your brain that are associated with bikes are activated, and this includes your memory of how to ride. So you climb on the bike and take off, never aware that your ability to do so is an experience that you've pulled up out of your implicit memory. When you remember how to kick a football, sew a particular type of stitch, or type on a computer, you are experiencing implicit memory. However, you usually don't experience it as *remembering*—you're just doing whatever it is that you're doing.[14]

It's the same way with emotional learning. When you smell the fragrance that your first love used to wear, you may experience a surge of emotions (depending on how things went in that relationship!). Your experience is one of *feeling*, but it's driven by your implicit memory—the connections your brain has laid down between your emotions and your sensory experiences. When you're presented with one piece of the puzzle, your brain naturally (and without your awareness) brings up the others. Sometimes you may also have conscious (explicit) awareness when this is happening, as in "I know I feel sad when I hear that song, because I remember hearing it on the radio the night we broke up." Often, however, you just experience it as "what I'm feeling right now" without understanding that much of what you are experiencing right now is actually *an echo of your previous experience*.

When I first really thought about what this meant, it blew me away. We tend to think that what we are experiencing right now—the information coming in through our senses—is *reality*. But actually, our sensory experience is just one part of what makes up our perception of the present moment. Our experience of reality at any moment in time is actually a combination of information coming *in* from our senses and information coming *down* from our implicit memories of similar situations in the past. Then this combination is *selectively filtered and pieced together* by those parts of our brains that deal with sense and emotion. Emotional memories laid down in the past can color our experience of the current moment and organize our minds in certain ways as we participate in the present.

Our implicit memory influences how we feel in response to the present, what aspects of the environment we attend to, and how we expect things to go—all of which helps to shape how we behave. Like I said, it's similar to a puzzle that our brains are trying frantically to put together by grabbing all the pieces that seem to fit in order to create a "reality" that makes sense to us. However, sometimes they force together pieces that don't really fit, and this can create interesting problems when combined with our sensitive threat systems. People and situations we've got no real reason to be angry with can trigger our threat response, because they have characteristics that our brains have connected with anger in the past—they may look, speak, or otherwise remind us of someone who treated us badly earlier in our lives, for example. In the moment we encounter them or interact with them, we can feel anger or irritation toward them. The emotion arises with our having little awareness that the anger has little to do with these people or the situation and everything to do with our pasts. We generally can't prevent this from happening, as it's just how our brains work. But once we're aware that it is happening (and it happens a lot), we can have some compassion for the others in the situation. It's *not their fault* that their behavior is stirring up all this learning from our past (even if they *are* being thoughtless or rude). We can also have some compassion for ourselves as well, reminding ourselves that it isn't *our fault* that our brains work like this, either. This awareness also gives us something else: an opportunity. If we can notice our shifts in mood and become aware that our tricky brains have allowed our threat systems to get rolling, we can do something about it.

TRIGGERS

This chapter has two purposes. The first is to help you begin to understand why you might have difficulties with anger when other people don't seem to. This understanding will come as you learn more about your attachment history, explore how you might have learned anger through your experiences, and recognize how this learning can play out in the present in the form of implicit memory. It's worth noting that you probably didn't choose any of these factors that contribute to your anger; but chosen or not, it's our job to deal with the anger and how it plays out in our lives. That's the second purpose—to help you begin developing awareness of the factors that cause *your* anger so that you can take on the job of working with it. Part of doing this is getting to know what may "trigger" your anger—what things may push your buttons or provoke you. You've learned to respond to these triggers with anger, and as you go through this book, you'll be learning alternate ways to respond to them that don't have the negative consequences that anger does. Let's take a moment to consider the things that trigger your anger.

Exercise 3.4: Exploring Anger Triggers

Think about the times when people or situations push your buttons. What sorts of things trigger your anger?

- When do you tend to get angry in your dealings with other people?

- What sorts of situations tend to trigger your anger?

FAULT AND RESPONSIBILITY

Several times in this book so far, I've stated that it is not your fault that you struggle with anger. If you're like me, you may have a hard time accepting this. I remember the first compassion focused therapy training I attended, when I heard Paul Gilbert talk about how many of our troublesome emotional reactions *weren't our fault*. I got a bit of a knot in my stomach, and I remember thinking, *Well, perhaps this is just a small part of the model...I can overlook this bit and take away the good stuff.* But over the course of the three-day training, he kept saying it over and over. As we continued through the training, I began to realize that this "It's not your fault" business wasn't just an aside; it was a core part of the Compassionate-Mind model and is a core part of the therapy model that flows from it (CFT).

Initially, I didn't like it. I mean, I'm not as familiar with how things work in the rest of the world, but I'm *American*, and if there is one thing we Americans are good at, it's assigning blame. "Not my fault? Well, whose fault is it? Because it's got to be *somebody's* fault!" Sadly for people in other parts of the world, it isn't just Americans who do this. In Western culture at least, we seem to be very good at assigning blame and shaming ourselves and other people, and this seems especially true with anger. It seems we are either blaming those who provoke our anger or shaming ourselves for having it. As I listened to Paul say, "It's not your fault," over and over, our tendency for blaming made sense to me. Again, it's got to be somebody's fault that we get angry, doesn't it?

Well, not so much. After giving it some thought and looking at the ways that our anger works, I truly believe that our anger really *isn't* our fault. Neither is it the fault of whoever or whatever provoked it. Yes, I'm a convert, and I'll try to explain the reasons why. What we mean when we say, "It's not your fault," is "It's not helpful to blame and shame yourself for things you didn't choose or for processes you didn't design." There are many factors that led to the way we experience and express our anger, very few of which were chosen by us or were under our control. I would argue that even the conscious decisions we make and the behaviors that we purposefully engage in when angry are not a sign of some fundamental flaw in us. As I discussed a bit earlier, when we're angry, even our decision-making and reasoning abilities can be impaired by our threat system as it narrows our vision and directs our thoughts in the attempt to protect us from real or imagined dangers.

I'm betting that some of you may feel a bit doubtful and resistant right now, and that a few others might be thinking, *This is all well and good, but…* You may find yourself wanting to argue against the idea that you're not to blame. You might even be getting a bit, well, angry. Perhaps that resistant feeling is based on the observation that, although you didn't choose your brain, your birth, your temperament, your childhood situation, or your caretakers, in fact you are reading this book because in your life, you've made some tragic choices. You've perhaps made choices that have harmed others and that have caused suffering for yourself and those you care about. But let me just say again: when we are fully in the grips of emotions like anger, when our threat systems have taken complete control of us, *we tend to make bad choices.* Our threat systems are good at producing misguided but powerful urges to protect ourselves, leading to flawed decisions—decisions made under conditions of significantly narrowed attention and a limited ability to think flexibly and solve problems. This is not an excuse. It is an observation.

This may be a difficult pill to swallow if you've learned other ways of relating to anger. Don't worry—I'm not letting you off the hook. There is a very important reason for the approach we're taking here. While it may seem strange to consider, the fact remains: if we stop shaming ourselves for experiencing anger, it frees us up to take responsibility for it. When we tell ourselves that our anger is somehow a reflection of something bad in us, we have two types of problems. We have the anger itself, but we also have the way the anger makes us feel about ourselves. When faced with this, it's easy to resort to blaming others; shaming ourselves; or ignoring, justifying, or rationalizing our anger. None of these reactions, driven by our deep fears about what our anger means about us, is helpful. In fact, shaming ourselves keeps us from working with our emotions in productive ways, because it keeps us focused on maintaining our self-image instead of working with the anger more effectively. When we stop beating ourselves up or pointing fingers, we will be better able to see clearly what needs to be done to improve our lives, and *to do it.*

I'm not saying that we aren't responsible for the decisions we've made when we're angry. Of course we are. If I'm careless and knock a cup of coffee all over my keyboard, which then causes my computer to blow up, it's only me that did that and it's my job to fix it. But blaming and shaming myself, getting angry, beating myself up, and then slamming about the house upsetting everybody else—these things just make the situation worse. Instead, we can learn to recognize what is happening, stay as calm as we can even though we're very frustrated, and try to be sympathetic to the difficulty. This then allows us to do the most important things—repair the damage we've done and learn to pay more attention next time. That is what I mean by "taking responsibility"—recognizing that our emotions can be very strongly aroused and learning how to work with them rather than letting them control us. So when I say that your anger isn't your fault, I'm not saying that it doesn't matter what you do. Rather, *it's precisely because* of all these factors you don't choose that you must work hard to understand yourself and take control of those things that you *can* change. As you will see, compassion creates the conditions for a profound sense of responsibility that arises naturally and is freely chosen, rather than being assigned or born of blame.

It also isn't particularly *useful* to get into a debate about things like fault or blame over the bad choices that we've made. The fact is that we've made them, and in this moment, we now have other choices to make. Are we going to devote our lives to the shame of having done those things or to blaming others for our bad choices? Are we going to endlessly debate whether or not those choices make us bad people? Or can we consider another choice, a choice to cultivate compassion toward the situation and everyone in it— toward ourselves, caught in the grip of an out-of-control threat response that we were unprepared to handle, and toward all those others who have experienced harm and emotional pain as a result of the situation and our anger? Can we allow ourselves to experience sorrow over the harm we've done and to channel that sorrow into making our best efforts to not do it again? Can we choose to work honestly, directly, and compassionately with our minds to change the habits and balance the emotions that led to those poor choices? Can we make better choices and commit ourselves to becoming the sort of people we want to be?

If you thought before you started reading this book that compassion is about something weak, soft, or fluffy—that it just means being nice all of the time—I hope you'll soon recognize that this isn't the case. Compassion involves making the difficult choices needed to take control of your mind and having the willingness to work directly with the thoughts and emotions that scare you the most. This takes determination, and it takes strength.

CONCLUSION

So far in reading this book, you've covered a fair bit of ground. You've explored anger, been introduced to a model of how your emotion-regulation systems work and interact, and explored a number of reasons why you've ended up having difficulties with anger. Hopefully, understanding these things can help you begin to overcome the emotional hurdles—the shame, self-criticism, and related avoidance—that may have hampered your previous attempts to work with your anger. You've also begun to look really closely at your anger so that you can understand where it comes from and the things that trigger it.

Going forward, you're going to learn a new way of organizing your mind. I will introduce ways that will help you work with the safeness system to restore balance to your emotions, so that your life isn't defined by anger or

controlled by your threat system or your drive system. You'll learn to cultivate compassion for yourself and for others, organize your mind in ways that
are strong enough to handle your difficulties, and put your focus squarely on
making life better for yourself and for those you care about. You'll learn skills
for cultivating this compassionate perspective that will help you become a
peacemaker—in your own life and in the world.

4

The Case for Compassion

The CFT approach to working with anger involves learning to organize our minds in different ways by developing what we call a "compassionate mind." In this chapter, we'll explore the meaning of "compassion" and discuss the mental qualities that we'll be developing as we learn to work with our anger.

THE HEART OF COMPASSION

As the Dalai Lama frequently points out, no one wants to suffer—we all just want to be happy.[1] So far, we've spent a good bit of time exploring how our anger can control us and that, despite our best efforts, we often find ourselves doing things that don't lead to happiness and actually produce the very suffering that we would prefer to avoid. But even these things we and others do—the ridiculous things, the irritating things, the maddening things—*these are all done in the attempt to be happy or to avoid suffering.*

Once we understand this, we can begin to see ourselves and other people differently. Thinking and meditating on this realization has long been a pathway to the development of compassion. Like it or not (and we usually don't like it), the normal course of a human life will involve tremendous suffering at various points: we will all become ill; we will all die;

we will all lose people we love; most of us will have our hearts broken—if not once, then several times; we will lose jobs; we will make mistakes that may have tragic consequences; and we will be faced with the reality that we all too often fall short of our expectations for ourselves. And we have to struggle with all of these challenges while equipped with tricky and often difficult human brains.

No one wakes up and decides, *I'm going to be an angry, miserable person today*. But often, we do things in the heat of anger and other emotions that cause us (and those around us) to be miserable. The key is to look upon our actions through the eyes of compassion, so that we can understand *why* we have behaved in such a way. Nevertheless, it can be hard to feel compassion for angry people—including ourselves!

One of my clients, Chris, was an adolescent referred for therapy because he had been fighting with others and had become hostile toward his care-takers, peers, and teachers. Chris had a hair-trigger temper, and he would often fly off the handle with little or no provocation. He was difficult to be around, as he became defensive and agitated so quickly that it was often impossible to have much of a conversation with him, even about random, neutral topics. He intentionally did things to irritate others, was a master at getting under your skin, and would frequently act aggressively. In short, he was easy to dislike. However, as I got to know Chris and established some trust with him (which took a while), I began to understand a few things about him. He lived with his grandparents because his parents had abused him and then ultimately abandoned him. Despite this, he was very protective of his parents and would speak no ill word against them. He often said that other people were not to be trusted and would hurt you if given the chance. He expressed deep fears of being abandoned, even as he pushed others away with his hostile and irritating behaviors (because, if you didn't trust people, they couldn't disappoint you). His anger was unpredictable and seemed to hit him out of the blue—once it kicked in, Chris felt out of control. He tried to turn this to his advantage, though. He took pride in his ability to fight well and said to me that it was the only thing he was good at. He was proud to consider himself one of the kids whom no one wanted to mess with.

When I took a closer look at Chris through the eyes of compassion, I could see how his behavior, however misguided, emerged from the combination of his background, his biological response to perceived threats, and the desire to protect himself, pursue happiness, and minimize suffering in his life. We also can see that the ways he attempted to protect himself actually created more suffering for him by driving away those people who might have been able to care for him and creating obstacles at home and at school.

It's easy to dismiss someone like Chris as a bully or a jerk—too easy. The difficult thing to do is to stop seeing Chris as "that irritating kid" and begin seeing him as a valuable human being who learned to cope with the very difficult life he had been born into (which was not the life that he or any of us would have chosen). The coping strategies he learned to protect himself came at the cost of his happiness. My role as a therapist was to help him learn to cope with his difficult life and his angry emotions in ways that wouldn't alienate him from everyone around him—ways that would work better for him and that might allow him to find happiness and contentment.

As challenging as it can be to feel compassion for others who are pushing our buttons and making us angry, it can be even *more difficult* to extend it to ourselves. This is particularly true when we see ourselves doing things that are harmful to our own lives and to people we care about. It's difficult to face and accept that we've caused such harm, but we must do this if we want to change. This is where compassion comes in—it helps us to have the courage to face those things in our lives that are most painful and to be kinder to ourselves as we go through the process of change. Compassion, as we've seen, isn't pink and fluffy. It isn't about just being sweet and nice all the time. It involves running into the fire to save the child, not running away and pretending that danger doesn't exist. In the case of this book, the fire is our anger, and the child is us.

SO WHAT EXACTLY IS COMPASSION?

The word *compassion* comes from a combination of two root words: *com*, meaning "together" and *pati*, meaning "to suffer."[2] Common definitions of compassion include two components, each of which is crucial. The first part is that compassion involves having sensitivity to suffering—noticing it and experiencing an emotional reaction when we are exposed to it. I like to define compassion as being moved by suffering and being motivated to help. I like the term "moved" because it evokes a sense of being *personally affected*—we are touched by the suffering; it affects us in a way that creates an emotional connection to the being that suffers (even when that being is me).

This brings us to the second component of compassion, which is the kind motivation to help. When we feel compassionate, we don't just passively observe someone as they suffer; rather, we want to do something about it.

Compassion, like anger, directs us toward the difficulty rather than away from it. With anger, the desire is to overcome, destroy, or punish. With compassion, we are sensitive to suffering and have a corresponding desire to be kind and understanding, and to somehow make things better—to help, or at least not to harm.

If compassion only involved sensitivity to suffering, it might have a lot in common with depression. If all we had was an emotional connection with suffering without the inspiring motivation to help, we could find ourselves wallowing in the negativity of the world and overwhelmed by the difficulties of life. That wouldn't be particularly helpful. To use a real-life example, this might be like swimming in the pain of a terrible breakup and refusing to ever enter another relationship because of the fear of being hurt.

On the other hand, if compassion included only kindness or being nice all the time, it would seem a lot like Pollyanna—dressed up in a pretty dress, naïvely repeating how wonderful life is, offering easy but superficial solutions while refusing to acknowledge the pain and difficulties we are faced with. Being kind and motivated to help without an understanding of the reality of suffering can lead to naïve avoidance or quick-and-dirty attempts to smooth things over that never really address the true difficulties of life. An example of this might be to hook up with someone else the day after that painful breakup or attempting to mask the feelings of pain with drugs or alcohol.

Compassion requires *both* sensitivity and a motivation for helpful action. Compassion knows that suffering means that there is something happening in our lives (or those of others) that demands attention, and the nature of this suffering can inform us about how we can help address it—about what the person who is suffering *needs*. When this wisdom is combined with the motivation to help, we suddenly have other options that can help us deal with difficult situations in positive ways. Compassion can give us the ability to engage in what Buddhists sometimes refer to as "skillful means"—being able to know and do exactly what needs to be done to best address the situation (even if that means simply holding a person's hand as she grieves).

Compassion is not about taking the smoothest road. It means being willing to risk discomfort in order to do the job correctly and completely. Compassion recognizes that difficult questions seldom have easy answers. Faced with a terrible breakup of a relationship, compassion recognizes the pain of the broken heart but also realizes that the pain will not last forever. Compassion takes into account the joys of life, the things that help us to feel better, as well as the suffering. In the case of this painful breakup, a compassionate perspective might help us find the wisdom to take advantage of other close relationships in our lives as we heal. Compassion would help us gradually begin to move into new relationships when we feel ready to do so and would help us know when the time is right. When faced with the pain of life, the threat system says, "This is bad—I need to fight or run away!" The drive system says, "Things will be better when I have that!" Compassion, intimately related to our safeness system, says, "Ah, pain. I recognize you. This is how life sometimes is. I will figure out what needs to be done to work with this, and I will bear it in the meantime."

Compassion is a strength that helps us find the courage to move toward difficulties so that we can do something about them—exactly the sort of courage that you are displaying by choosing to work with your anger. In the rest of this chapter, we'll look at ways that compassion organizes our minds and how different this is from the way our minds are organized by anger.

HOW COMPASSION ORGANIZES OUR MINDS

Remember how our different mood states (like anger) and the three emotion-regulation systems can organize our minds? Well, compassion can help us take control of the way our minds are organized in ways that help us cope more effectively with the difficult emotions and struggles we will face in life, as illustrated in figure 4.1.

Figure 4.1: Organizing the Mind in Different Ways
Reprinted from *The Compassionate Mind* (London: Constable and Robinson, 2009) with permission.

Next, figure 4.2 illustrates what we call "The Circle of Compassion" and depicts various aspects of what we call "the compassionate mind":

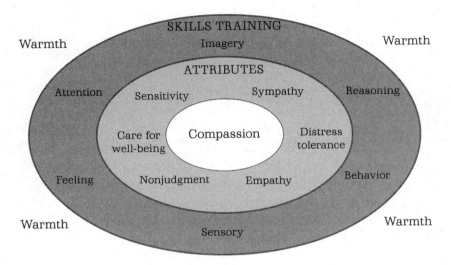

Figure 4.2: The Circle of Compassion
Reprinted from Gilbert, 2009 with kind permission from Constable and Robinson

Attributes: What a compassionate mind is like.

Skills: The things that we'll be doing to develop the attributes of compassion.

Environment: Where all of this takes place—an environment of warmth.

ATTRIBUTES OF THE COMPASSIONATE MIND

The first aim of this book is to give you practical tools you can use to work with anger; the second aim is a bit broader and more ambitious—the development of your compassionate self and the ability to approach life in a way that allows you to work with your anger *and* build a happy life. This life will be filled with good relationships and actions that reflect your deepest values and priorities. This may seem like a big task, and in some ways it is. But we don't need to do it all in one try, or even very quickly. Not at all. Instead, we'll aim to tackle it one small step at a time. Let's start by considering the attributes featured in the inner ring of the "Compassion Circle."

Motivation

A compassionate mind is motivated by the basic desire to care for the well-being of ourselves and other people. This caring mentality is already within us—it's part of how our brains work. If we've struggled with anger, though, we may not have had much experience of this caring motivation. It's hard to care if we are constantly feeling threatened and angry. Interestingly, one reason we may feel threatened so often is that we don't relate to ourselves in caring ways. The parts of your old brain that trigger your emotions often can't tell the difference between external threats (for example, someone else telling you that you're a terrible person) and internal threats (like telling *yourself* that you're a terrible person). *The shame we create by beating ourselves up is "mental gasoline" that fuels our anger.* Cultivating the motivation to care for our own well-being can help stop the internal cycle that keeps our threatened, angry minds in operation. The motivation to care for ourselves allows us to replace feelings of blame with questions like, "What do I need in order to handle this better?"

A compassionate mind also experiences a motivation to care for others. Being motivated to care for the well-being of others is a powerful antidote to anger, which is associated with the urge to harm. One way we can help ourselves manage our anger is to become more sensitive to the negative consequences that our angry behavior can create. We already do this when we refrain from snapping at the boss at work, even though we may be very irritated with him. We know that if we let nasty remarks go, it could cost us our jobs. By developing a caring motivation toward other people and keeping this motivation at the front of our minds (rather than buried as a value we deeply hold but often do not live), it makes it much harder to give our anger free reign to harm them. When we truly relate to others from a position of caring, we're much less likely to act in ways that harm them because we're aware of the suffering that it will cause them, and we aren't willing to risk that consequence. We know it isn't worth it.

Another reason for cultivating the motivation to be caring of others is that it naturally produces good relationships. When we act out of this motivation, we tend to naturally stimulate the safeness systems of others. Instead of becoming someone they feel threatened by, we can instead become the person who helps them to feel safe. They will then react to us with more warmth, in ways that are more positive and that help us to feel safe and accepted as well.

Sensitivity

Sensitivity means being open to signs of suffering in ourselves and in other people. Often, anger emerges when we are faced with difficult emotions that we'd rather not feel. Examples include lashing out when we are criticized by others in order to avoid feeling embarrassed or becoming frustrated and angry with our children as a way of masking the worry we feel when they're struggling. Anger emerges from threat, and these emotions seem to threaten us psychologically (*What if I really am no good at my job? What if my child isn't bright enough to make it in school? What if I'm a bad parent?*). Sensitivity means being willing to notice the difficult feelings behind our anger and being honest with ourselves about how we feel when we're faced with the inevitable difficulties of life. It means being able to say (at least to ourselves), "That really hurt my feelings" or "I'm really worried that my son won't have a good life" or "I'm terrified that I'm becoming an emotionally abusive parent."

Instead of distracting ourselves from our worries and pain by allowing our threat systems to fill our minds with anger, compassion helps us to open our awareness to our fears and challenges so that we can then work to improve the situations that cause them. It's about being aware of how we are hurting and then treating ourselves with kindness, forgiveness, and openheartedness.

As with compassionate motivation, sensitivity to the suffering of others can be an antidote to anger. While our angry minds may relish the idea of harming others, they may not feel so eager to do so if we allow ourselves to really become aware of others' circumstances and their own pain. Ultimately, I suspect most of us (when we aren't trapped in a threatened state of mind) don't want to cause others to suffer. At least I'm betting that *you* don't—or you probably wouldn't be reading this book. As we become aware that our actions are producing real suffering in others—that *it isn't just about us*—we can be prompted to step back and reevaluate our actions, to detour from the track that our threat system has placed us in.

The sensitivity of compassion can also take the form of *vigilance*: looking out for things that trigger our anger and signs in our bodies that let us know the dominoes of anger have begun to fall. The sooner we notice that we're getting angry, the more likely we'll be to do something about it before our minds are captured by our threat systems. This awareness is the first step in catching our anger before it gets out of control. When applied to the suffering of others, this vigilance can also work with our caring motivation to help us transform ourselves. Our increased awareness of suffering in others creates more and more opportunities for us to put our compassion into action—to help them, which research shows can improve our own mental health as well.[3]

Sympathy

Sympathy is the emotional extension of our caring motivation. It is being moved in the face of suffering, the emotional reaction we feel when we see someone struggling or in pain. Perhaps you've seen television programs showing people whose homes have been destroyed by a natural disaster, or learned of children who were abused or starving. Perhaps you've had friends who have had their hearts broken, lost their jobs or homes, developed cancer, or worked very hard for something but fell short of their goals. When we hear of things like this, we often experience a sense of sadness or concern. We understand the pain of life, and a part of us hurts for them—we don't want to see them suffer. Sympathy can be a great motivation for positive action; look at the outpouring of donations in the face of earthquakes and hurricanes across the globe and the number of people who donate time and money to help others.

We can direct this sympathy toward ourselves as well, opening to the realization, *This is hard. Right now, my life is difficult.* We can allow ourselves to feel some sadness or brokenheartedness about it, and some kindness. Instead of blaming ourselves for having a hard time, we open our hearts to the difficulty of it. This is very different from how we may usually relate to suffering: by ignoring it, denying it, or quickly attempting to distract ourselves from it. Even anger is an example of suffering that we can allow ourselves to be moved by. Anger isn't fun, and it can get in the way of our pursuing happiness. While anger might feel briefly empowering, we know that in the long term, it can cause us tremendous suffering. In softening our hearts toward our own suffering, we can fuel our motivation to do something about it. Recognizing how hard it has been for us to have to deal with the consequences that out-of-control anger has caused in our lives, we can strengthen our commitment to do something about it. Sympathy is *not* pity, which has a quality of looking down on the person who is suffering.[4] Sympathy is opening ourselves to the emotions that naturally emerge when we acknowledge the fact that we all struggle and encounter pain and hardship.

Distress Tolerance

As you've read previously, a compassionate mind doesn't shy away from pain. Distress tolerance is the ability to experience difficult emotions as they happen, accepting that these feelings are a normal part of human life. As we learn to open ourselves to the reality of suffering and difficult emotions in order to work with them, we also learn to tolerate the discomfort that these difficulties create. At first, this might not feel natural—our habit may be to avoid working with anger and other painful emotions that contribute to it because we feel we can't bear it. In fact, it's true: we do have powerful reflexes and habitual reactions that pull us back from pain, such as when we jerk our hands away from a hot stove. Remember, our threat systems operate from a "better safe than sorry" mode.

However, the habit of attempting to avoid pain at any cost can create real problems in our lives. CFT practitioners refer to these threat-based behaviors that can reduce discomfort in the short term but create troublesome long-term consequences as *safety strategies*,[5] which include such behaviors as acting out in anger and aggression when we find ourselves frustrated or embarrassed. When we're unable or unwilling to tolerate emotional discomfort, we can find ourselves doing all sorts of unhelpful things to try to avoid it.

One of my clients, Richard, had this habit and told me that when a colleague questioned his decisions, he would feel threatened and insecure, afraid that the person would see him as incompetent. In response, he would quickly become heated and verbally aggressive. Faced with this, his colleagues would back down and end the encounter, which caused Richard to feel some short-term relief. However, this strategy set the stage for lots of long-term problems. First, he became known as someone who was difficult to deal with, and his colleagues began to keep him out of the loop. He began missing out on opportunities to be involved in important projects that would have furthered his career. Additionally, his reactions prevented him from taking advantage of what was actually help from his colleagues. Threatened by his feeling that they were questioning his competence, he shut them down before they could offer suggestions that would have improved the projects he was working on. Later, when he learned to work with his anger, Richard learned to tolerate the distress (feelings of insecurity, fears of being incompetent) he felt in response to his colleagues' constructive criticism. Once he could do that, he found he didn't feel the urge, or the *need*, to respond with anger. Remember, anger emerges when we feel threatened, and that involves discomfort. In order to work through such situations, we must learn to tolerate that discomfort, giving ourselves room to develop helpful ways of responding.

Distress tolerance allows us to work *with* difficult feelings instead of rushing to avoid them. You probably already do this in some areas of your life. After all, most of us have had to tolerate some discomfort when we've pursued goals in our lives. For example, if you lift weights or work out in other ways, you have learned to tolerate the discomfort and pain of the exercises in order to benefit from a healthier body. What we're doing when we develop our compassion is like a workout for the mind and brain.

A compassionate mind recognizes that sometimes we can't get rid of our discomfort, but instead must *change our relationship* to it and learn that we can tolerate difficult feelings. In this book, we'll examine a number of strategies for doing just this. Instead of habitually running away or going on the attack when we're faced with difficult or painful situations, we can learn to recognize and accept them as a fundamental part of the human experience, to approach them with the calm confidence that, *I can work with this, too.* And it doesn't matter what "this" is.

Empathy

The nature of empathy is similar to that of sympathy; however, whereas sympathy is about allowing ourselves to feel moved in the face of pain and struggles, empathy is about *understanding* what we and other people are feeling. Empathy involves accepting whatever emotions are being felt or expressed, and attempting to understand where those emotions are coming from and why they are valid.

Can you recall a time when you were trying to explain how you felt about something and the other person said something like, "It sounds like you feel _____," and they got it exactly right? How did that feel? In my experience, it feels great to be understood when I'm struggling, even if that understanding comes from me—from within myself.

Much of my work at Eastern Washington University involves training psychology students who are learning to be masters-level therapists, and we consistently work on the development of empathy. After all, if you can't develop empathy, you probably aren't going to be much help to your clients. One prompt I often use is a question: "How does it *make sense* that your client feels as she does?" If we're feeling something, there is a reason for it, a reason why the mind is responding in this way. When we empathize, we drop the tendency to be judgmental and instead seek to understand what we and other people are feeling, and the reasons why we might be feeling this way, in this situation. *How does it make sense that I/she/he might be feeling this way right now?*

Imagine that you have a good friend who is very close to her mother. Now imagine that her mother has been diagnosed with a rapidly advancing form of cancer and dies suddenly. Consider how your friend might feel. How would you try to understand her reaction to her mother's death? You might mentally put yourself in her shoes, imagining what it would be like if your own mother died, drawing upon your own experiences of losing people you loved. You might consider what you know of your friend and of her relationship with her mother in order to understand how her response might differ from your own. Most importantly, you would *listen* to her, allowing her to express her emotions in her own way, perhaps occasionally reflecting back what you're hearing to make sure that you are really understanding what she's saying. In addition to drawing upon our own emotional experience, there is a cognitive (thinking) component to empathy, as we consider the emotional experience of the other person and how it fits into the story of her life.

Cultivating empathy and compassion toward others is very important as we learn to work with anger. Our threat systems reduce the actions of other people into very simple terms, usually defensive ones (*He cut me off because he's a jerk! Let's get him back!*). If we work to deepen empathy, we come to realize that there can be very complex causes for the emotions and behaviors of others—causes that often *don't have anything to do with us.* The willingness to step out of your threat system and put yourself into other peoples' shoes can take the wind right out of your anger. Once you begin to understand how other people feel and the reasons why they act as they do, you'll often discover that there just isn't much to be angry about. You can find yourself feeling compassion for them instead, as you connect with times when you've felt and behaved in similar ways and the reasons why you did so. Remember, *no one wants to suffer—we all just want to be happy.*

We can also direct empathy toward ourselves. For many, this may sound a bit strange, as empathy is often discussed specifically as understanding the emotions of others. However, we often don't take time to consider and understand our *own* emotions (and this is particularly true with anger). Why? Because we're too busy avoiding them! When we look closely at anger, for example, we often find that there are a whole host of other emotions lying just underneath the surface. We may see that we use anger to avoid feeling things like shame, embarrassment, insecurity, vulnerability, fear, and heart-break. We cultivate hatred and anger toward the partner who left us so that we don't have to face the pain of being left or the fears that we weren't good enough for that person. My client Richard snapped angrily at his colleagues so that he didn't have to experience the fear that he wasn't good at his job or that others didn't respect him.

The problem is that anger doesn't solve those problems or deal with those emotions—it just shouts over them and often creates more difficulties. In this book, you'll begin to learn how to have empathy for yourself—to understand what you're feeling and how it makes sense that you would feel that way. One way you can begin is by learning to "listen" to yourself. You can practice this by doing things like paying attention to what you're feeling in your body, and perhaps writing in a journal about how you feel and going back to read it later.

Nonjudgment

Nonjudgment involves relating to our experiences and those of other people without condemnation. Our minds often rush to place things into categories, often with the labels "good" and "bad" on them. A compassion-ate mind lets things be *as they are* and instead seeks to understand them. It recognizes that emotions, for example, are inherently neither good nor bad—they just *are.* Our compassionate selves recognize that emotions we experience as unpleasant are products of our threat systems, which ulti-mately are just trying to protect us. When we recognize this, we can learn to stop the labeling process that can turn challenging emotions or embar-rassing life circumstances into the shameful feeling that there is something wrong with us. We can just let things be as they are (*Oh, look—there goes my threat system again. I'm really feeling ticked off*).

To be nonjudgmental doesn't mean that we don't have preferences, that we don't need to behave better, or that we won't work to change things. Instead, it is the recognition that before we can really address difficulties in our lives or challenges with other people, we need an honest understanding of just what is happening right now.[6] It's about figuring out exactly what is on our plates before we decide whether or not we're going to eat it and recognizing that just because you don't care for brussels sprouts, it doesn't mean that they're "bad" (and they might even be "good" for you!). If we look at Richard again, we can see that he couldn't deal with his anger because he thought he was justifiably angry because his colleagues were jerks—of course he should be angry, right? Once he was able to look nonjudgmentally at their comments, he saw them for what they were: well-meant, constructive criticism. Looking then at his own reaction, he could accept that their comments caused him to feel threatened because he was afraid they didn't see him as competent. With support, he became able to work with the issue that fed his anger—those feelings of insecurity that kept his threat system on high alert. When we allow ourselves to see things just as they are and resist the urge to label them, we are better able to see them clearly. In this state, we can learn to recognize what things are better left alone and which ones we need to change.

SKILLS TRAINING

We won't get into the outer ring of the circle too deeply here, because the rest of the book is pretty much devoted to helping you develop these skills for working with anger and developing your compassionate mind. What I did want to mention, though, is that skills training in compassion-focused therapy takes a number of different forms. This variety helps you take advantage of the many ways that your brain works. You can work with attention and with your senses to increase your awareness of the things that trigger your anger. You can begin to relate to your emotions and experiences with acceptance, confidence, and clarity. You'll use imagery to balance your emotions by learning to stimulate your safeness system and practice new ways of dealing with your emotions—anger in particular. You'll use your thinking and reasoning to discover new ways of working with difficult situations, explore qualities you'd like to develop, and build new habits that reflect these values. Finally, you'll work to create and cultivate more positive emotions in your life and train your brain to respond more effectively to challenges.

Just as the different aspects of the threatened mind interact to keep us in a state of anger, so, too, can we take advantage of how our attention, reasoning, imagery, emotions, senses, and behaviors interact to shape other states of mind. Learning to work with these different aspects of our minds gives us flexibility—it allows us to find and use different tools for working with anger—and, as a result, opens up our options. We're all a little different, and some of us will really like one method while some will like another. The point is to find what works for *you*.

WARMTH

Moving to the outside of the compassion circle, we see the word "warmth." What this means is that a compassionate mind and our efforts to develop it occur in a context of warmth, kindness, and self-acceptance. In learning to direct warmth toward our efforts to work with our anger, we remind ourselves that our experience of anger is not our fault, and attempt to give ourselves encouragement for choosing to work with it more effectively. Warmth allows us to recognize that the efforts we are making to work with anger are courageous ones and are evidence of our good-heartedness.

It can be helpful if you engage other people in your efforts to work with anger. Let them know what you're doing and ask for their support (if you have someone who can be truly supportive). In our prison groups, one of the most powerful parts of the program is the warmth and encouragement that participants receive from one another—the kindness and validation. In the beginning, this can be a difficult gift to give ourselves, particularly if we're used to criticizing and shaming ourselves. However, learning to be kind to ourselves is worth the effort.

CONCLUSION

Many of us have failed in our attempts to deal with our anger. We may have decided *From this point on, things will be different* time and time again. But then we've been unable to maintain the changes we were trying to create in our lives, soon going back to doing the same old things. There are good reasons why this happens. *Deciding to change is an important beginning, but the decision itself is not the change.* You can decide to become a physician, but if you don't then attend medical school, you won't make it very far. If your car broke down, you wouldn't expect to be able to fix it if you had no understanding of how the engine works, without tools or training. Yet this is exactly how we often approach the process of working with difficult emotions and behaviors. We assume that if we just want it badly enough, we will change. *This is why we fail.* Simply having the motivation to change is a great start, but it isn't enough—we need to practice strategies that work.

In this book, my goal has been to help remedy this situation by providing you with two things. The first is an *understanding* of your anger and how it works within your mind. In the second half of the book, the goal is to give you the *tools* you need to change things. In this chapter, you were introduced to the idea of compassion and how you can use it to organize your mind in ways that are very different from what you've seen with anger. In the following chapters, you're going to discover how to use compassion to manage your anger.

5

First Steps

In the first part of this book, we examined the power of anger, the ease by which it is triggered, and the way it flows through us to direct our thoughts and actions. From here on out, you'll practice skills that will allow you to develop your compassionate mind so that, over time, you'll learn to engage the world in ways that are different from those dictated by your anger. The idea is to work with your mind to weaken your habitual anger responses and to cultivate ways of feeling and responding that are driven instead by compassion, concern, and the motivation to help both others and yourself. Do you have a notebook and pen nearby? Now may be a good time to get them, as we'll be proceeding through a few exercises as we move through this chapter.

You might think of this chapter and the next one as "preseason training." I'll introduce ways for you to keep yourself motivated—to keep you going when the going gets a bit rough. You'll also learn soothing-rhythm breathing, a technique that helps you slow your body and mind down, and prepares you to shift into a compassionate mode of relating to yourself and other people. In chapter 6, you'll learn about "mindfulness," a skill that will help you to observe how thoughts and emotions arise in your mind, helping you to dampen the flame of anger before it grows into a forest fire.

THE COURAGE TO CHANGE: COMPASSIONATE MOTIVATION

In learning to work with your anger, your motivation will tend to wax and wane depending on what is going on in your life and many other factors. However, you can stimulate your motivation by considering what you have to gain. In *The Compassionate Mind*,[1] Paul Gilbert asks us to imagine being offered ten dollars to regulate our anger for a week. Would you do it? What about a hundred dollars? A thousand dollars? Perhaps a cool million? The idea is that, at some point, the incentive will be so great that you will absolutely commit yourself to the goal of regulating your anger. Perhaps money isn't the motivation. What if you knew that the rewards for handling your anger were less stress, more happiness, better relationships, and perhaps the ability to better live in accordance with your values? The key is to recognize that it is possible to manage your anger and to find ways of committing yourself to this effort—for example, by considering what you have to gain by succeeding. Let's explore some factors that may help keep you motivated.

Exercise 5.1: Exploring Motivation

Consider the way your anger has played out in your life.

1. How has your anger negatively impacted your life? How has it been in the way? What don't you like about your anger?

2. How might your life be improved if you learned to work with your anger more effectively?

3. What specific improvements would you like to see in your life as a result of working with your anger? What are the incentives that can motivate you to keep going, even when it seems difficult?

One of the things that can help motivate you as you pursue your goals is to consider your *values*—the deeply held ideas you have about the sort of person you want to be and the sort of life you want to lead.[2] It may be that you've thought about the sort of person you'd like to be and, in order to be that person, decided that you'll need to get a better handle on your anger.

Not everything that we value can motivate us equally. Some things work better than others in terms of how likely they are to help us lead happy lives filled with good relationships—the kind that help us to activate our safeness systems and balance our emotions. For example, we could value money ("'I want to be unbelievably rich") and spend our lives in the pursuit of material gain while alienating those we love—but in the long term, that value probably wouldn't lead us to happiness. Let's take a moment to consider those things we value and see where compassion fits in with them.

To give you a structure for doing this, I've set out a practical exercise for you to complete in your journal. I've also included an example of a completed exercise adapted from a client named David.

DAVID'S EXAMPLE

Sample Exercise 5.2: The Sort of Person I Want to Be

Take a moment to consider the sort of person you would like to be. Imagine that you have died and that the people you love most are at your funeral. Imagine the eulogy they have put together: "She/He was so _____."

If you had lived according to your deepest values, what words would you want them to say? Come up with three words to finish that sentence.

1. *Strong*

2. *Kind*

3. *Loving (especially as a father)*

In your notebook or journal (what I'll call your "Compassion Practice Journal"), write a more detailed description of the type of person you'd like to be. What qualities would you like to have? How would compassion manifest itself in your life? How would you like others to describe you? How would you like others to feel when you're around? What would you like to think about yourself? What feelings would you like your days to be filled with? What goals would you like to pursue? Try to really connect with those things that you value, and bear in mind that some of them may be buried so deep down that you may not think of them often. Use this as an opportunity to reconnect with them now.

Next, ask yourself if your anger fits in with the sort of person you want to be. Then ask yourself if compassion fits. For example, I began working with my own anger because I wanted to be a better father and husband and to help my son learn ways of managing his emotions so that he wouldn't struggle with anger as an adult the way I sometimes have. Consider the following questions:

- How does your anger help or get in the way of your being able to live according to your values? *My anger creates lots of problems for me because I end up being irritable with the people I care about. I don't treat them as well as I'd like. It keeps me focused on the things that are wrong and distracts me from the things I value, such as achieving my targets at work or having an easy relationship with my young son, who is full of energy and always wants to play football with me when I come home from work.*

- How might compassion for yourself and other people help you to live a life that reflects the sort of person you want to be? How might it help you improve your relationships with others? *I hope that compassion for myself would help me stop being so defensive when things don't go my way, and to focus on the things that really matter and all the good things that do come my way. Compassion for others would help me keep in mind that my actions affect them and that they have their own reasons for doing things.*

Exercise 5.2: The Sort of Person I Want to Be

Take a moment to consider the sort of person you would like to be. Imagine that you have died, and that the people you love most are at your funeral. Imagine the eulogy they have put together: "She/He was so _____."

If you had lived according to your deepest values, what would you want them to say? Come up with three words to finish that sentence.

1. _____

2. _____

YOU MAY ALSO LIKE...

Healing the Angry Brain: How...
   by Ronald Potter-Efron

Depression For Dummies
   by Laura L. Smith

Taking Charge of Anger, Second Edition:...
   by W. Robert Nay

Beyond Anger: A Guide for Men: How to...
   by Thomas Harbin

Anxiety & Depression Workbook For Dummies
   by Charles H. Elliott

title and only if defective. NOOKs purchased from other retailers or sellers are returnable only to the retailer or seller from which they are purchased, pursuant to such retailer's or seller's return policy. Magazines, newspapers, eBooks, digital downloads, and used books are not returnable or exchangeable. Defective NOOKs may be exchanged at the store in accordance with the applicable warranty.

Returns or exchanges will not be permitted (i) after 14 days or without receipt or (ii) for product not carried by Barnes & Noble or Barnes & Noble.com.

Policy on receipt may appear in two sections.

Return Policy

With a sales receipt or Barnes & Noble.com packing slip, a full refund in the original form of payment will be issued from any Barnes & Noble Booksellers store for returns of undamaged NOOKs, new and unread books, and unopened and undamaged music CDs, DVDs, and audio books made within 14 days of purchase from a Barnes & Noble Booksellers store or Barnes & Noble.com with the below

3. _____

In your notebook or Compassion Practice Journal, write a more detailed description of the type of person you'd like to be. What qualities would you like to have? How would compassion manifest itself in your life? How would you like others to describe you? How would you like others to feel when you're around? What would you like to think about yourself? What feelings would you like your days to be filled with? What goals would you like to pursue? Try to really connect with those things that you value, and bear in mind that some of them may be buried so deep down that you may not think of them often. Use this as an opportunity to reconnect with them now.

Next, ask yourself if your anger fits in with the sort of person you want to be. Then ask yourself if compassion fits in. For example, I began working with my own anger because I wanted to be a better father and husband, and to help my son learn ways of managing his emotions so that he wouldn't struggle with anger as an adult the way I sometimes have. Consider the following questions:

- How does your anger help or get in the way of your being able to live according to your values?

- How might compassion for yourself and other people help you to live a life that reflects the sort of person you want to be? How might it help you improve your relationships with others?

As a threat response, anger keeps us trapped in the experience of feeling threatened and focused on negative aspects of life—things that cause us to be unhappy. As we saw in the first few chapters, when we're in the grip of anger, we're less able to think clearly, to form and maintain good relationships, and over time, we can be more likely to have major health difficulties.

If we can learn to change the way we respond to perceived threats and use compassion to understand more clearly why we and other people behave as we do, we can begin to live with more ease and comfort. Compassion allows us to understand the sources of suffering in our lives and then helps us to alleviate the pain we feel because of them. As we've discussed, anger can be thought of as a form of suffering—this often-misdirected threat response causes real pain and problems in our lives. As I mentioned in chapter 4, compassion can help us develop sympathy for ourselves: *How difficult it's been to live with my anger.* When we open our hearts to the difficulties that our anger brings into our lives, we can begin to commit ourselves to changing the ways we deal with it: *My life would be much better if I could free myself from this anger. It's worth the commitment to do so.*

At the end of the day, what do you have to lose? You can always go back to being angry—you can't lose it, as it's a part of how everyone's brain works. The real question to ask yourself is: *Is it worth it to experiment—to see if my life can be improved by learning new ways of coping with my anger? Is worth it to see what could happen if I began to look at myself and other people from a compassionate point of view?* The idea here is to find ways to really motivate yourself to make the effort to work with your anger so that you can stick with it when things get tough. Imagine what it would be like if you succeeded.

USING COMPASSIONATE ATTENTION WITH AROUSAL: SOOTHING-RHYTHM BREATHING

How and where you direct your attention is incredibly important in shaping your mental state. In this section, you're going to learn how to focus your attention in ways that will help you prepare your mind for compassion and counteract the arousal that fuels your anger. A compassionate mind is a calm mind, and while our angry states of mind are fueled by physical arousal and tension, our compassionate states of mind thrive when we've slowed ourselves down a bit. To do this, we'll use a technique called *soothing-rhythm breathing,*[3] which will lay the groundwork for cultivating compassionate characteristics such as empathy, the ability to be nonjudgmental, and the ability to tolerate distress. Soothing-rhythm breathing works with our breath and posture to gently shift our emotional state when we're feeling threatened. Here are some tips for developing this practice.

Breathing

The idea is not to *control* your breathing, but to slow it down a bit and allow it to fall into a rhythm that is comfortable and soothing. You breathe in and out through your nose, observing your breath as it slowly leaves your body during the exhalation.

Posture

The aim is to slow down your body and mind but also to be alert (not to fall asleep!). In order to do this, it's best to get into a posture that will support you. Sit upright in a comfortable chair with your back straightened in a dignified posture, the soles of your feet flat on the floor in front of you, with your knees parallel and roughly as wide apart as your shoulders. Your arms will be relaxed and your hands placed gently on your thighs or held open and together in your lap, as if you were holding a small rice bowl, with one hand resting inside the other. As you continue to practice soothing-rhythm breathing throughout the day, you may want to use it at times when you're standing. If so, stand up straight instead of slouching. If you are lying down, lie down on your back, with your body straight instead of curled up.

Facial Expression

It's useful to adopt a gentle smile while you are practicing soothing-rhythm breathing and many of the other exercises. Relax the facial muscles, let your tongue drop from the roof of your mouth, and allow your jaw to drop open slightly. Then begin to let your mouth turn upward into a smile you feel comfortable with—one that gives you a feeling of friendship, as if you've just seen somebody you like. Research shows that the way we position our bodies and form facial expressions affects our mental state.

Don't Worry about Becoming Distracted

You *will* sometimes become distracted as you do the exercises in this book. *This is okay.* It's just how our minds work, and we'll discuss this in greater detail in the next chapter, when we cover mindfulness. For now, if you notice that thoughts or sensations have taken you away, you can refocus by just gently bringing your attention back to the feeling of your breath. The key is to use the breath's natural rhythm to slow your mind and body down. That won't happen if you're getting all uptight because you're worried about doing it "right." There is no doing it "wrong." You're simply allowing your body to breathe—and if you're not doing *that* right, you won't be alive to worry about it!

Sit Up Straight and Smile: Does Posture Matter?

For decades, our parents and teachers have often told us, "Sit up straight!" and "Smile!", aware of the importance of having an upright posture and a pleasing expression. Why?

Well, a growing number of studies have examined the effects of different postures and facial expressions on our mental state. One study examined "power posing."[4] The researchers experimented with different body postures and their possible affects on hormonal responses, feelings of power, and risk tolerance. In this study some participants engaged in "high-power" poses, which were more expansive (taking up more space) and open (keeping their limbs open and uncrossed); other participants adopted "low-power" poses, adopting slumped and closed (arms and legs crossed) postures. Participants in each group engaged in two poses for one minute each—one standing and one seated. The results showed that posture did indeed matter. The researchers examined levels of testosterone (a sex hormone related to feelings of power and dominance) and the stress hormone cortisol, both before and after the posture manipulation. Both types of poses significantly affected the participants' hormone levels, measured by sampling their saliva. High-power poses led to *increases* in testosterone and *decreases* in cortisol. In contrast, low-power poses had the opposite effect, causing *decreases* in testosterone and *increases* in cortisol. These changes were reflected in participants' psychological states. Individuals in the high-power poses felt more powerful and more tolerant of risk than those who had engaged in low-power poses. Posture matters!

Other research shows that smiling helps, too. In one of my favorite studies,[5] participants were asked to watch a cartoon while holding a pencil either between their teeth (which encouraged smiling) or between their lips (which prevented it). Those who were able to smile rated the cartoon more favorably (funnier) than those who were prevented from smiling.

Practice When It's Easy

Like most skills, soothing-rhythm breathing requires practice if you're going to use it effectively. This skill can help bring some calmness and relaxation to any part of your day, but it can also be used specifically to reduce arousal when you notice that you're becoming angry. As you might suspect, calming yourself when your threat system is doing its best to get you worked up isn't the easiest thing to do. For this reason, you want to become very familiar with soothing-rhythm breathing, to establish it as an automatic behavior that you can just shift into when you need it, without having to think about it too much. Just as athletes practice extensively before the big game, you can practice soothing-rhythm breathing when you don't have a lot of distractions and aren't upset. Once you've found a comfortable breathing rhythm and are familiar with the exercise, you can apply it to many different situations, even when your arousal is up.

Don't Fight It

Allow your breath to fall into a natural, soothing rhythm—don't try to force anything. Experiment with different rates of breathing until you find one that feels natural and relaxing. A good starting point can be to breathe in for three seconds, holding the breath for three seconds, and letting go of the breath for three seconds. Members of our prison anger groups have told us that focusing on the counting helps distract them from the angry thoughts that fuel their arousal. It's also worth mentioning, on the other hand, that some people find that focusing on their bodies creates discomfort for them, which in turn can actually increase their tension and arousal. If this is the case for you, don't force it. However, it would likely be useful to explore other ways of slowing down your mind and body. For example, you might just sit quietly or direct your attention toward something else that you find relaxing, perhaps imagining listening to the rhythmic sound of waves coming in on a beach. Ultimately, the key is to find a way to focus your attention that helps you slow and relax your body, and create a calm state of mind. The idea is to find something that works for you.

Exercise 5.3: Soothing-Rhythm Breathing

For this exercise, you'll want to find a relatively quiet place where you can sit undisturbed for ten minutes or so.

- Sit upright in a dignified posture, with your back straight, the soles of your feet flat on the floor in front of you, and your knees about shoulder-width apart. Gently rest the palms of your hands on your thighs or cup them in your lap. You can close your eyes or direct your gaze to the floor a few feet in front of you, allowing it to soften (unfocus) a bit.

- Gently bring your attention to your breath, noticing it entering your body, expanding your diaphragm, and gently lifting your abdomen.

- Allow your breathing to fall into a natural rhythm, a bit slower and deeper than you usually breathe. A good place to start is about three seconds as you inhale, a brief pause, and then about three seconds as you exhale. Experiment with different breathing rates to find one that feels natural and soothing to you—this is the key.

- As you breathe, allow your attention to settle on the exhalation. Follow the rhythm of the breathing, resting as you inhale and, again, watching as you exhale.

- You'll sometimes become distracted. This is very normal, and it's okay. Just gently refocus your attention on the breathing and the calm sensations that come with it. Focus on the feeling of slowing down, as if there were a rhythm of breathing within you that gives you the sense of slowing—like a fast-flowing river slowing as it feeds into a wide lake.

- Spend at least thirty seconds on this (more if you wish) simply focusing on the soothing rhythm of your breathing. The soothing will come from the sense of slowing within.

- When you finish, take a moment to reflect on your experience. How does your body feel right now? What did you notice during the exercise?

- Once you've practiced this exercise a few times when you've been seated, try using it in other situations—perhaps while you're waiting in line at the store, at the bus stop or when you're on the train, or when you have a few moments between tasks at work. Just allow your breathing to fall into the comfortable rhythm that you've become familiar with, and for thirty seconds or so, allow your attention to simply follow your breath as you inhale and exhale.

THE COMPASSION PRACTICE JOURNAL

The odds of whether or not this book will help you are directly related to whether or not you *actually do the exercises.* It can be tempting to simply read books like this and skim over the exercises. In my experience, that can help us feel better while we're reading, but it usually doesn't produce lasting change.

It can help to keep track of the exercises as you do them throughout the day. I've included below a simple form for this; you may wish to copy it in your journal. I've completed an example of what a Monday entry might look like:

Day	Type of Practice and How Long	Comments: What Was Helpful?
Monday	10:30 a.m.—soothing-rhythm breathing (SRB): 2 min. 2:45 p.m.—SRB: 1 min. 8:37 p.m.—SRB: 2 min.	Helped me slow down between meetings. Figured out I could practice during TV commercials!

I encourage you to use this or something similar to keep track of your compassion practice. As you can see in the above example, doing so can help you discover new uses for exercises (slowing down and centering yourself between tasks at work) and find new times to practice. Also note that, although in this example soothing-rhythm breathing was practiced three times during the day, it only took a total of *five minutes* (although you could certainly do more). We'll cover a good number of exercises, but don't be overwhelmed—you'll likely find that practicing doesn't take that much time. Doing brief exercises several times during the day works great!

Compassion Practice Journal

Day	Type of Practice and How Long	Comments: What Was Helpful?
Monday		
Tuesday		
Wednesday		
Thursday		
Friday		
Saturday		
Sunday		

Adapted with kind permission from the Compassionate Mind Foundation (www .compassionatemind.co.uk).

CONCLUSION

This chapter has set the stage for you to begin to your work with anger so that you can handle it more effectively. We began by looking at the issue of motivation and the recognition that you can work to increase your motivation when it begins to run low; for example, by reminding yourself of what you have to gain by handling your anger better. You also considered your values and how your anger has affected your life and those of people around you. You can choose to commit yourself to at least trying to change. The essence of compassionate reasoning is opening yourself to the idea that you will encounter difficulties, but that you can work with them in constructive ways.

You also learned about soothing-rhythm breathing, a skill that is designed to help you reduce angry arousal and that can be used any time you want to slow yourself down. SRB will help you shift from a mind state that's focused on responding to threats to a more compassionate frame of mind. In this way, you can prepare yourself to draw upon the compassionate skills you'll be learning in the rest of the book. In the next chapter, we'll begin to explore mindfulness, which will help you develop other aspects of your compassionate mind.

6

The Cultivation of Mindfulness

Before we proceed, I'd like you to do a little exercise. Take a moment to notice how your body feels right now. What's the temperature like? Are you warm or cool? Notice the way your body feels as it comes into contact with various surfaces—the chair or bed, the floor. Are you comfortable?

Next, turn your awareness to your internal bodily experiences. Do you notice any muscle tension or relaxation? Hunger? Are there any other sensations that stand out to you?

Notice your breath flowing in and out of your body, the rise and fall of your abdomen as you inhale and exhale. If you feel any unpleasant sensations, simply label them for what they are—pain, tension, or itchiness. Observe your body for a few moments.

Try to be aware of the information coming in through your other senses. What do you hear? What do you see? Try to be curious and to notice things without judging them or trying to change them. Just observe whatever you see, hear, feel, and smell. Stay with these experiences for a bit.

Now turn your awareness to your thoughts. Are you thinking, *Ten more pages and then I'll get a snack?* Or, perhaps, *How does he expect me to pay attention to all this other stuff while I'm reading?* Try to notice these thoughts without getting caught up in the content—they are just what you happen to be thinking right now.

Open your awareness to your emotions. How do you feel? Irritated? Content? Confused? Curious? Notice these emotions as *mental experiences*—as events that are occurring in your mind. Observe without judging, just as you observed the information coming in from your senses. Simply be aware that this is what it's like right now.

This is it. This is your life. This is what your life feels like. It is this moment, unfolding before you in the form of bodily sensations, sensory experiences, thoughts, feelings, motivations, and imagery. And this moment is where our lives occur—it is the *only* place our lives occur. We can think about the past. We can anticipate and plan for the future. But we can only live right now.

Our experience of life is directly shaped by the ways we direct our attention in the present moment. You've perhaps heard the phrase, "You are what you eat." I'm more likely to say, "Your life is what you attend to." There are lots of things going on in the space of every moment—both in our heads and out there in the world—and the things we pay attention to and the *way* we pay attention to them can have a great effect on how we feel. As we've seen, anger tends to keep our attention focused in ways that keep us angry. But there are other ways of paying attention, even when we're angry, ways that give us more power to step back from our anger and exert some influence over our emotions. Directing your attention to *this moment* in the way that you just have—with curiosity and without being judgmental—is the essence of mindfulness. The way you began the chapter was a method of "checking in" and was your first mindfulness exercise.

Mindfulness exercises are rooted in practices developed by Buddhists over two thousand years ago. These practices were used to stabilize and focus the mind as meditators worked to free themselves from suffering and the factors that cause it. More recently in the West, mindfulness has been adapted and successfully applied to the treatment of pain and distress that accompany a variety of medical conditions and to emotional difficulties such as depression and anxiety.[1, 2] The person most associated with applying mindfulness practices in the west is Jon Kabat-Zinn, who developed the Mindfulness Based Stress Reduction (MBSR) program in the 1970s to help patients cope with stress, pain, and illness. Dr. Kabat-Zinn defines mindfulness as "paying attention in a particular way: on purpose, in the present moment, and nonjudgmentally."[3] When we are being mindful, we are connected with what is happening *right now*. We observe the things that are happening in the world, our bodies, and our minds *as they are* without judging, condemning, or getting lost in them.

Mindfulness is different from the ways many of us have learned to go about our lives. Instead of bringing our awareness fully to what is happening right now, we may spend much of our time lost in thought—replaying the past, fantasizing about the future—as the present passes us by. Have you ever had the experience of turning off your car when you've arrived somewhere and becoming aware that you have no memory of driving there? Have you ever been in the middle of a conversation, looked at the other person, and realized that you have no idea what he just said? Many of us spend large amounts of our lives lost in our heads and traveling through the world on automatic pilot.

Learning mindfulness helps us learn to stay connected with the present moment. In contrast to the examples of "mindlessness" above, you've probably had experiences of being completely present and absolutely engaged in whatever you were doing. For example, I enjoy playing the guitar, cooking, mountain biking, and teaching statistics because these are activities that easily keep me engaged. Sometimes when I'm doing these things, I so completely focus my attention on them that it seems as if I have no other thoughts; I'm not easily distracted while I'm doing them, either. Mindfulness can have this quality, combined with the awareness that we're *choosing* to focus the spotlight of our attention on these experiences or activities. This way of paying attention stands in contrast to how strong emotions like anger may focus our attention very powerfully but in ways that we don't choose and may not even be aware of. Here's an exercise that will help you begin to explore what mindful attention is like.

Exercise 6.1: Mindful Eating

Find a quiet place where you won't be disturbed and a small piece of food that you enjoy. Something healthy would be good, like a bit of fruit or vegetable—perhaps a grape, berry, raisin, olive, carrot stick, or slice of orange.

- Hold the food in your hand and take a moment to study it. Imagine that you have never seen anything like this before and are discovering it for the first time.

- Turn it in your fingers. Notice how it feels.

- Look closely at the food. Notice its different qualities (smooth, shiny, and so on).

- Smell it. Notice any sounds that are made as you move it about.

- Notice any thoughts you have about the food. What are you thinking?

- Notice any feelings you are having, any desires. Do you want to eat it?

- When you have finished studying it, slowly place the food in your mouth.

- Notice how it feels in your mouth. Observe the texture of the food.

- As you begin to chew, notice how it tastes. Do you experience different flavors at different places in your mouth or on your tongue?

- Observe your behavior. Are you chewing quickly or slowly?

- Once again, notice your thoughts and feelings. Are any evaluations, judgments, or preferences coming up (*I like this, I don't like that*)?

- As you finish, allow yourself to notice your thoughts and feelings about the exercise. Did you enjoy it or not? What was the experience like for you?

- You might consider repeating the exercise with a food that you feel neutral about, or one that you don't particularly like.

Hopefully, doing that exercise gave you a taste (sorry, I couldn't resist!) of what it's like to be mindful of your experience of eating. I'd encourage you to try eating an entire meal mindfully and see what it's like. People often report that they enjoy their food more and that they eat less when they practice eating mindfully. If you're like many of us, this can be very different from the way we usually eat—distractedly shoving food into our mouths as we think about what we need to do next or stare at the television.

Although this exercise used eating as an example, it's also possible to bring mindful awareness to almost any activity you engage in, like doing the dishes, gardening, or cleaning up the garage. The key is to slow down a bit and focus the spotlight of your attention directly on whatever you're doing, opening your awareness to all aspects of the experience. We can walk mindfully, noting the feeling of our feet touching and leaving the ground, the feeling in our muscles as we maintain our balance and move ourselves forward. You can be mindfully aware of a particular sense, like your hearing, as you nonjudgmentally observe all the sounds that come in through your ears. Practicing mindfulness can be particularly fun when you fully direct your attention to something that you find pleasurable, like the feeling of hot water in a shower, bath, or tub; the taste of a food you enjoy; or the sound of a piece of music you particularly like.

As we've seen, we often go through the world in a state of mind*less*ness, with our minds on automatic pilot. When you are in the grip of anger, the automatic pilot driving your attention is none other than your threat system. It keeps your awareness fixed on experiences and thoughts that fuel your anger and your sense of being threatened. As we've seen, our powerful threat and drive systems can dictate the focus and content of our attention, thoughts, imagery, motivations, emotions, and bodily experiences so that we become lost in experiences like anger and completely lose contact with the present.

Learning mindfulness can help us recognize this process as it happens and step out of it. In contrast to the threat system, which grabs hold of our attention and focuses it (as well as our thoughts, emotions, and so on) on the object of our anger, our compassionate minds can *choose* where we place our attention. Being mindful doesn't mean that we don't experience emotions like anger. Rather, mindfulness recognizes emotions and thoughts for what they are—events in the mind. From the perspective of mindfulness, we can *observe* both external and internal experiences without being caught up in them. We can recognize that mental experiences such as thoughts and emotions are not necessarily reality: just because I have the thought *I can't do this* doesn't make it *true*. In terms of emotional impact, there's a big difference between really believing *I can't do it* and having the mindful awareness that *I was just thinking, "I can't do this." Hmm...I seem to be doubting myself a bit.* Recognizing thoughts and emotions as mental experiences gives us a bit of distance and perspective—some space in which to operate. One of my favorite bumper stickers is, "Don't believe everything you think." As we go about the business of working with anger, we can come up with other helpful sticker-slogans, like "slow it down," and "give things some space."

When we are mindful, we can bring our attention to the present moment in a way that is curious and nonjudgmental about what we discover. We can notice and investigate the quality of our experiences (for example, the way anger feels in our bodies) as if we are studying them out of curiosity: *Oh, this is what it's like*[4]...*this is what my anger feels like. No wonder I have such a hard time calming down—things are really moving in there!* When we are mindful, we open ourselves to the variety of human experience (not just the pleasant stuff) and accept all of it without clinging to it or pushing it away. In chapter 3, we looked at how our anger is often rooted in avoidance, grasping, or clinging and how easily we become upset because we want things to be different from the way they are now. Our mindful, compassionate selves are able to accept and tolerate difficult situations and to *work with things as they are, not just how we'd prefer them to be.*

That doesn't mean we won't work to change things. By reading this book, for example, you're specifically working to change how you respond to threats and your tendencies to become angry and express anger in unhelpful ways. We can draw upon our compassionate motivation to make things better. Mindful acceptance actually helps with this, as we learn to stop fueling our anger and discontent with thoughts such as, *It's all going wrong! This is awful!* or *I hate this!* When you *do* lose awareness and slip back into those ways of thinking (and you will), you can always find it again by noticing those thoughts for what they are: *Ah...angry thoughts! I recognize you! You're trying to keep me locked into my anger. What a delightfully tricky brain I have!*

Exercise 6.2: Mindfulness of the Body

Take a moment to direct your awareness to your body—to *notice* and *explore* what your body feels like. For each of these exercises, you'll want to find a quiet space where you won't be disturbed.

1. **Body Scan.** Direct your attention to the top of your head. Notice what it feels like. Gradually bring your attention down to your forehead, nose, cheeks, jaw, mouth, and then to the back of your head, neck, and shoulders. Work your way down your body—down your arms to your hands, down your chest to your stomach, waist, buttocks, sexual organs, legs...

all the way down to your toes. As you slowly move down, spend time with each part of your body, pausing for a number of seconds at each part. Focus your attention closely on that portion of your body and get to know what it feels like.

2. **Open Bodily Awareness.** Take a moment to connect with the overall feeling of your body. Open your awareness to your whole body. Do any sensations stand out from the others? Does any part of your body call for your attention more than others? (For example, *I'm now aware that my feet are cold and that I'm getting hungry.*) Allow your attention to move to those sensations, wherever they are. Really study them, as if you might have to explain the sensations in specific detail to someone who has never felt them before. Try not to judge the sensations as good or bad—even if they are painful. Just be curious. What are they like? What qualities do they have? Spend time with one sensation and then allow your attention to shift as other sensations stand out to you.

3. **Working with Discomfort.** In this exercise, you'll bring your awareness to a point of mild discomfort, such as an itch, or perhaps the cold feet or mild hunger I noticed a few moments ago. Select an area where you experience some mild discomfort but not severe pain. Allow yourself to be open to this sensation and accept it. This sensation is neither bad nor good—it's just a bodily sensation. Bring your attention to the discomfort and really study it. What are its different qualities? Does it tingle, ache, sting, or burn? Does there seem to be a temperature or color associated with the sensation? Try to also notice any thoughts or feelings that come up. If you notice yourself desiring to scratch or rub the area, you can do so, but mindfully observe what that feels like, too. Alternatively, you can choose to *not* scratch or rub it for now, and observe what it feels like to refrain from doing so. This is one way we can learn the compassionate quality of distress tolerance: *refraining from acting out in anger can be a lot like choosing not to scratch an itch.* It's possible to observe an experience without reacting to it. See if you can direct some kindness toward the area, imagining that it is surrounded in warm acceptance—as if you are relaxing and opening to the experience rather than tensing and trying to push it away.

In his book *The Wise Heart: A Guide to the Universal Teachings of Buddhist Psychology,*[5] Jack Kornfield describes the acronym "RAIN," which stands for Recognition, Acceptance, Investigation, and Nonidentification—all of which can be applied to a practice of becoming mindfully aware of our anger. We can *recognize* our anger—notice that it's happening: *This is just the sort of situation that tends to set me off. I'm getting angry right now. I can see the signs of anger coming up in my body.* We can *accept* our experience without pushing it away or being judgmental about what is happening: *I'm getting really worked up right now.* We can mindfully *investigate* our experience and take a closer, deeper look at what is going on. And we can engage in *nonidentification,* which means that we realize that our anger is not *who we are,* but instead it is simply *an experience we are having.*

As we mindfully explore our experience, we can use the spider diagrams featured in the previous chapters as a guide for our investigation—bringing our awareness to experiences happening in our bodies, noticing where our attention is drawn, observing our desires—what we are motivated to do and what we are feeling, thinking, and doing. We can study these experiences and describe them to ourselves: *My heart is racing and my stomach is in a knot. I'm angry, and my thoughts keep going back to what I could say to her. I want to lash out, to hurt her feelings the way she hurt mine.* Simply observing these experiences can give us a bit of distance from them. The recognition that *we are not the anger* can help us step back from it. A metaphor that we in CFT circles have borrowed from Buddhist traditions is that you can put mud (or poison) into water and the water will look cloudy, but the mud and the water are not the same thing. The mud can be removed or allowed to settle, and the water will again be clear. Our minds are the same way—they can be contaminated by anger, but the anger is merely an experience that colors the mind. Our minds can again become clear as we help them to settle.

MINDFULNESS: A WORKOUT FOR THE BRAIN

A growing body of research shows that persistent mindfulness practice can produce changes in the function and structure of the brain. In 2011, Britta Hölzel and her colleagues published a study that used magnetic resonance imaging to examine changes in the brains of people who had taken an eight-week course of Mindfulness Based Stress Reduction (MBSR).[6, 7] The study compared sixteen people in the mindfulness program with a control sample of seventeen others who did not practice mindfulness. Participants in the MBSR program attended a weekly two-and-a-half-hour group meeting in which they participated in a number of mindfulness-based training exercises, including body scans, mindful yoga, and "sitting meditation," which uses mindfulness to focus on the breath and other sensory experiences. Additionally, participants in the mindfulness group spent an average of twenty-seven minutes per day engaged in mindfulness practices during the course of the study.

Results from the study revealed that the individuals in the mindfulness condition showed significant increases in brain gray matter concentration in the left *hippocampus*, an area of the brain that is involved in cortical arousal and emotion regulation. Increases in gray matter were also observed in other parts of the brain: the *posterior cingulated cortex* and the left *temporo-parietal junction* (two structures involved in processes related to self-awareness) and clusters in the *cerebellum*, which is also involved in helping us regulate our emotions. These changes were not observed in the control group. What is the take-home message? By choosing to engage in mental activities such as mindfulness and compassion practices, we can potentially *change our brains*. The ways our tricky brains work can cause us difficulties, but this doesn't mean we're helpless to affect things. More and more, we are learning that practicing mindfulness is a workout for the brain, developing the abilities (and the parts of our brains) that will help us manage our emotions and function better in the social world.

MINDFULNESS OF THE BREATH

With mindful breathing, we bring our attention to the breath and keep it anchored there, observing the breath as it enters and leaves our bodies. We can settle our attention wherever we feel the breath most clearly, perhaps at the point at the end of our nostrils where the breath enters and leaves the nose or on the rise and fall of our abdomen, just below the rib cage. There are a number of reasons for choosing the breath as an anchor point for practicing mindful attention. As we learned in the preceding chapter, the rhythm of the breath can be soothing to us as we attempt to focus our attention. Additionally, the sensation of breathing stands out so that we can easily find it, but it's subtle enough that it requires some effort to keep our attention there. Also, the breath is always there; if we're alive, we can always turn to the breath.

Mindfulness of the breath can be both simple and challenging, basic yet profound in its impact. The essence of the practice is straightforward: we bring our attention to our breath and attempt to keep it there. When our attention inevitably wanders off because we've been distracted by thoughts, feelings, or other sensations, we refocus our mindful attention by noticing that we've been distracted and then gently bringing our attention back to the breath. We notice and return, over and over again. Simple, right? Well, it is simple, but it's not easy. Keeping our attention on the breath is actually a lot more challenging than we may anticipate. Our minds are used to being very active—thinking and doing and remembering and imagining. They may struggle with the experience of stillness and the attempt to stay in the present moment, not being used to staying in one place for extended periods of time. So, when we begin to observe the breath, our minds almost immediately will begin to carry us away. We become distracted by thoughts, memories, noises, bodily sensations—the list goes on and on. This happens very frequently when we're learning mindfulness. Sometimes, we notice the distraction right away and can bring ourselves right back to the breath. At other times, we'll get completely lost in thought and may stay there for almost the entire session.

The fact that we get distracted when we're learning mindfulness can be very frustrating—we may think we *should* be able to keep our attention perfectly centered on our breath, and may get angry or frustrated when we can't. We may even think there is something wrong with us that prevents us from doing it; we may feel that we just don't have the right minds for it. Can you see what's happening here? Our threat systems are activated by the sense that we're failing at something we think should be easy, which then causes frustration, arousal, and a variety of other thoughts that make it even more difficult to be mindful.

Luckily, you can prevent yourself from getting caught up in this sort of difficulty if you keep a few things in mind. First, you want to approach the process of learning mindfulness, well...mindfully. Remember—being mindful means being curious, accepting, and nonjudgmental about whatever is happening in the present moment. Allow yourself to observe whatever is happening, *including* feelings of distraction, frustration, and self-doubt. You can even choose to draw upon some compassionate understanding, kindly encouraging yourself to do this surprisingly difficult task. In the next chapter, we'll dive into developing our compassionate minds, which will help with this. When we approach learning mindfulness in this way, the frustration of *I can't do this!* becomes an observation: *Wow! I've got a very busy mind today!* Compassionate thinking helps us to remind ourselves that everyone gets distracted during mindful breathing exercises, particularly when we're starting out. It's not your fault. (If you've read the first half of the book, I bet you knew that one was coming.) Your mind has spent decades learning how to be busy. The fact that it takes some practice to settle it down is *not* a sign that something is wrong with you. It's completely normal.

Another point to understand is that *we can't lose* when we're practicing mindfulness. We actually need our minds to become distracted during our practice so that we can learn to notice when it happens. Every thought, emotion, or experience that takes us away from the breath is an opportunity to practice noticing movement in our minds—learning to notice when our attention is captured by these experiences—and to practice bringing our attention back to where we want it. Notice what happens when you do this. When you observe that you've been distracted by thoughts or emotions, there is a shift in awareness that pulls you out of the daydream and back into the present moment. This awareness is the essence of mindfulness. In learning to catch your anger early, being able to notice these movements in your mind and body can be a real advantage. This ability can help snap you out of your angry state of mind, allowing you to observe your angry thoughts and emotions as mental events without your behavior being dictated by them. If you never have distractions, how will you learn to notice your thoughts and emotions as they arise?

Despite all of that, we're almost guaranteed to become frustrated sometimes during our mindfulness practice. Given our current purpose, this is also a good thing. Tibetan Buddhist teachers often refer to "taking adversity as the path," which means that *we can't learn to work with a difficulty unless we sometimes have that difficulty.* This is one reason why distress tolerance is an important component of a compassionate mind and why it's crucial for learning to deal with anger in more effective ways. Developing distress tolerance gives us the ability to accept temporary discomfort as a part of life and to endure the discomfort that comes with being angry while refraining from acting on the anger. Frustration during mindfulness practice gives us an opportunity to learn how to sit with a mild form of anger, to tolerate it, and to work with it. We can observe the frustration as a mental experience and gently bring our attention back to the breath. We could even shift the focus of our mindful attention from our breath to the frustration itself. Doing this, you would accept that *This is how I'm feeling right now,* taking a perspective of curiosity as you examine your frustration, as well as the thoughts, motivations, and bodily experiences that go with it. Most folks who stick with mindfulness practice learn early on how to observe the thought *I don't want to do this. I'm going to get up,* even as they keep on practicing, knowing that this is just another thought.

Exercise 6.3: Mindfulness of the Breath

As with the previous exercises, find a quiet place where you won't be disturbed. You might want to get a timer or set an alarm (something with a pleasant tone, not a jarring one) to let you know when your session is done.

- Sit in an upright position, with your back straight and the soles of your feet flat on the floor. It's all right to lie down if you need to, but that can sometimes cause drowsiness.

- If you like, you may close your eyes. Alternately, you can keep them open and allow your gaze to drop—perhaps to a spot on the floor—and then "soften" your gaze, allowing your eyes to unfocus a bit.

- Allow yourself to become aware of your breathing. Just notice the sensation of the breath entering and leaving your body.

- You're not attempting to control your breathing—just let it take on a rhythm that is comfortable for you. There will be variations from breath to breath. Just notice them.

- Follow the pathway of your breath: in through the nose, filling your lungs, raising your abdomen, and back out again.

- Bring your attention to the point at which the sensation of the breath stands out most strongly to you. Often people observe the rise and fall of their abdomens, just below the rib cage, or attend to the breath entering and leaving at the tips of their nostrils. The key is to find the spot that works best for you.

- Once you find a spot, let your attention rest there, observing your breath. You're just setting your attention there, not clamping it down. Gently observe your breath.

- Thoughts, feelings, and sensations will distract you and take you away from the breath. When this happens, simply notice that it has happened and gently bring your attention back to the breath. Notice and return. Notice and return. This is the practice, and you'll do it many times.

- Optional: When you notice that a thought, feeling, or sensation has taken you away, you can choose to briefly label what it was that you noticed. For example, if you're thinking about something, simply note to yourself, *Thinking*, and return to the breath (other labels might include *Listening*, and so on). You can also briefly congratulate yourself when you notice the distraction as you learn to observe the movement of your mind.

Mindfulness is a skill, and just like any other skill, it needs to be practiced. You can take some actions to increase the likelihood that you will follow through with your practice and benefit from it. First, when you begin to do the breathing exercises, it's good to start small. In our anger groups, the first assignment is to practice for at least two minutes per day for the first week. We move up to five minutes the second week and ask members to maintain a five-to-ten-minute daily mindfulness practice (encouraging them to go longer if they choose) as we begin introducing other, compassion-based practices into the routine. Other programs encourage people to practice for longer, say twenty to thirty minutes per day, and that is wonderful. I encourage you to do this if you'd like. In my groups, I tend to keep it a bit briefer than that and encourage folks to do it more often—several times a day, if possible.

The idea is to keep yourself motivated so that you keep practicing. Even if you find yourself very motivated in the beginning, I'd recommend doing shorter sessions several times a day, even just "checking in" with the present moment for a few seconds. I know countless people who've started out very excitedly and enthusiastically with long mindfulness meditation sessions, only to burn out a few weeks later and stop altogether. Try to structure your practice so that you'll keep doing it. While I won't be giving you any "rules" for your practice, there is one very practical guideline from Buddhist master Yongey Mingyur Rinpoche that has guided how we've structured things in our groups: "short periods, many times."[8] I think this is good advice for our purposes because it helps us bring mindfulness into many aspects of our day. The goal is to gradually cultivate an open awareness of the unfolding process of our lives, so that we spend more time engaged in the present moment and less time lost in thoughts and emotions that contribute little to our happiness.

I find it useful to set aside time for a mindful breathing session every day for a consistent length of time. I do twenty or thirty minutes in the morning, just before or after a small breakfast (depending on how hungry I am!), and I also practice a variety of very brief mindfulness exercises at different times throughout the day. It's useful to pick times of day when you're mentally alert—it's much harder to be mindful when we are struggling to stay awake. There are lots of ways to briefly introduce mindfulness into the day so that you can develop the habit of connecting with the present moment. For example, you can commit to eating at least one mouthful mindfully every time you have a meal or snack. When walking, you can do so mindfully—if only for a few steps. If you have a few minutes free, you can do a quick body scan, moving your awareness across your body, spending a few seconds on each part as you go. Or you can simply bring your awareness to a particular body part while doing things like washing dishes, bathing, or using the toilet (if this sounds odd, recall that you're learning to nonjudgmentally observe *all* of your experiences). You can combine your mindfulness practice with the soothing-rhythm breathing exercise, connecting to the calming rhythm of the breath for thirty seconds or so whenever you get the chance. Several times a day, you can do a quick checking-in exercise like the one we began this chapter with (and which is included as exercise 6.4). Again, the idea is that you're trying to *establish the habit* of mindful awareness so that, eventually, you just naturally find yourself connecting with the present moment in this way—and are more likely to notice when angry thoughts or emotions begin to carry you away.

Exercise 6.4: Mindful Checking In

The goal of this exercise is to bring you quickly and efficiently into the present moment and to establish the habit of noticing what is happening in your body, thoughts, and emotions. It takes just a few moments, and you can do it at almost any time (except while driving—then keep your attention on the road!). As you do this exercise, remember to direct your attention in a warm, nonjudgmental way. You are simply observing what your experiences are in the moment:

- Bring your attention to your body. Notice how it feels.

  - What is the temperature like?

  - Notice the points of contact between your body and other objects.

  - Is your body tensed or relaxed?

  - Allow your attention to be drawn to any bodily sensations that stand out to you.

  - Notice the information coming in through your other senses— what sights and sounds are you aware of?

- Bring your attention to your thoughts.

  - Observe your thoughts as mental events.

  - Notice the content of your thoughts—what are they about?

  - Notice the rate of your thoughts—are they coming quickly or slowly?

- Bring your attention to your emotions and motivation.

  - What emotions are you feeling? Which emotions stand out?

  - Notice the different emotions that can be present at one time and how they're related to one another.

  - Notice your desires—what do you feel motivated to do?

- Try to observe the relationships between your bodily experiences, thoughts, and emotions. Which ones go together?

Here's a summary of some tips for learning and maintaining a mindfulness practice:

- Start small and gradually increase the amount of time you practice.

- Establish a routine of doing mindful breathing at a consistent time of day, at a time when you tend to be mentally alert.

- Have fun! Bring mindful awareness to a variety of different activities throughout the day. Don't let it get boring.

- Get in the habit of mindfully observing your body. Learning to bring awareness to sensations in the body can help you step out of the inertia of an emotion and observe it. In this way, you gain a sense of distance from it and avoid being trapped in thoughts that continue to fuel your anger.

- Bring mindful awareness to activities that can be pleasurable.

- Check in with yourself and your experience several times per day.

- Remember that there's no way to fail. Your mind *will* become distracted, and learning to notice this is part of the reason you are learning mindfulness. Just keep coming back to the focus of your mindful attention. Remember: *notice* and *return*.

MINDFULNESS AND WORKING WITH ANGER

Mindfulness prepares us to access our compassionate minds as we relate to the experiences of our lives with calmness, curiosity, openness, and acceptance. This is opposite to the way anger organizes our minds. Where our angry minds seek to reject and harm, mindfulness accepts and embraces. Where anger judges, mindfulness observes. When faced with difficulties, anger narrows our attention and locks our minds into a flurry of threat-related thoughts, images, and bodily sensations. Mindfulness observes all of this mental activity for what it is and allows us to step out of our threat-driven mind-set, broaden our attention, and see all aspects of the situation.

We can see that mindfulness gives us many tools that we can use to work compassionately with specific anger episodes and that fit with many of the skills we'll be developing in the rest of the book. As we learn to notice movement in our bodies and minds, we can wisely recognize the signs of anger before we become caught up in them. Our anger motivates us to act in destructive ways, but if we relate to the anger as just another mental event, we can disengage from it and refrain from engaging in our habitual and destructive angry behaviors. The ability to mindfully observe our bodily experiences can help us to *accept* and *endure* the discomfort associated with anger and refrain from the urges it produces. As we practice mindfulness, we gain greater control over our attention. This control will help us to redirect attention in more useful ways—for example, finding ways to get our safeness systems going and the creation of compassionate thoughts and behaviors. Finally, as we practice connecting with the present moment in different ways, we will slowly *establish new patterns* in our brains—patterns associated with a compassionate willingness to engage with whatever life presents us rather than falling into anger every time something doesn't go our way.

CONCLUSION

Learning mindfulness gives us a way to connect with our experiences that is open, accepting, and nonjudgmental. It can help you learn to control your attention and to participate directly in your life, rather than being captured by your thoughts and emotions or going through life on automatic pilot. Research shows that mindfulness can be beneficial to us on many levels, potentially improving our physical health, helping us to deal with difficult emotions, and even stimulating growth in our brains.

Mindfulness is a valuable tool that can help you work with your anger in more effective ways, and like any valuable skill, it takes time to cultivate. The key is to establish mindful awareness as a *new habit*. I'd recommend mindfully checking in with yourself before and after doing the other exercises we'll cover in the rest of the book. This will increase your awareness of how the practices affect your thoughts, emotions, motivations, and behaviors. Getting in the habit of observing your state of mind gives you countless opportunities to shift your mental perspective. In the next chapter, we'll do exactly that as we focus squarely on developing the perspective of the compassionate self, which will provide a framework for organizing the work we'll be doing for the rest of the book.

7

Compassionate Imagery: Developing the Compassionate Self

I n this chapter, we'll use imagery to begin developing what I call the "compassionate self." As we've seen, our brains and bodies can respond to mental experiences (thoughts, fantasies, and imagination) in ways that are similar to how they respond to external situations. We've seen how imagery can impact our mood and overall mental state—imagining situations that threaten or anger us can keep us angry for hours at a time. In the same way, compassionate imagery can produce entirely different patterns in our brains, organizing our minds in ways that are helpful rather than harmful. Many of the exercises included here are reminiscent of mind-training techniques that have been used for thousands of years.

USING IMAGERY

Before we jump into the practices and exercises, let's consider how to work with three potential obstacles that sometimes come up when we begin to use imagery: having a wandering mind, feeling as if you "can't do" imagery, and not having time to practice.[1]

The Wandering Mind

Our minds will sometimes wander during these imagery exercises, just as they do when we practice mindfulness. Sometimes they wander a *lot*. The key to managing this is to simply accept that our minds will sometimes wander, and that it's okay. The routine is to bring your attention to the imagery exercise and, when you observe that your attention has wandered, to gently bring your attention back to the imagery. Remember, becoming aware that your attention has wandered helps you learn to notice movement in your mind—a valuable skill to have when you are working with anger.

"I just can't do imagery!"

We may tend to think that mental images are like Polaroid pictures in the mind, but for many of us, mental imagery may simply consist of fleeting, fragmented images or simply of "having a sense" of something. To help you understand, let's take a moment to do some brief imagery exercises:

- Think about your favorite meal.

- Now bring to mind a recent drive or ride that you've taken, perhaps to work.

- Think about the summer holiday you'd like to take this year.

Don't rush. Just give yourself a bit of time to think about these things, noticing what happens in your mind. Those fleeting impressions of favorite foods, the journeys you took and houses you passed on the trip to work, the beach or mountains of your vacation spot—all of those impressions were created through mental imagery. To a greater or lesser extent, we can all engage in imagery—say, by imagining a meal in such a way that it impacts our bodies and minds, perhaps by making our mouths water.

These imagery exercises aren't about creating vivid or sharp mental images—they are about having a *mental experience* that can impact your state of mind. And if you find that you have difficulty creating or maintaining vivid images in your mind, it isn't a problem. The key is to focus on the experience and to notice any feelings that might come with it. As I've mentioned, my mind tends to be very auditory—I can play songs in my head like a jukebox, but I struggle to *picture* anything. One technique I sometimes use is to imagine what it would be like if I could picture whatever it is I'm imagining.[2] You don't want to get caught up in being judgmental about your ability to visualize. It's better to simply notice when you think, *I can't really imagine this very well,* and recognize it as just another distracting thought to be aware of as you gently bring the spotlight of your attention back to the imagery.

Not Having Time to Practice

Many of us have very busy lives and may feel as if we don't have any time to set aside for practice. However, practice doesn't need to be really time consuming—it can take up as little as thirty seconds of your time. Additionally, if we really look at how we spend our days, there are often lots of small pockets of time that we could potentially use—while sitting on the train on the way home from work, during a commercial while watching television, that sort of thing. It's also useful to find convenient ways to remind yourself to practice, possibly with a tiny note by the bedside or in your lunch box, or by using a cell phone alarm. It can help to keep a small stone or some other small object in your pocket so that you'll be reminded every time you reach in your pocket. When you notice it, you can practice thirty seconds of soothing-rhythm breathing and then spend possibly a few minutes on one of the imagery exercises. Instead of a pebble, I use a one-pound coin, as it's the perfect size and reminds me of England, where I first learned about CFT.

To identify the "pockets of time" I've mentioned, you could keep a record of how you spend your time for a week, and then review where you might be able to create space for practice. You may discover time that you hadn't been aware of before. Often, we may *feel* as if we have no time yet also spend several hours per day watching television programs that we aren't terribly fond of or surfing the Internet. If this is the case, it may be possible to find ten or twenty minutes in the day for imagery practice. We can be creative in looking for times and places that are great for compassionate-imagery practice; for example, we can practice in the bath, in bed before we get up (what we in CFT circles sometimes call "compassion under the duvet"), or for a few minutes during the lunch break at work. Remember, "short periods, many times."

Finally, if you really don't have *any* time to yourself, it's worth putting some effort into changing this, as this lack of time may be contributing to your struggles with anger. Stress tends to turn up the volume on our difficult emotions. Sometimes making the effort to create a bit of space in our lives can make a world of difference.

CULTIVATING THE COMPASSIONATE SELF

We'll be looking more closely at the qualities of the compassionate self shortly, but for a moment let's begin by briefly *imagining* that you have them. What would it be like to have a sincere desire to be helpful? To possess a sense of calm confidence and the courage to face difficulties? To have wisdom drawn from life experiences and the ability to be in control of your mind, rather than having it controlled by anger or any other particular emotion? You can create a vision in your mind of how you'd like to be—of a "compassionate self." Your sense of self can be *practiced* and *developed* in the way that you practice and develop other qualities that you'd like to have. For example, if you wanted to be a good tennis player or guitarist, you would spend time hitting the ball on the tennis court or practicing chord changes over and over. Gradually your body and mind become familiar with the things you need to do to be a better tennis player or a better musician, as those new brain patterns begin to "wear in." If your goal were to solve math problems, you'd need lots of practice to train your mind to work in those specific, analytical ways.

Once you've connected with a compassionate motivation—for example, to be helpful and caring—you can move on to practicing and developing these qualities so that they become a greater part of who you are. Once again, the idea is to get into the *habit* of bringing forth these qualities in ourselves, so that we can have a greater sense of well-being and purpose, feel that we have more control over our lives, and contribute to the happiness of those people around us. The compassionate self is capable of taking anger and turning it into respectful assertiveness, defined by wisdom and strength. Nelson Mandela is a good example of someone who chose to take a compassionate focus and, as a result, became a powerful leader.

The compassionate-self exercises are about beginning to develop a new identity for yourself based on the qualities of compassion. Why is it important to do this? Well, much of how we think, feel, and behave is related to how we see ourselves. If we see ourselves as being "angry" people, we're more likely to act out of anger, to accept our angry behaviors as simply part of who we are, and to use that as an excuse not to change them. Alternatively, the development of a compassionate self-image can set us up to think and behave as someone who is compassionate and who doesn't want to harm others or ourselves. It can help us to *take responsibility* for changing angry behaviors that don't fit with the sort of person we want to be.

All the imagery exercises will begin in the same way: you'll start by taking an upright, dignified posture, assuming a seated position when first learning the exercises (although later you can feel free to do them standing up or lying down), and relaxing your facial muscles. You'll slow yourself down a bit, engaging in thirty seconds or so of soothing-rhythm breathing, which helps prepare your mind for the calm, thoughtful perspective of compassion and teaches your brain to associate SRB with the qualities of your compassionate mind. Remember how we looked at classical conditioning in chapter 3? By consistently doing soothing-rhythm breathing immediately before each of the compassionate-imagery exercises, you'll be teaching your brain that this way of breathing and compassionate ways of thinking and feeling go together. Then, in the future, the combination of this learning and the slowing effects of the breathing can work together to help you shift into a compassionate state.

To relax your facial muscles, begin with the forehead and work down, allowing your jaw to drop slightly. Allow the edges of your mouth to turn upward slightly. Keep going until you arrive at a smile that you feel is gentle, warm, and friendly. It should be a comfortable and natural expression— the kind that you might have if you felt completely at peace with yourself, completely safe. This is not an exaggerated, cheesy smile, or a too-friendly "creepy guy at the bar" smile. You're just taking advantage of the subtle way your facial muscles can send messages to your brain that can tend to improve your mood.

As you do the compassionate-self exercises, it can be useful to approach them as if you were a method actor who is studying your character by mimicking his posture, manner of speaking, and facial expressions, as well as by imagining how the character *feels*, *thinks*, and *is motivated to behave*. It doesn't matter if the method actor actually resembles the character he is portraying—he imagines what it would be like if he were that person.

We'll be taking this approach as well, and it may help us avoid the potential obstacle of thoughts such as *I can't do this! How can I imagine myself as a compassionate person? I'm nothing like this!* It *doesn't matter* if you feel that you have these qualities or don't. Just imagine what it would be like if you did have them. Allow your mind to explore this way of being without judging or second-guessing your efforts. The key is simply to approach the exercise with the motivation to begin developing the innately compassionate aspects of yourself. This motivation should grow increasingly as you continue to practice so that it gradually becomes more than just acting a role. The idea is for it to become a greater part of your identity, a part of yourself that you feel is worth developing.

If this seems far fetched, let me say that I've used these exercises in a prison environment, and the power of learning to nurture and connect with our compassionate selves can be profound. Earlier in the book you met Wade, who was regularly abused as a child, was imprisoned for violent offenses, and had developed such a threatening persona that even other prisoners tended to avoid him. One day during our CFT for Anger group, Wade reported that he had received a letter from his ex-wife asking him to relinquish his legal rights to his children so that her new husband (whom she had left Wade to be with and whom Wade had violently attacked before entering prison) could adopt them. A hush came over the room as the gravity of the situation hit our all-male group. As a father, I can imagine few things more difficult than signing away rights to my son, and Wade had frequently shared his caring and concern for his own children. For Wade, this issue brought up tremendous pain and turmoil—reopening the wounds of his divorce and his own childhood, highlighting the pain of being in prison and unable to care for his children, and bringing up feelings of being inadequate as a father.

The first time he read the letter, all of this surfaced in the form of anger: he was overcome with rage. After a few minutes, though, something happened. He told us, "I just sat down, defeated, staring at the floor. I just sat there and breathed for about forty-five minutes. And then my compassionate self kicked in, and I knew I had to sign that letter." It took him over a month to sign it; he spent the time thinking, going over the situation in his mind, trying to figure out what would be the best thing for his children. Once he'd created space for his compassionate self to emerge and not be bullied and tossed out of the way by his angry self, he was able to connect with his would feel, think, and behave as a result. Select different qualities in different practice sessions:

- **Sensitivity.** Acknowledging suffering without being overwhelmed by it.

- **Sympathy.** Allowing your calm and confident compassionate self to be touched by the suffering of yourself and others.

- **Empathy.** Being able to put yourself in the shoes of others (and yourself) and understand why they feel the way they do—how it makes sense that they might feel this way.

- **Generosity.** Feeling the compassionate motivation to give.

- **Forgiveness.** Being able to let go of grudges and hurt caused by others (and yourself).

- **Playfulness.** Allowing yourself to be lighthearted, even in the face of difficulties.

Consider other compassionate qualities you'd like to have.

To develop this practice, you might *imagine that you are looking at yourself from the outside.* See your facial expressions and the way you move in the world. Note your motivation to be thoughtful, kind, helpful, and wise. Hear yourself speaking to others, noting your compassionate tone of voice. See others relating to you as a compassionate person. See yourself relating to other people in this compassionate way that you're developing. For the next thirty seconds or so, playfully and gently enjoy watching yourself being a compassionate person in the world, and note how other people relate to you as this person.

When ready, return your attention to the present moment, bringing your compassionate presence into the world. As you develop your practice, you can imagine yourself having all those qualities you've been practicing. This way, when you focus on activating your compassionate mind using the skills in the rest of the book, you'll have a sense of the kind of person you're working to become. The more you practice slowing down and imagining being this person, the more easily you may find that you can access these qualities in yourself and the more easily they will be able to express themselves through you. Over time, your compassionate self can simply become your, *self.*

CONSIDERING SELF-COMPASSION

CFT emphasizes bringing compassion into our relationships with all beings, including *ourselves*, and focuses on self-compassion as a pathway to good mental health.[3, 4, 5] In chapter 4, we looked at the way compassion involves being sensitive to suffering, and having a kind motivation to help. While we may tend to think of compassion as extending these qualities to others, *self-compassion* involves extending this kind sensitivity, understanding, and helpful motivation to ourselves and to our own suffering. In many cases, we may tend to treat ourselves much more harshly than we treat others and may deny ourselves the kindness that we unthinkingly give to other people. With self-compassion, we recognize that we are also worthy of this kindness, which we then give to ourselves.

Psychologist and self-compassion researcher Kristin Neff[5] defines self-compassion as involving three components:

1. Extending kindness and understanding to yourself rather than harsh self-criticism and judgment

2. Seeing your experiences as part of the larger human experience rather than as separating and isolating

3. Holding your painful thoughts and feelings in balanced awareness rather than overidentifying with them

This definition helps us recognize our struggles in a larger context—that of the common human experience—and guides us to relate to these challenges in more helpful ways.

In CFT, we approach self-compassion by particularly emphasizing the nature of the human experience. By now, you are familiar with the CFT approach to self-compassion: the idea that we all have tricky, evolved brains that create difficulties in our lives and that we all just find ourselves here, doing the best we can in the face of often challenging lives. When we recognize the difficulties and suffering that we and others will inevitably face simply as a result of being born human, we see that directing kindness and patience toward ourselves is not only helpful; it's really the only approach that makes sense. However you choose to approach it, the idea behind self-compassion is that, instead of relating to ourselves with harsh judgments, self-criticism, and shame, we give ourselves the same compassionate kindness and patience that we would direct toward others that we dearly care about. Doing so can help us shift out of the patterns of shame and self-blame that keep our threat system on high alert, providing continuous fuel to our anger.

THE COMPASSIONATE SELF IN ACTION

Once we become acquainted with the compassionate-self practice and how it feels to imagine ourselves with these qualities, we can focus our thoughts and attention on other exercises designed to deepen the experience of feeling compassionate and to stimulate our safeness response. For the following exercises, begin by shifting into the perspective of your compassionate self. Take an upright, dignified posture, spend about thirty seconds in soothing-rhythm breathing, and image yourself with the compassionate qualities emphasized in the compassionate-self exercise. Imagine yourself as the sort of person who is kind and is motivated to be helpful, as someone who has a calm sense of confidence and authority, a sensitive emotional perspective, and the wisdom that comes from a wealth of life experiences.

The first practice is called "Deepening Compassion," and the idea is to awaken and really familiarize yourself with the compassionate wish to flourish and to be free from suffering and the emotional experience that goes with it. You'll focus your compassionate wishes on someone whom you care about, for whom you naturally and easily feel a strong sense of warmth and affection[6]. For example, you might choose to imagine a friend, partner, child, or even an animal. It shouldn't be someone whom you have mixed or negative feelings about (for example, a partner whom you love very much but with whom you've also had a lot of recent conflict). If you pick someone but find yourself feeling a lot of resistance, feel free to shift to someone else for whom the feeling of kindness and compassion flows more naturally.

Exercise 7.2: Deepening Compassion

Begin by accessing your compassionate self: take an upright, dignified posture with your face relaxed and smiling slightly. Start with thirty seconds of soothing-rhythm breathing. Imagine yourself as someone who is kind and is motivated to be helpful (thirty seconds). Imagine having strength and a sense of authority—the calm confidence to work with difficulties (thirty seconds). Next, imagine having wisdom and insightfulness (thirty seconds).

Now bring to mind someone you care about. This should be someone you naturally have affection for, for whom caring arises fairly naturally in you. It could be a friend, partner, child, or an animal—someone for whom it's easy to have kind, nurturing feelings.

Hold this person (or being) in your mind's eye. Focus your compassionate feelings on them and bring to mind the kind wish for them to prosper—to be happy and free from suffering. Extend this wish to them and really try to *feel it*. Name them in your mind as you breathe in, and say the following as you breathe out:

- "May you be *free of suffering*." (Pause for ten to thirty seconds.)

- "May you be *happy*." (Pause for ten to thirty seconds.)

- "May you *flourish*." (Pause for ten to thirty seconds.)

- "May you *find peace*." (Pause for ten to thirty seconds.)

For the next minute or longer, if you can, continue to say these phrases (out loud or silently) as you visualize this being you care about. With each phrase, focus on the wish you are directing toward them. Attempt to feel the wish that they be free of suffering, happy, and able to flourish and find peace. After each phrase, wait a few seconds. Really let the meaning sink in as you sincerely direct this wish to the person you care about. If you can't remember these specific phrases (or have other compassionate wishes that you prefer), just use the ones that you recall.

When you're ready, let the image fade. Spend a moment or two reflecting on the feelings that have arisen in you while you have focused your compassion on this being. Notice how it feels in your body. Remember, this is a practice designed to awaken feelings that we may not connect with all that often, so it may take time to really feel it.

After practicing the deepening compassion exercise a few times, you'll become familiar with how it feels to extend compassionate wishes to someone you care about. For those of us who have struggled with anger, this exercise can sometimes bring up difficult emotions. For example, if we've caused pain to the person we're visualizing, we may experience guilt or shame. This is normal, and it's a sign that we're beginning to connect with compassion for that person. (If we didn't feel compassion toward them, we likely wouldn't care if we'd caused them pain or not.) If you notice this happening, try to mindfully observe those thoughts and emotions as mental events, occurring because you are connecting with the compassionate wish that the person or animal be happy, and gently bring your attention back to the phrases. If you continue to struggle, I'd strongly suggest that you choose another object of compassion. The idea is to pick someone (perhaps the family dog!) for whom compassion easily arises so that you can practice it, and become very familiar with what it feels like. By doing this, you aren't letting yourself off the hook for the pain you've caused—you're working to develop states of mind that will help you treat that person better in the future. People you've hurt won't benefit if you get caught up in punishing yourself. But they (and everyone you interact with) will benefit from your development of kindness and compassion. Once this exercise comes to you more easily, you can move on to extending your compassion to slightly more challenging targets.

As you've perhaps noticed, these exercises build on one another, and you'll begin each by briefly connecting with the compassionate qualities of the mind by doing the compassionate-self exercise. In the following exercise, you'll first connect with your compassionate feelings by first directing them to someone you care about as you did in the preceding exercise, and then you'll extend those compassionate wishes to a new target—*you*. This may seem like a lot to do in a single exercise, but it takes just a few minutes to progress through the preceding exercises, and the total practice can be done in well under ten minutes, particularly after you become used to it.

Exercise 7.3: Compassionate Focusing on the Self

Begin by moving through the Compassionate Self and Deepening Compassion exercises, taking a few minutes to assume the posture and qualities of the compassionate self and then visualizing someone you care about and extending compassionate wishes to that person. Focus on your compassionate feelings and your sense of kindness, calm confidence, and wisdom. Connect with the deep wish that this person be happy and free from suffering, focusing on how this feels.

Now create a picture of yourself in your mind's eye, as if you were looking at yourself from the outside. Don't worry if you can't produce a vivid image—if the image doesn't come easily, you can instead place one hand flat on your chest at the level of your heart, and one just below, on your abdomen. The idea is to get a sense of connecting with yourself. Focus your compassion on yourself as a human being who has arrived in this world, one who just wants to be happy and to avoid suffering, a person doing the best you can as you're faced with difficult feelings and life circumstances. Keeping your compassionate, friendly expression and a sense of your warm voice, imagine directing the following phrases toward yourself:

- *May I be* free from suffering. (Pause for ten to thirty seconds.)

- *May I be* happy. (Pause for ten to thirty seconds.)

- *May I* flourish. (Pause for ten to thirty seconds.)

- *May I* find peace. (Pause for ten to thirty seconds.)

For a few minutes, continue to say these phrases (out loud or silently) as you visualize yourself in your mind or attend to the feeling of your hands on your torso. With each phrase, focus on the wish that you're directing toward yourself. Attempt to *feel* the wish that you will be free of suffering, happy, able to flourish, and at peace. After each phrase, wait a few seconds, really letting the meaning sink in as you sincerely direct this wish to yourself. Again, if you can't remember these specific phrases (or have compassionate wishes that you prefer), just use the ones that you recall.

If you find yourself resisting (for example, feeling as if you don't *deserve* to be happy or free from suffering), remember that we're working with our minds in ways that will help us to improve ourselves and our ability to manage anger—this goal has *little to do with what we may or may not feel we deserve*. Our shame keeps us locked into our threatened, angry states of mind, so it's time to learn to *let it go*. You can notice and compassionately acknowledge these thoughts, gently let them go, and bring the focus back to your kind, confident, and wise compassionate self. Notice what feelings arise as you direct these kind wishes toward yourself and how it feels in your body.

Directing compassionate wishes to yourself can feel a bit strange or uncomfortable in the beginning, particularly if you usually relate to yourself with anger, shame, and self-criticism. Some resistance and discomfort is perfectly normal as you begin to shift the way you think and feel about yourself. You may fear that you don't deserve kindness, that directing compassion toward yourself will make you weak, or that it may let you off the hook for the things you've done. Directing these kind thoughts to the self can also bring up feelings of heartbreak if the exercise reminds us of affection and support we never received. When this happens, you can draw upon the skills you've been building: you can mindfully observe the feelings while refraining from judging them; you can access your kind, wise, compassionate self; you can recognize your shame and difficult feelings for what they are—*suffering*—and a sign that in fact you *do* need compassion. You can withhold judgment, directing sympathy and kindness to yourself as you struggle with these feelings. You can also attempt to develop empathy for yourself, working to understand how it makes sense that you feel this way. So when these emotions come up, gently bring your attention back to your compassionate self and reconnect with the attributes you're working to develop—kind concern, confidence, and wisdom. Then return to the phrases. Just like the previous exercises, the key to the practice is to notice and return, over and over again.

Sometimes, the emotions that come up can be so overwhelming and paralyzing that they prevent us from continuing in the exercises entirely. This is a sign that you may benefit from a therapist who can support and guide you as you go through this process. Part of the wisdom of compassion is recognizing when we need help and then getting it.

USING IMAGERY TO ENGAGE YOUR SAFENESS SYSTEM

So far in this chapter, you've worked using imagery to help you connect with your compassionate self. In the chapters to come, we'll explore how we can use the perspective of our compassionate minds to help us view situations that anger us in new ways and discover new approaches for responding to these situations. However, when we find ourselves hijacked by anger, the arousal and emotional inertia of the threat response can make it very challenging to shift our minds in this way. It's hard to think flexibly and compassionately when we are driven by our threat systems. We'll address this by using some imagery exercises that can help us activate our soothing system and bring some balance to our emotions.

You took the first step in this direction when you learned soothing-rhythm breathing, which helps you slow your body and mind down, helping to counter the physical arousal and the racing thoughts that fuel (and are fueled by) anger. Now you'll try using imagery exercises to direct your attention away from the thoughts and fantasies that keep your anger going.

"DON'T THINK OF A WHITE BEAR!"

One strategy you may have tried in attempting to manage your anger is to simply stop thinking about it. Does this work?

It turns out that the answer seems to be, "Not really." In 1987, memory researcher Daniel Wegner and his colleagues examined the effects of *thought suppression*: attempting to avoid thinking about specific topics.[7] They divided the participants in their study into two groups, and one (the "initial suppression" group) was instructed to avoid thinking about a white bear for five minutes. The other group (the "initial expression" group) was given opposite instructions: they were told to try to think of a white bear. Both groups were instructed to ring a bell every time they thought of a white bear during the five-minute period. Afterward, the group instructions were reversed—the initial suppression group was asked to think of a white bear for five minutes, and the initial expression group was asked not to.

The results revealed that members of both groups continued to think of white bears at a rate of more than once per minute even when asked not to, but the group that was *most likely* to think about white bears was the thought suppression group—the one that had at first been asked not to think of them. In fact, this group thought of white bears *more often* than the participants who had been told to think of them from the outset.

Furthermore, rates of "white-bear thoughts" in participants who'd been asked to avoid thinking of them *increased* over time once they were no longer attempting to suppress their thoughts. In every other condition, the rates of white-bear thoughts gradually decreased over the five-minute periods. It seemed that initially attempting to not think of white bears actually set participants up to be preoccupied with them later, in a way that increased over time. The researchers called this the "rebound effect."

In a second study, an additional condition was added. A third group of participants was instructed to avoid thinking of a white bear but was told, "If you do happen to think of a white bear, please try to think of a red Volkswagen instead." This strategy worked: giving participants something else to think about seemed to block the rebound effect. These participants didn't tend to think about white bears more as time went on in the way that the others had.

The results of this study mean that it doesn't work to simply try to avoid thinking about something that has made us angry, because this may actually make us *more likely* to stew over it later. If we want to move on, we'll need to focus our attention on something else. Specifically, we're going to bring our attention to imagery and thoughts designed to help calm and balance our emotions so we can come back and address the situation from a compassionate perspective (rather than one that is controlled by our threat systems).

These exercises are not about soothing away anger or trying to suppress it by distracting ourselves and forever avoiding the situations that led to it. A growing body of research indicates that *avoidance of difficult emotions doesn't work*. Rather, our goal is to step away from the anger and bring a bit of balance to our emotions so we can come back to the situation that has activated us, addressing it from the perspective of our compassionate selves. This isn't avoidance—it's working with the spotlight of our attention to help us approach difficult situations from a perspective that is driven by a compassionate motivation to help rather than by our automatic threat responses. We shift away momentarily, center ourselves, and return when we're ready.

YOUR IDEAL COMPASSIONATE IMAGE

Our next exercise will focus on the creation of your "ideal compassionate image."[8] Like other exercises that help us direct compassion toward ourselves, this exercise is designed to help us counter feelings of shame and self-doubt or of feeling judged, disliked, or criticized. We do this by imagining a perfect (or ideal) compassionate nurturer who accepts, understands, and values us.

Sometimes we can initially feel strange imagining someone who relates to us in this way. We may even feel anxious or saddened, thinking, *I don't have anyone in my life who relates to me like this*. Apart from religious entities, the truth is that none of us truly has a perfect nurturer—someone who purely accepts us, understands our inner thoughts, feelings, and motivations; someone who will never condemn us regardless of the circumstances. Real people can't do that. The key to remember here is that our emotional minds *respond to our imaginations*, and we're using this observation to help change the way we think and feel about ourselves. Recall that our safeness system is linked to experiences of affiliation—cues of safety, acceptance, and kindness that we receive from others. The goal of this exercise is to use your imagination to stimulate such experiences. The fewer actual people you have in your life who provide this kindness and acceptance, the more important it is to learn to do it for yourself.

To begin, consider what qualities you would like your compassionate image to have—perhaps complete acceptance of you no matter what, a deep concern and affection for you, or a sense of kinship and belonging. For example, if you feel that you don't deserve compassion, imagine that your compassionate image understands this concern and helps you with these feelings. If you don't feel understood, you might imagine your compassionate image as being completely understanding. The idea is that your compassionate image is a match for *you*—possessing qualities that are perfectly designed to meet your needs and help with your own particular struggles. This being understands the human condition very well, perhaps because it has been through difficulties itself. It understands that we all just find ourselves here— we are born, grow up, and somehow become the people we are—equipped with a tricky brain and with feelings and problems that we didn't choose and that we may not have been prepared to deal with. Sometimes we may find ourselves avoiding our problems or even doing things out of anger that make them worse. Your ideal compassionate image understands that this is part of the struggle of being a human being. Your ideal compassionate image will always try to help you become more compassionate to yourself and others and will never criticize you.

If you find yourself struggling with this practice, start by just imagining a compassionate voice that tells you the sorts of things you would say to comfort a friend whom you dearly cared about. The idea behind all of these exercises is to find a way to start directing compassion toward yourself and to allow yourself to receive it, to feel cared about, respected, and valued.

Exercise 7.4: Your Ideal Compassionate Image

As with the other exercises, begin by assuming an upright, dignified posture, relaxing your face and allowing your mouth to form a slight, warm smile. Spend about thirty seconds in soothing-rhythm breathing, allowing your breath to fall into a slow, soothing rhythm:

- Keeping in mind the qualities we've considered, begin to visualize your ideal compassionate image. Consider what this being would look like. Would you want that person to be old or young? Male or female? Perhaps nonhuman, such as an animal or a part of nature? When you think of this being, notice what comes to mind; over time, you may find that different images will come and go. Don't try to hold on to them, just see what happens and go with what is helpful to you. If your ideal compassionate image were to communicate with you, what would their tone of voice sound like? Imagine their facial expression—the way he or she smiles at you or shows concern for you. Spend the next thirty seconds imagining your ideal compassionate image, one that's perfect for you in every way.

- If you'd like, you can imagine your compassionate image coming to you in the safe place you'll be developing in exercise 7.7 later in this chapter. Once you're familiar with that exercise, feel free to bring that place to mind. Imagine that your image is coming toward you to meet you and that you are moving toward her. Feel this being's pleasure as he or she smiles at you. Imagine them being with you, either standing in front of you or perhaps sitting or standing beside you. Spend thirty seconds imagining this scene.

- Take a few moments to consider any other sensory qualities that are associated with your ideal compassionate image. Focus on your sense of its presence and the feeling of having this compassionate being with you, supporting you. Focus on this for thirty seconds.

- Imagine how your compassionate ideal became compassionate. Maybe they've had many experiences of pain and suffering, of doing good and bad things but has learned how to dedicate themselves to the compassionate path. The idea is that this ideal compassionate being deeply understands the suffering and pain of humanity and can completely understand your own personal struggles. This being's wisdom comes from inner knowledge of the pain and suffering that is a part of life. His or her deepest wish is to offer you complete compassion and understanding. Spend the next thirty seconds considering this aspect of your compassionate ideal image.

- Now imagine that your compassionate image has certain qualities. Begin by focusing on the sense of safety, kindness, and warmth you feel when you are with your compassionate image. Imagine what it would be like to feel completely safe with this being (it doesn't matter if you do or don't feel safe—the key is to imagine what it would be like *if you did*). Notice the feelings that would arise in you. Spend thirty seconds in this way.

- Now focus on the sense of this being's maturity, authority, and confidence. This being is not overwhelmed by your anger, pain, or distress, is not put off by the strange things that can go on in your mind. It remains present, enduring these experiences with you. Imagine what it would be like to be with such a compassionate being, one who's there just for you, conveying a calm sense of strength and confidence and helping you to experience these qualities as well. Spend thirty seconds or so imagining this.

- Imagine your compassionate image also having great wisdom that comes from experience and dedication. A part of this wisdom is reflected in this being's kindness, calm confidence, and deep desire to be helpful and supportive. Imagine the profound wisdom enabling them to truly understand your struggles, hopes, and fears. Imagine that this being passes this wisdom on to you. Spend thirty seconds in this way.

- Now focus on your compassionate image having a deep commitment to you. Imagine that, no matter what, this being is fully accepting of you and committed to supporting you in becoming more compassionate to yourself and others and getting better at coping with life. This being's kindness, acceptance, and commitment to you are freely given, and there is nothing you could do that would cause him or her to reject you. Spend thirty seconds imagining this.

- Keeping your friendly facial expression and breathing in a soothing rhythm, imagine your ideal compassionate image speaking to you in a warm voice, conveying deep wishes and commitment to you:

  - "(Your name), may you be free of suffering."

  - "(Your name), may you be happy."

  - "(Your name), may you flourish."

  - "(Your name), may you find peace."

  Spend one minute imagining this.

- When you're ready, allow the vision of your compassionate image to fade and bring your awareness back to the present moment.

COMPASSION FLOWING INTO US

In this practice, we imagine that compassion and peace, visualized as a healing light, flows into us from an outside source. You can imagine these compassionate wishes coming from your ideal compassionate image, from some aspect of nature, from all the kind beings in the universe, or from a spiritual source from your own faith tradition if you have one. It doesn't really matter what the source is—the important part is that in your imagination you can accept these kind wishes flowing into you.

Exercise 7.5: Compassion Flowing In

Again, spend about thirty seconds doing soothing-rhythm breathing and access the kindness, wisdom, and confident authority of your compassionate mind:

- Imagine that, outside of you, a source of great kindness and compassion sees that you're struggling and directs its efforts to help you. Imagine it directing great compassion, peace, and kindness to you.

- Imagine that this great wish for you to be happy takes the form of light—any color you'd like—and that this light flows into you through the crown of your head (or, if you like, at the level of your heart).

- Imagine this light flowing into your body, accumulating at the level of your heart, and slowly filling you. As it flows in, you experience a sense of great compassion, peace, and kindness spreading through you. When this light contacts pain in you—physical or emotional—it simply surrounds this pain and gently holds it in warmth and compassion.

- Imagine being completely filled with this light and being completely filled with this sense of compassion, peace, and kindness. You feel completely safe and comfortable.

BRINGING COMPASSION TO PAIN

In this next exercise, we use our imaginations to direct compassion to our own pain. For example, this could be the pain of embarrassment or regret from having spoken harshly to a loved one, or even the physical pain of an ingrown toenail (ouch!). We can also use this compassion to target feelings of resentment and hurt we feel toward others, feelings we may have simply been trying to ignore. We imagine sending compassion out to this pain and surrounding and holding the pain with acceptance and kindness. We're not covering the pain up or pushing it out. The light-visualization portion of the exercise is optional—some people like visualizing the light, and some don't. Just find the way that works best for you. The key is that you're directing compassion toward a part of yourself that is hurting or suffering.

Exercise 7.6: Sending Compassion Out to Pain

Again, spend about thirty seconds doing soothing-rhythm breathing and access the kindness, wisdom, and calm confidence of your compassionate self:

- Take a moment to reflect on an experience of physical or emotional pain in your life. It can be a physical hurt; the emotional pain of anger, regret, sadness, disappointment, or embarrassment; or any other pain that you feel.

- Imagine sending compassion and kindness to this pain, accepting it as a part of your life experience, holding it in warmth, safety, and kindness, and soothing it.

- If you like, you can imagine these kind wishes originating as a point of light at the level of your heart (imagine what color it would be). Imagine that this is the light of compassion, peace, and happiness, and that it pulses with the rhythm of your breathing. Imagine that this light extends out to your pain and gently surrounds it, warmly holding it and accepting it as a part of your current experience.

- Observe what happens to the experience of your pain as it is held in your kind compassion. Keep in mind that you aren't trying to rid yourself of it—the pain isn't bad; it's just an experience you're having in this sometimes-challenging life.

THE SAFE-PLACE EXERCISE

As we've seen, anger is driven by the experience of feeling threatened—our brains perceive threats and activate us to respond. As long as our attention is focused on the threat experience, our anger is likely to continue. The goal of this imagery exercise is to construct a mental experience that is completely free from all feelings of threat. You'll be mentally creating a "place" that is safe, comfortable, and soothing—a place where you are welcomed and valued. This exercise is specifically designed to stimulate your safeness system, and it is unique to you. Some people imagine being at a beach, smelling the water and feeling the wind in their hair, or in a beautiful forest, watching the sun shine down through the trees. Other people prefer to use places from their memories. There are no rules for what your safe place should be, apart from being a place where you feel safe, comfortable, and welcome. There can be other people or animals there if you like, or you can be alone. I have several safe places: one involves walking alone on a beach, with the sun on my face and the salty smell of the ocean in the air; another is entirely different—a favorite pub in Birmingham, England, surrounded by old oak beams and furnishings, welcoming faces, and the tasty aroma of steak and ale pie at my table. Experiment to find the mental space that works best for you. Your safe place *welcomes you*, and *it's glad that you're there.* It takes joy in your presence. When you are there, you can imagine your cares, anger, and experience of feeling threatened melting away, replaced by the soothing sense of being valued and accepted.

Exercise 7.7: Constructing a Safe Place

Begin by assuming an upright, dignified posture, relaxing your facial muscles and allowing your mouth to form a warm, slight smile. Allow your breathing to slow, and spend thirty seconds or so doing soothing-rhythm breathing.

When you are ready, allow yourself to imagine being in a place that is comfortable and soothing, where you are filled with a sense of safety and calm comfort. This is *your* place, filled with comforting sights, sounds, and experiences:

- Imagine the details of this place. What do you see? Hear? Smell? Feel? Really try to form a mental experience of what it's like here.

Spend a few moments (thirty seconds to a minute, or longer if you like) imagining what this place is like.

- Are there other beings (people, animals) here? If so, imagine that they are welcoming you, value you, and are glad you're here.

- Imagine that this place itself takes joy in the fact that you are here, that this place itself welcomes you, accepts you, and is happy to have you.

- Spend as long as you like imagining and exploring this safe, comforting place. If thoughts intrude or distract you, mindfully notice them as distractions (attempting not to judge them or get caught up in them) and bring your attention back to your safe place. It's okay to resist the pull of the angry thoughts, despite how urgent they may feel. This urgency is simply a quality of threat emotions. Don't worry—you can go back and attend to these later, when things feel a bit more balanced. For now, it's all right to stay in this soothing space for a bit and allow yourself to feel safe, comfortable, valued, and calm.

CONCLUSION

In this chapter, we've covered a number of imagery exercises designed to help you activate your safeness system and begin developing the qualities of your compassionate self. Because our emotional minds can respond to imagined experience in ways that can be similar to how they respond to the experiences in the external world, imagery is a powerful tool for helping us to cultivate states of mind that we wish to have. Instead of using your mind's ability to imagine and fantasize to fuel your anger, as you likely have in the past, you're learning to use it to calm yourself and develop compassionate qualities.

As with any skill, the key is to practice as often as you can, and brief practice periods work just fine. You can shorten the exercises to suit your time period. For example, you don't have to go through all of the attributes in the compassionate self or ideal compassionate image exercises every time. Instead, you can focus on the attributes that will be most helpful to you in that moment (or even choose a particular one to focus on for a day or week) and also on the general sense of yourself as a compassionate being or of the compassionate being that accepts and supports you. Keep in mind that you can spend more time on the different parts of the exercises if you'd like, and you don't need to create sharp images in your mind—fleeting impressions are fine. You will likely find that you enjoy some of the exercises more than others. It's fine to spend more time with those exercises that work best for you, sometimes returning to the others to develop them as well. It can be useful to use the Compassion Practice Journal introduced in chapter 5 to keep track of your progress.

Copies of this log and guided audio (MP3) versions of many of the exercises can be found in the "Working with Anger" section at www .compassionatemind.net.

8

Working Compassionately with Anger: Validation, Distress Tolerance, and Exploring Your Emotional Self

We've explored the ways that anger works in our minds and seen how compassion can serve as its antidote. We'll now look at how we can bring compassion to our own experiences of anger. As we do this, it will be useful to have a specific example that demonstrates the various things we'll be discussing.

A CASE EXAMPLE: SHEILA AND JOSH

Over the past several years, Sheila had developed significant anger around her relationship with her twenty-five-year-old son, Joshua, an on-again, off-again university student who had spent the past six years or so moving in and out of different jobs and academic programs but making little progress toward a career. Sheila, a fifty-one-year-old single mother, raised Josh by herself even while maintaining a high-achieving career in advertising, and she worked very hard to give Josh a good life and pay for his education. She loves her son dearly but found herself frequently filled with anger and frustration at his life choices. "I'm just furious with him. He spends his time lying around, playing video games, and hanging out with his friends. He can't keep a job, and because he can't decide what he wants to do with his life, he won't finish his degree. He won't do anything to help himself. I've worked myself nearly to death for the past twenty-five years to give him these opportunities, and he's throwing it back in my face!" Sheila went back and forth between being angry at Josh and being angry at herself, because she interpreted his situation as being her own fault: "It was *my* job to raise him and give him the tools to succeed—clearly, I failed!" Her interactions with Josh became increasingly tense and snappish, which she was somewhat mindful of: "Now, it's like I'm angry as soon as I think of him. If I look at caller-ID when my phone rings and I see that it's him, I'm angry before I even pick up the phone. I just know that he's going to tell me about his latest screwup and expect me to bail him out."

Sheila was convinced that if she had been able to provide Joshua with a male role model, things would be turning out differently for him. At times when her shame got the better of her, she attempted to "help him" by sending him money, even when he hadn't asked for it (and several times, even when he told her not to send it). Sheila felt trapped in a cycle of anger, disappointment, fear for her son's future, desire to control his behavior, and shame.

Looking back, we see that what Sheila is going through demonstrates the ways that anger can fuel itself in our minds. She interprets her son's behavior as signs of negative personality traits on his part—laziness, ingratitude—and of her failure as a parent. She spends lots of time ruminating over what's made her angry with her son and herself, focusing on both his "failures" and hers. As a result, she's oblivious to the signs of success in his life (or her own successes with regard to him). She feels embarrassed during conversations with colleagues, some of whose children are attending medical school or already have budding careers. She indulges in tragic fantasies about Joshua's future—that he will be chronically unemployed and alone, that he will move back in with her, that others will judge her based on his failures. Sheila harbors strong desires to control Joshua, to coerce or force him to live his life in a way that meets her standards. As we move through the next couple of chapters, we'll use Sheila's case as an example that will show us how we can bring the skills of compassion to counter the ways that anger plays out in our minds.

GETTING TO KNOW YOUR ANGER RESPONSE

I've prompted you several times to consider your anger, the factors that tend to trigger it, and how you tend to feel, think, and behave when angry. Becoming familiar with anger in this way paves the way for working with it compassionately, because we gain a sense of what there is to work with. It also allows us to begin anticipating situations that are likely to trigger anger in us and to plan how to approach them. The anger monitoring form introduced in this chapter is designed to help you *get in the habit* of mindfully observing your anger and then to generate compassionate alternatives for dealing with it and the situations that trigger it. Let's take an initial look at what the form will help you examine.

Situation/Trigger

Briefly describe a situation that provoked anger or irritation in you. What threat was involved? Describe the context as well ("I was late, and the people in front of me were dawdling").

Your Response Emotions

What feelings did you have during the situation? Often when we feel anger, there are other emotions going on as well. Use specific terms (anger, irritation, rage, embarrassment, shame, fear, sadness, excitement, and so on).

Thoughts

What things did you tell yourself? (For example: *I can't let him treat me with such disrespect! She was probably just in a hurry.*) How did your thoughts fit with your anger? Did they fuel it or calm it?

Behavior

What did you do? What actions did you take?

What Does Your Compassionate Self Say?

Think about your wise, kind, confident, and compassionate mind that you connected with in the compassionate-self exercise. What would it think or say? How would your compassionate self approach this situation?

What Would Your Compassionate Self Have Done?

If it were in control, how would your compassionate self behave in this situation?

Outcome

How did it turn out? What helped in the situation? What did you do that worked? What got in the way of handling the situation the best you could?

The idea of the anger monitoring form is to have a structured way of examining how anger plays out in our lives. If we use the form, we can begin to see patterns in the situations that trigger our anger and in how we respond. This can help us anticipate and plan for how we will deal with similar situations in the future. The form also prompts us to use our compassionate minds to come up with alternatives to our habitual responses to anger, which we'll be looking at in the rest of this chapter. I've included a blank monitoring form later, as well as an example drawn from Sheila's work on her own anger.

Sample Anger Monitoring Form: Sheila's Example

The purpose of this form is to help you become familiar with the situations that tend to provoke your anger and the ways you tend to respond. It also aims to help you generate compassionate alternatives. Pick one time during the week when you experienced anger, rage, or irritation.

Situation/Trigger: *Phone call from Joshua. He told me he was changing his major yet again, this time to art.*

Emotions: *Anger and worry. I also felt hopeless and inadequate as a parent, like it's my fault that he can't get his act together.*

Thoughts: *Well, that adds another year of college. He's never going to get a decent job! Why can't he just stop screwing around and get to work? This is my fault. My parents would never have put up with this.*

Behaviors (What did you do?): *I snapped at him and told him that I was getting sick of it and that he needed to get his act together. I also told him there weren't any good jobs for artists.*

What does your compassionate self say? *He isn't doing this just to frustrate me. He's trying to figure out his life. Josh is a grown man who can make his own choices. I don't have to agree with all of his choices to love and support him.*

What would your compassionate self do? *Call him back and apologize. Assertively express my concerns in a way that doesn't attack him. Work with my own emotions so that I can accept his decisions.*

Outcome: *I ended up calling him back and apologizing. I'm still struggling with his decision, but I'm not as angry.*

Anger Monitoring Form

The purpose of this form is to help you become familiar with the situations that tend to provoke your anger and the ways you tend to respond. It also aims to help you generate compassionate alternatives. Pick one time during the week when you experienced anger, rage, or irritation.

Situation/Trigger:

Emotions:

Thoughts:

Behaviors (What did I do?):

What does your compassionate self say?

What would your compassionate self do?

Outcome:

COMPASSIONATE VALIDATION OF ANGER AS A THREAT RESPONSE

This chapter's first exercise aims to help us overcome the self-criticism and shame that can keep us from dealing with anger. Shame and self-criticism about our anger and its consequences can create great pain in us, prompting us to either ignore our anger altogether or to justify our angry behaviors as we attempt to avoid facing the harm and difficulties that they have caused. As a result, instead of seeing the anger itself as the issue, we experience hostility toward ourselves, other people, or the situations that trigger it. This tendency only fuels the habitual process of anger. We'll explore ways of dealing with trigger situations, but the *first* thing we'll attend to is the anger itself. We're intentionally shifting our focus from whatever the situation is (the battle) to the way that anger plays itself out time and time again in our lives (the war). Difficult situations will come and go, but out-of-control anger can create problems in many different areas of our lives. Once you're able to manage the way you respond to feeling threatened, you'll be much better equipped to deal thoughtfully and compassionately with whatever situation has triggered your anger. When things in your life go badly (as they sometimes will, despite your best efforts), you'll be able to stop yourself from making them even worse.

We need to find a way to take responsibility for our anger that doesn't cause us to feel ashamed, "bad," attacked, self-righteous, or contemptuous. In doing this, we'll want to mindfully recognize when we begin to justify, deny, push down, or blame our anger on others, and use those observations as reminders to refocus on compassion instead. Keep in mind that while we *didn't* choose to have threat systems that produce anger, we can recognize the suffering that our anger causes us and other people, and we *can* choose to connect with the compassionate motivation to help ourselves manage anger better. In this exercise, you'll remind yourself again that anger is your brain trying to protect you and that the reaction isn't your fault, and you'll commit yourself to working with anger more effectively.

This exercise can be done at any time. As with all of the exercises, it helps to practice when it's easy, so it may be a good idea to start by dealing with minor irritations.

Exercise 8.1: Compassionate Understanding of Anger as a Threat Response

Take a dignified posture, slow your breath, and bring to mind the characteristics of your compassionate self: imagine yourself taking on the qualities of a confident, calm, and wise person who is motivated to be supportive, understanding, and helpful. Feel those qualities in you as you breathe. Create a friendly expression on your face and imagine your tone of voice to be firm, kind, and understanding. Imagine yourself speaking compassionately. Spend a few moments imagining yourself from the outside, observing your compassionate self. Now imagine what it would be like to bring these qualities to this situation you're having difficulty with:

- Using your mindful awareness, observe the experience of your anger. Observe the thoughts and fantasies that fuel your emotional experience. Notice how your anger feels in your body, what sensations are associated with it.

- Observe your feelings and the motivations you have to act in certain ways.

- Consider what other emotions might be present alongside the anger. You may or may not be acknowledging these emotions in this situation (for instance, sadness, embarrassment, disappointment, and so on).

- Observe the quality of these emotions—how they direct your attention, perceptions, and motivation. Notice the angry thoughts and fantasies you are having and how they fuel your emotional response to threat.

- Remind yourself that all of these experiences are products of your threat system, your brain's attempts to protect you because it has perceived a danger to you. You didn't *choose* for your brain to respond in this way, and it isn't your fault. Your anger is not a sign that you are a bad person *or* that someone else is. It just means that your sensitive threat system has been activated. This can happen for many different reasons.

- Direct compassionate thoughts toward yourself: spend at least twenty seconds or more with each one as you breathe slowly, and hold on to the image of your compassionate self.

  - Empathy: Consider how it makes sense that you might experience anger in this situation and that it is unpleasant for you.

  - Encouragement: *These feelings are hard to take, but I've dealt with difficult situations in the past. I can work with this.*

  - Commitment: *Now that I've noticed my anger, I don't have to let it control me. What skills can I use to work with these feelings?*

- Bring to mind the reasons why you are choosing to work with your anger compassionately. Commit yourself to doing so.

- Allow yourself to feel good about your efforts: *I'm taking responsibility for my anger rather than letting it control me.*

Let's consider how this compassionate approach played out in Sheila's case. As she connected with her kind, wise compassionate mind, she realized that her reaction made sense—of course she would be frustrated and angry when she perceived a threat to her son's future and to herself as a parent. At the same time, she began to recognize that her anger only served to fuel her darkest perceptions of her son as a "failure," which exaggerated the negative aspects of his situation and ignored his positive qualities. For example, Josh actually spent much of his "lazy" time at home working on art projects, several of which had been featured in a recent show at the university gallery. She began to recognize her anger, fear, and desires to control Josh's life as indications of how much she cared about him, even though this created distance between them. She came to understand that although there were real concerns to be had about her son's future, much of her frustration was driven by values she had inherited from her own parents, and she recognized her tendency to compare herself to her colleagues and use their children's "success" as a measure of her parenting competence.

Anger is often like this—our threat systems personalize things and make them about *us*, even when the reality is that we may be relatively minor players in a situation that is playing out in *someone else's* life. Sheila also noticed that her anger had somewhat poisoned her relationship with Josh, making it hard for him to share his feelings and concerns honestly with her because he feared her disapproval, and prompting him to push back against her efforts to control him.

TOLERATING DISTRESS AND DISCOMFORT

When we consider the circle of compassion I introduced in chapter 4, we see that distress tolerance is a primary attribute of a compassionate mind. Compassion involves bringing ourselves into contact with suffering and enacting a kind motivation to help. Bringing ourselves face to face with difficult emotions and life situations is simply uncomfortable. It just is. But we can spend so much time and effort attempting to *avoid* discomfort that we forget that we can actually *tolerate* a good deal of it if we need to.[1] Again, most of us have at some point tolerated discomfort or distress in the pursuit of a goal—the pain of working out or running, the frustration of practicing a skill over and over to get it right, the irritation of studying for an exam when we'd rather be doing something more enjoyable.

Learning to tolerate discomfort and distress can help us work with anger, particularly if we tend to act out or are passive-aggressive. As an emotion, anger naturally produces a strong desire to act (aggressively), and this desire can be experienced as tension or discomfort. Sort of like an itch, it doesn't hurt exactly, but there is a strong experience of discomfort combined with the sense that the discomfort will go away if we act on the angry urge. Since working with anger often means refraining from acting out our angry, hostile, aggressive, or passive-aggressive urges, we need to learn to tolerate this discomfort. The idea is to find strategies that will help you to accept and tolerate discomfort as simply a part of working with anger, to remind yourself that you *can* do it, and to soothe yourself a bit until the wave of your anger has passed. Feel free to use any other strategies that you've found helpful as well.

Let's take a look at some of the wide variety of strategies that we can use to help ourselves tolerate distress. In chapter 6, for example, I introduced mindfulness, a powerful distress-tolerance skill that helps us understand that we are capable of observing our anger and discomfort without having to act on the urges that come with it. In fact, there are a number of skills that can help you to tolerate this discomfort:

- You can mindfully *observe* your anger-related discomfort without acting on it, accepting it for what it is—an activation of your threat response. When using mindful observation to deal with discomfort, it can sometimes be useful to keep bringing your attention back to your bodily experience. Just observe discomfort in an accepting, curious way.

- You can use soothing-rhythm breathing to counteract the angry arousal in your body, to slow yourself down a bit.

- You can use your compassionate mind to coach yourself through the discomfort.

- You can talk with a supportive friend or family member who can listen well, understand how you are feeling, and offer helpful suggestions (the kind that help you feel calmer and don't fuel your anger).

- You can use distraction to reduce your sensation of discomfort by temporarily bringing your attention to something that slows you down or soothes you (the safe-place exercise in chapter 7 or other imagery exercises we've covered).

- You can look at the anger event through the eyes of the compassionate self rather than stay in an angry mode of observation. The meaning of the event (and your reaction to it) can change when you view it from a compassionate perspective.

- Also, you can imagine the anger event from a third perspective: how might someone who cares about you (for example, your ideal compassionate other) think about this and help everyone in the situation? How would that person see the situation differently? Research shows that we stay angry if we simply ruminate about the situation, but we can reduce our anger if we can reconsider it from a different perspective.[2]

Let's return to our case example. Sheila noticed that she experienced significant discomfort whenever she was reminded of her son Joshua's situation, either in her thoughts or in conversations with him. It was particularly difficult for her when Josh told her of his decision to study art. For Sheila, this created a flow of extremely distressing thoughts: that he would be forever poor and unemployed, that he didn't respect her advice, and that she had failed to instill the value of hard work in him. These thoughts produced lots of emotional discomfort (anger, fear) in her, as well as the urge to yell at him. She wanted to "set him straight," a strategy that hadn't helped in the past. What it had done was create an uncomfortable distance in their relationship.

With some effort, Sheila found that when these thoughts came up, she could mindfully notice them and the distress they produced and then use a number of strategies for working with them. She found that spending time with a supportive friend helped a good deal. When her friend wasn't available, she found that she could compassionately coach herself through: *It makes sense that you feel this way, but you can make it through this, and you'll be better able to cope when you've calmed down a bit.* She also wrote a compassionate letter to herself so that she could read it in such situations (chapter 12) and found the safe-place (chapter 7) exercise useful at these times.

DISTRESS-TOLERANCE STRATEGIES

There are a number of strategies that can be useful for tolerating the distress of anger and the discomfort of refraining from how you normally (or habitually) behave when you're angry. Experiment with a number of strategies and find the ones that work best for you:

- Soothing-rhythm breathing (chapter 5).

- Mindful awareness, particularly of the breath and body (chapter 6).

- Self-coaching by shifting into the perspective of your compassionate self or imagining your ideal compassionate image (chapter 7). Imagine what this person might say to you to help you through. Remember, the key thing here is the *emotional tone* of these thoughts—keeping your well-being in mind, being kind, and having a deep and genuine wish to be helpful to yourself. Here are some examples:

- *This is uncomfortable, but you've lived through lots of things that are uncomfortable. You can do this.*

- *Remember why you're doing this.*

- *Ride out the wave. This won't last forever.*

- *This discomfort is a sign that you're succeeding. As with the pain from a workout, you are developing your mental muscles so that they can work with anger, and it will get easier in the future because of this effort.*

- *Keep going, one moment at a time.*

- Bringing to mind your compassionate motivation (chapter 5).

- Compassionate-imagery exercises (chapter 7), such as:

  - Safe place

  - Ideal compassionate other

- Compassionate-thinking exercises (chapter 9).

- Compassionate letter to yourself (chapter 12).

- Broadening your perspective by considering interdependence and the unintended kindnesses of others (chapter 12).

- Compassionate behavior, such as:

  - Conversations with supportive others

  - Distraction through positive experiences

  - Enjoyable songs, movies, quotes

  - Walks or enjoyable exercise

  - Humorous Internet movie clips (my favorite clip is called "Baby Monkey Going Backwards on a Pig!")

  - Be creative!

The idea is to find strategies that help you to accept and tolerate this discomfort as simply a part of working with anger, to remind yourself that you *can* do it, and to soothe yourself a bit until the wave of your anger has passed. Feel free to use any other strategies that you've found helpful as well.

EXPLORING EMOTIONS BEHIND YOUR ANGER

As we've seen, emotions like anger, anxiety, and compassion involve very different motivations, thinking, and ways of experiencing and interacting with the world. It can feel as if we have different selves: an angry self, an anxious self, a happy self, a sad self, a self-critical self, and, of course, a compassionate self. These perspectives can sometimes compete with one another, as reflected in the classic image of the person with a little angel on one shoulder and a little devil on the other, each offering very different advice. In any given situation, we can experience a number of competing emotions and motivations that can pull our minds in different directions. The problem is that, due to the "better safe than sorry" way that our brains have evolved, our threat systems are often capable of overwhelming the better angels of our nature.

One way to gain some understanding and control is to step back and explore the perspectives of our different emotional selves, giving priority to the compassionate self. We'll do this in the next exercise. The idea is to explore the ways that your different emotions experience the situation, but to do so in a mode of curiosity, as a kind, nonjudgmental observer. We'll be exploring the perspectives of anger, anxiety, sadness, and compassion in turn, examining how the situation appears from these different viewpoints. If you find yourself becoming overwhelmed by these emotions as you explore them, break away from the exercise, do some soothing-rhythm breathing, and shift back to the perspective of your compassionate self. Try to have a friendly interest in what these different parts of you think, feel, and want to do. If needed, you can always shift into a soothing exercise like the safe-place practice (chapter 7) in order to center yourself. The goal is to gain a clearer understanding of how different emotions play out in your mind, allowing yourself to explore them without criticism and learning to shift into the perspective of your compassionate self even in the face of other, threat-based emotions.

As we do this, we want to establish the compassionate self as a kind "emotional authority," sort of like the captain of a ship. The job of this compassionate captain is to make sure that all the other passengers (angry self, anxious self, sad self, and so on) are allowed to have their say. As they do, we accept and reassure them while using the compassionate self's kind, wise, and confident presence to work with the situation. We can imagine that, when faced with a stormy sea, the angry self might get mad: *I knew it was a terrible idea to get on this ship! Who's responsible for this mess? Let's string 'em up!* The anxious self might get lost in worry: *Oh my goodness, we could all die! I can't handle this!* The sad self might become hopeless and mournful: *I'll never see my loved ones again. It's all over for me.* In contrast, the compassionate captain knows that stormy seas (life's difficulties) simply happen sometimes, and that although it's not fun and can sometimes be scary, the captain can draw upon wisdom and experience in guiding the ship to safety. Our compassionate selves can understand the perspectives of our angry, anxious, and sad selves, understanding that *it is our nature* to experience and express these emotions, and working to bring comfort and balance to ourselves as we work our way through difficult experiences. In this way, we can bring acceptance to the various emotions we feel (rather than shame and self-criticism), even as we work to move beyond their limited perspectives.

To prepare for this next exercise, take out a pen and a sheet of paper and draw lines on the paper to divide it into four squares. Label the first square "Angry Self," the second "Anxious Self," the third "Sad Self," and the final square "Compassionate Self." Let's start with Angry Self in the top-left square:

- Consider a challenging situation that you've been dealing with, perhaps something that has recently caused you to be upset.

- How does your angry self view this situation? Spend a moment thinking about the typical thoughts you have when you're angry—thoughts of unfairness, being dismissed, or rejected. For instance, thoughts may sound like, *People don't care, People shouldn't get away with this, I have to show them,* or *People take advantage.* By now, you're probably familiar with the sorts of thoughts you have when you're angry. Write them down in this space.

- When you're ready, consider how your anger *feels.* Where is it in your body? Does it seem to move? How would you feel if that anger built up in you?

- Now think about the urges for action that come with your angry feelings. If your anger were totally in charge, what would it have you do? Notice how the threat system tries to control your behavior.

- Consider: What does your anger *really want*? Deep down, what would your anger like to have happen? What would happen if it were in complete control?

The idea is to get some insight into the core thoughts, feelings, and desires for action that go with your anger system or "angry self."

Exercise 8.2: Exploring Different Aspects of the Emotional Self

_____ Self

Thoughts and Imagery. What thoughts are you having as you feel this emotion? What are you imagining?

Bodily Experiences. How do you experience this emotion in your body? For example, does it hurt? Is there an experience of tightness, tension, sinking, or temperature? How does it feel?

Motivation. What does this emotional self want to do? What behavior is it trying to motivate you to do?

Desired Outcome. What does this emotional self want to happen? How does it want the situation to turn out? What would happen if it was in complete control?

Let's see how this exercise can work by looking at how Sheila responded to Josh changing his course to study art. First, she wrote from the perspective of her angry self:

I'll tell you what my angry self thinks. It thinks that he's spent six years in and out of university just so that he can choose a degree that prepares him to be unemployed! *It says that after all I've put into raising him and saving for his education, I'm going to be stuck supporting him for the rest of his life. My anger thinks that this is just another way for him to avoid having to do any actual work—that he's so lazy! My heart is racing, my stomach is tensed up, and my jaw is tensed—I feel like I could explode! I feel like smacking some sense into him, cutting him off, and telling him not to call me until he's graduated and found himself a decent job. What my anger really wants to do is take complete control, to force him to study something worthwhile and get himself into gear.*

Now let's look at the anxious self. In the top-right square, you'll have written the subheading "Anxious Self." Take a moment to think about the event that made you angry, and focus on any feelings of anxiety or fear that went through you. What were you concerned about? You may have lots of different thoughts: *This is getting out of control, I might regret this, Maybe something is wrong with me.* Just try to notice those anxious thoughts in the background of your mind and write them down as you do. When you're ready, move on to thinking about how anxiety feels in your body. How would you feel if that anxiety built up in you? If your anxiety were totally in control, what would it want you to do? How might it make you behave? Deep down, what does your anxious self really *want?*

The voice of Sheila's anxious self came from a very different perspective than did the voice of her angry self:

The voice of my anxious self is rather loud. It tells me that Josh just isn't going to make it, that he'll end up unemployed and alone, that he hasn't learned to support himself, and that I won't always be there to do it. What will happen to him? It worries me that he won't have a happy life and that it will be my fault—that I didn't give him the tools he'll need to succeed. My anxious self is scared of my angry self. I'm worried that my anger is driving him away from me. I'm worried that he sees all my attempts to help as efforts to control his life, and that he'll resent me for it and won't want anything to do with me. My body is filled with this restlessness—butterflies in my stomach and all jittery. I feel like if it doesn't stop, I might go crazy. My anxious self wants to just ignore the situation and run away. But, really, what it wants is to know for sure that everything will be all right—for Josh to have a great life and to know that I've done a good job at raising him.

Another aspect of the self that we sometimes don't want to think about when we're angry is the sad self. Before continuing, perhaps take a moment to slow things down and focus on the breath. Then, when you're ready, consider the subheading "Sad Self" in the bottom left-hand square. Take a moment to think about the event that angered you, focusing on any sad thoughts that are related to this event. These might be thoughts such as *I've failed, I don't want things to be like this, I'm pushing away the people I care about, I feel so alone.* Sometimes the sad self has thoughts that seem hopeless, that make us feel as if there's nothing we can do or that things won't change. For this exercise, just note these sad thoughts in the square so that you can understand where they're coming from. When you're ready, move on to thinking about how sadness feels in your body. Note how it's quite different from the energized angry feelings, that there is often a sort of heaviness with sadness. How would you feel if that sadness built up in you? How would it play out in your body? If your sadness were totally in charge, what would it want you to do? Deep down, what does your sad self really *want*? Try not get too pulled into sadness—remember, the aim is just to explore the perspectives of these different parts of your emotional self, as Sheila does below:

> *I've got a lot of sadness around my relationship with Josh. My sad self thinks that as hard as I tried, I failed in being a good mother to him. It thinks that I should have given him a father and that he's going to have a terrible, difficult life because I didn't give him what he needed. It thinks that I should never have had him, because I'm not strong enough to care for him. My sadness is lonely and thinks that there is no one who really loves me. It tells me that Josh doesn't love me because I keep harassing him all the time. In my body, my sadness feels tired, old, and achy. It wants to curl up in bed and never get up again, or maybe to just go to sleep and die. Deep down, my sadness just wants to stop feeling, to stop hurting. It just wants it all to stop.*

It can be quite sobering to explore our emotions in this way, because we can become tuned in to different parts of ourselves that anger usually blocks out. Many of my clients have discovered that behind their anger, there is actually a lot of sadness and anxiety that they are trying to avoid. They report preferring the powerful feeling of anger to the vulnerable experiences of sadness or anxiety, and that they use anger to keep from having to feel these emotions, or because they've been taught that it is okay for them to feel and express some emotions but not others. If we are unable or unwill-ing to tolerate sadness and anxiety, anger can feel like the only response we have left.

After using this exercise to explore different emotions and why we may choose to avoid them, we can also consider how they can interact. How does your angry self feel about your anxious self? Is it annoyed by your anxiety or even contemptuous of it? How does your angry self feel about your sad self? Now switch perspectives. How does your anxious self feel about the angry and sad selves? For example, do you find yourself being scared of your own capacity for anger? Finally, how might the sad self feel about the angry self and anxious self? It's worth taking a bit of time to explore the ways these different emotions can organize our minds and lead us to make critical judg-ments about ourselves as we observe our different emotions.

You can probably see that these threat-based selves are often in conflict with one another and might even dislike one another. Some people can be so anxious about expressing anger that they retreat into passive coping: keeping their anger locked up so that it can never really develop into mature assertiveness. However, their fantasies, resentment, and irritation still bubble inside and cause them great distress. Other people work so hard to avoid experiencing anxiety and sadness that the angry self always takes center stage and runs the show. *All* of these threat-based emotions can be power-ful, often unpleasant, and difficult to work with. This is why it's so helpful to develop the compassionate self as a kind, wise, and confident perspective that will allow us to work with our challenging threat emotions and the situations that provoke them. In this exercise, we've reserved the bottom right-hand corner of your page for the voice of your compassionate self.

By now, you are familiar with how to access your compassionate self. Begin by breathing slightly more slowly and deeply; feel your body slowing down. As you do this, imagine yourself as a deeply compassionate being: kind, wise, and confident. Create a friendly facial expression and imagine your kind, confident tone of voice. When you feel you are ready, take a moment to think about the situation that angered you, but focus on thoughts you have when you're being helpful and compassionate. Note how the sense of slowing associated with the compassionate self feels in your body. If that feeling (associated with a sense of confidence, wisdom, and warmth) were to grow inside you, how would that feel in your body? If your compassionate self were totally in control, what would it want you to do? Consider for a moment, deep down: what does your compassionate self really want?

Don't rush the exercise. Spend time reflecting and being curious and open to new discoveries. You will gradually discover that the compassionate self thinks, feels, and wants to act very differently than the angry, anxious, and sad selves do. Sit back and look at the angry self through the eyes of the compassionate self. Do this with the anxious self and sad self as well. What does the compassionate self think and feel about these other parts of you? Can the compassionate self recognize that these parts of you have their own points of view that are not to be ignored but need help to be more balanced? As your compassionate self recognizes that these emotions are just a part of you, how would it help them? For example, might it help the angry self and anxious self to learn to be more assertive? Might it reassure the anxious self? Might it help the sad self to feel loved?

Paul Gilbert developed these ways of working with different emotional selves with a focus on building our compassionate capacity to deal with these inner voices, so that we can gain more emotional balance. You'll also see that while the anxious, angry, and sad selves can be frightened or contemptuous of each other, the compassionate self is like the kind, authoritative parent or captain who can take different points of view and is not in a battle with the other parts of the self. This is why we see this self like an inner authority: it can create space for the difficult, threat-based emotions we experience in a way that is both accepting and assertive. We can see that Sheila's angry, anxious, and sad selves were focused on several key threats: her son's livelihood, how others perceived her as a mother, and threats to her relationship with Joshua, whom she loves very much. Let's see what her compassionate self had to say:

> First, my compassionate self would say that it makes sense that I would be scared about Josh's future and frustrated with his choices. It's a difficult economy right now, and I'm his mother—I love him and want him to have a good life. I was also raised to believe that it's very important to be a high achiever and to make lots of money. My compassionate self recognizes that much of my sadness comes from feeling unloved. When I was growing up, my parents only seemed to love me when I did what they wanted, and they often expressed very harsh disapproval when I didn't. There is a part of me that has a hard time feeling loved, even now. My compassionate self also helps to reassure me as I deal with my anger, anxiety, and sadness, by helping me to see other parts of the situation. Although I get really worked up about it, I have to admit that Josh

always seems to find his way through things. He pays his own rent and some of his tuition, and we've been able to keep him from having to go into debt. He calls me every weekend and even sometimes tries to reassure me that he'll be all right. He's kind, so I must have done something right. And he did seem very happy about changing his course of study. I want him to be happy, and I guess there are jobs out there for art teachers and things like that. When I access my compassionate self, my body calms down, and I feel comfortable. My compassionate self sees my angry, anxious, and sad selves almost like children. They're important, but they don't understand the whole situation, and my compassionate self is like the parent who can help them see things more clearly. The goal of my compassionate self is just to do the best I can to help, both with Josh and with my own emotions. It wants all of us to be happy.

In summary, the goal of this exercise is to explore the perspectives of your competing threat-based emotions and allow them to express the thoughts, concerns, physical experiences, and motivations that drive them. Then take a few moments to shift into the perspective of your compassionate self and respond from this perspective of a kind, wise authority who is motivated to understand and help *everyone* in the situation.

THE "TWO CHAIRS" TECHNIQUE

One way to explore the perspectives of your different emotional selves is to use the "two chairs" technique commonly used in Gestalt therapy[3] and other therapy approaches. You'll need to find two chairs and place them so that they are facing one another. One chair is the "angry chair," and when you're in it, you speak directly (and out loud) from the perspective of your anger. You let your anger roll—expressing how your angry self feels and why it's angry. When your anger has had its say, you get up and move to the opposite chair, speaking from the perspective of your compassionate self—again, letting it roll, expressing how it feels and what it would say, with kindness and concern for the angry self. This shift in perspectives from anger to compassion is the key to our approach in working with anger, and most of the exercises in this book are designed to help you make this shift in various ways.

CONCLUSION

In this chapter you've begun to explore ways of bringing compassion to your experience of anger. I've highlighted practices designed to support a compassionate approach to working with anger. These practices will also help you recognize anger as a manifestation of your threat response that evolved to protect you, but which is ill suited to many modern-day difficulties. You've begun to understand how to refrain from engaging in problematic, anger-driven behavior by accessing your compassionate mind and by giving yourself permission to experience and explore whatever feelings you may have. Doing this work requires you to develop tolerance for your distress—to accept and endure the discomfort that is associated with your anger and with resisting the action urges that accompany it. In the next chapter, we will explore how we can use compassionate thinking to further understand our anger and work with it in helpful ways.

9

Working Compassionately with Anger: Mentalizing, Compassionate Thinking, and Problem Solving

It's easy to see our anger as being provoked in a very direct way by things that happen in the *outside world*. It can feel as if other people just keep doing things that make us angry. If we view our anger in this way, it can seem as if there is no other way we could have reacted, and we may find ourselves feeling justified and self-righteous. However, if we look closely, we can see that anger is much more complex than this. As we've seen, the angry state of mind involves much more than how we feel and behave—it also involves our attention, thinking and reasoning, imagery, and motivation. In this chapter, we'll focus on ways we can use thinking and reasoning to work with our anger and with the situations that trigger it.

MENTALIZING

One important quality of the compassionate mind is that it can help us do something the British psychotherapist Peter Fonagy has called "mentalizing."[1] Mentalizing involves looking at our actions and understanding where they come from in terms of desires, feelings, needs, beliefs, and reasons.[2] When we mentalize about other people, we see that their actions stem from their own feelings, desires, and beliefs, and this applies to ourselves as well. Mentalizing helps us to spend less time on automatic pilot and to be better able to see past the appearance of things. We begin to understand our behavior as the result of the different things that are going on in our minds.

Let's consider the example of Sheila and her son, Joshua. We can imagine how Josh might react to his mother's anger at him. If Josh doesn't think about the situation from his mother's point of view, he may dismiss her as an angry, controlling person who isn't worth dealing with—or he might just get angry right back at her. On the other hand, if he's good at mentalizing, he may consider that his mother has had a difficult life and that it's been tough for her to raise him on her own. He might see that she becomes angry partly because she's worried for him and wants the best for him, and that she would take joy in seeing him do well. This might help him understand that his mother could have acted in the opposite way and just not bothered with him at all. He may begin to see that her anger is in part a reflection of her care and hopes for him. And yes, he could also recognize that maybe she *is* a bit controlling, but that this may be a part of her personality that has little to do with him. Mentalizing helps us see that we (and others) are driven by a range of complex feelings and desires. We can see that if Josh can mentalize a bit, really thinking about his mother's feelings and needs, he ends up with a totally different perspective that may help him to behave more kindly toward her.

You will probably not be surprised to hear that slowing down and trying to engage with our compassionate selves can help us mentalize, which in turn can enable us to take responsibility for our anger and the actions we engage in when we're angry. Rather than look to other people and situations as the source of our anger, we can look inward and find that our anger *isn't* caused by external factors. It's a product of our own reactions—our experience of feeling threatened in response to those factors.

Imagine that someone has spoken rudely to you. Some days, perhaps when you've had little sleep and are feeling irritable, or when you attach a hostile meaning to the other person's rudeness, you may tend to get angry.

On other days, when you're feeling a bit more centered, you may simply be confused or maybe even compassionately wonder if the person who's being rude is having a bad day himself. Even if *we* do get angry every time someone is even a little bit rude to us, lots of other people don't. Why the differences in these reactions? If we look closely, we can see that our anger is rooted in a whole range of experiences occurring *within our own minds*, such as thoughts and beliefs like, *People should always treat me with respect.* If we look even more deeply, we may even see that we feel threatened or embarrassed by the person's rudeness, or that perhaps we interpret it as meaning that we are not worthy of respect or kindness, or that we're unlikeable. As human beings, we are very sensitive to these sorts of social threats, even as our typical threat emotions (anger, fear/anxiety) are poorly equipped to handle them. But if we take the kind, confident, and wise perspective of our compassionate selves, we can courageously look inward for the roots of our anger, be they thoughts or emotions like fear, embarrassment, indignation, or jealousy. Knowing that anger is a threat response, we can look closely at ourselves and ask, *What is the threat that my anger is responding to?*

LEARNING TO PAUSE AND ASK YOURSELF QUESTIONS

A key question to ask yourself is, *Why do I act this way when I am angry?*

We may act very differently in different situations. At work, some people may find themselves covering up their emotional reactions, saying nothing to the boss who is being unreasonable or behaving passive-aggressively behind their colleagues' backs. In contrast, at home they might be openly hostile toward their spouses. Each of these reactions to anger—suppression, passive-aggression, and hostility—can be examined in terms of the mental states that go along with them. Each of them is associated with certain feelings, ways of reasoning, and underlying desires and motivations. By considering the thoughts, motivations, and emotional reactions that underpin our feelings and behaviors, we can begin to understand *why* we and other people act the way we do. This information can be very helpful as we work with our anger.

Accessing the inner authority of our compassionate selves helps us to slow down and ask these questions with genuine interest and concern. There are good reasons to believe that if we feel socially safe,[3] we can then mentalize more easily. The experience of feeling threatened seems to impair our ability and willingness to look inward and examine our own thinking, feeling, and motivations. Shifting out of the certainty of our anger and into the inquisitive perspective of the compassionate self helps us to slow down and really look at the thoughts and feelings behind the anger. Instead of shaming and blaming ourselves or other people for our reactions, the compassionate self asks questions that direct our attention to our internal experience:

- *How am I interpreting this situation? What does this mean about me? What does it imply for my future? What does it imply that others are thinking about me?*

- *How does it make sense that I would feel threatened by this situation?*

- *What feelings are coming up in me right now?*

- *Are there other feelings I'm not acknowledging here?* (See "Different Aspects of the Emotional Self" in chapter 8.)

- *What is my greatest fear if I don't act on my anger? What's my greatest fear if I do?*

- *What are the motives and desires in me that are being served by my anger?*

- *What do I need to feel safe? What would help me to feel less threatened?*

Mentalizing helps you direct empathy and sympathy to the part of yourself that feels threatened and to accept and work with those feelings rather than direct your anger at outside sources (or at yourself). You can shift your perspective from, *How do I get back at them for being so rude to me?* to *How do I help myself to feel safe in this situation?* Like it or not, people *will* sometimes be rude to us, sometimes for reasons that may often have nothing whatsoever to do with us and even if we magically found a way to be perfectly nice all of the time. So we have to take responsibility for how we respond when it happens by learning to *understand and work with the roots of anger in our own minds.* As the Buddhist saying goes, "It's easier to put on shoes than it is to carpet the world."

In the following exercise, you'll practice mentalizing. I like to think of this process as an extension of mindfulness—we are looking deeply into the feelings, desires, and reasoning that produce our angry behavior. You'll begin this exercise by using soothing-rhythm breathing to slow down your body and mind, and you'll access the kind, wise, confident authority of your compassionate self. The idea is to help yourself feel safe so that you can look closely at the mental experiences that fuel your anger and angry behaviors.

Exercise 9.1: Mentalizing

Begin by doing thirty seconds of soothing-rhythm breathing, slowly breathing in, holding the breath for a few seconds and then slowly breathing out. Then, go ahead and access the qualities of your compassionate self. Open yourself to experience a kind motivation to help, the wisdom to draw upon your life experience, and the confident authority to work with difficulties. If you are struggling to bring up a sense of safety, feel free to engage in any of the other practices that have helped you to do this (for example, the safe place or the ideal compassionate image).

Now, bring to mind a recent experience of anger. Acknowledge the situation that triggered this, and bring your attention to your reaction:

- Consider how you felt when you experienced anger or irritation. What was it like?

- What did you do in response to your anger? How did you express it (or not)?

Focus on your experience of anger and the behavior that followed it, and explore the mental factors that led you to react this way:

- What motivations or desires contributed to your reaction? What were you pursuing or seeking to avoid?

- Consider your response to the situation that triggered your anger. How did you make sense of this situation and assign meaning to it? What thoughts did you have about the causes of your anger? How did your reasoning impact the situation? Did it magnify your anger or help to alleviate it?

- What other feelings were present in response to this situation? How did they contribute to your reaction?

- Revisit the questions you considered in the mentalizing section earlier in this chapter.

When we shift into the perspective of our compassionate selves and bring our attention to the mental processes that contribute to our anger, we can begin to understand it in a much deeper way than the "He did this, so I did that!" reasoning of our threat systems. While we consider this, let's again return to the example of Sheila and Joshua.

As Sheila looked closely at her angry interactions with Josh, when she would insult his judgment and ridicule his choice to study art, she found that the hurtful things she said resulted from all sorts of things going on in her mind. "I felt ignored, taken for granted, and afraid he was going to be forever unemployed and have a miserable life. I had this desire to bully him into doing what I wanted. I justified this by telling myself that I knew what was best for him and that he obviously didn't. Underneath all of that were fears that I'd done a poor job parenting him, and the desire for him to have a good job and a happy life. I felt he needed me to tell him what to do and motivate him to work hard so he could succeed, that this was how I could be a good parent to him. I guess I thought that if I worked on him hard enough and persistently enough, he'd change his degree to something more marketable, work hard at it, graduate, and get a good job. I was sure he'd come back and thank me when it was all over." As Sheila looked more closely at the thinking and emotions that led to her ongoing conflict with Josh, she discovered that the conflict had more to do with her reasoning, assumptions, desires, and fears than with any behavior on Josh's part. When Sheila began to examine her impact on Josh, she could see that, in fact, her criticism and suggestions likely had a very different effect on him than she had hoped. Her responses served to undermine him rather than improve his confidence, weakening rather than strengthening their relationship. This understanding was helpful to Sheila, and she decided to shift her strategy from trying to control Josh to working with her own fears and to changing the things she did that drove wedges into their relationship.

WORKING COMPASSIONATELY WITH ANGRY THINKING

As we've discussed, when something triggers our threat systems, we tend to magnify and personalize the situation. If someone cuts us off in traffic, for example, we can feel personally attacked—as if that person did it intentionally to endanger us, or because she just doesn't care about our well-being. We tend to assign very negative motives to the people involved, and we may generalize these negative intentions to others as well. We've seen some of this with Sheila, whose anger was fueled by thoughts that other people judged her negatively because of her son's behavior. She also personalized his life choices as acts of defiance against her. In chapter 1, we also saw the example of Steve, whose angry thoughts extended to many areas of his life as he perceived his colleagues and family members as hostile, unappreciative, and lazy. In both of these cases, these thinking patterns fueled the fires of their anger.

Compassionate-thinking exercises are derived from cognitive therapy (where "cognitive" means "thought"), developed in the 1960s by psychiatrist Aaron T. Beck.[4] *Cognitive therapy* involves examining the thoughts and underlying beliefs that fuel negative emotions and behaviors, noting their irrational, exaggerated quality and replacing them with more logical, evidence-based alternatives. Dr. Beck observed that patients who struggled with various psychological difficulties experienced specific sorts of negative thoughts. For example, depressed patients tended to experience very negative thoughts about themselves, the world, and the future. He also noticed that these thoughts affected the patients' emotions and behavior in particular ways. Observing the ease with which such thoughts would arise, Beck labeled them "automatic thoughts," which he noted were often irrational and involved the sorts of exaggerations and generalizations that we observed in the cases of Sheila and Steve.

Over the following decades, this therapy became very popular and was combined with learning-based strategies for changing behavior, leading to what is called cognitive behavioral therapy, or CBT. Over the years, CBT has been applied to the treatment of many psychological disorders and is now supported by a great deal of research.[5]

Newer therapies have focused less on the content of the automatic thoughts and beliefs that drive our problems (for example, whether or not they are accurate, correct, or rational) and assert that the problem isn't so much that we *have* irrational thoughts but that we *accept them as being true*. These newer therapies often use mindfulness approaches like the ones I introduced in chapter 6, and they focus less on changing the content of our thoughts and more on changing *our relationship* to the thoughts. The idea is that we learn to observe our thoughts rather than just buying into them, understand them as mental events (rather than as reality). By doing so, we weaken the hold that these thoughts have on us. A number of therapies incorporate this approach to working with thoughts, including mindfulness-based cognitive therapy[6] (MBCT), dialectical behavior therapy[7] (DBT), and acceptance and commitment therapy[8] (ACT).

The approach we take in CFT is a combination of those described above. Our goal is to learn to notice the thoughts that drive our anger (along with the other aspects of our responses), to mindfully observe them as mental events arising from our threat systems (rather than treating them as facts or reality), and to replace them with alternative, compassionately helpful thoughts. Like mindfulness-based approaches, we will avoid spending much time looking at whether or not our angry thoughts are accurate or rational. Instead, we're simply aiming to relate to them as mental events that serve the purpose of fueling our anger. To deal with our anger more effectively, we'll also learn to replace them with alternative, compassionate thoughts designed to reduce our anger in the present and to develop the habit of thinking compassionately in the future. The key is that when we generate alternative thoughts, we try to infuse them with the compassionate qualities of warmth, wisdom, strength, and caring.

"WHAT WOULD MY COMPASSIONATE SELF THINK?"

In order to shift our minds from angry, threat-driven thinking to compassionate thinking, we can learn to identify the specific thoughts that tend to drive our anger and to consider and generate compassionate alternatives. Let's compare and contrast angry thinking to compassionate thinking.

Angry Thinking	Compassionate Thinking
Narrowly focuses on the threat or object of our anger	Broad, considers many factors in understanding a situation
Inflexible and ruminative	Flexible, problem solving
Activates our threat systems; fuels anger	Activates our safeness systems; helps us to feel comfortable and at peace
Directs hostility toward others and ourselves	Directs kindness toward others and ourselves
Judgmental and critical	Noncritical and empathic
Focuses on dominating or punishing	Focuses on helping ourselves and others, finding solutions that benefit everyone and harm no one

Angry thinking has an interactive relationship with the threat system—it's fueled by the threat response and it fuels the threat response in turn, keeping things going long after the situation that provoked it is over. If we allow our behavior to follow our angry thoughts, it often leads to negative consequences. In contrast to anger, which is very narrowly focused on what the brain perceives to be an immediate threat, compassionate thinking takes a broader view. It recognizes that all of this happens in the context of an ongoing life in which we (and others) will sometimes have to face discomfort and disappointment, and that we'll also have to face the consequences of our actions. A compassionate perspective understands that everyone involved in the situation wants to be happy and free from suffering and that we all are struggling with the same things—tricky brains, life challenges, and competing goals. Although our goals, strategies, and habits may sometimes clash, compassion recognizes that this doesn't make us enemies—just fellow beings working through our lives in different ways. When harm is being done (for example, when we or others are being abused), a compassionate perspective helps us recognize the need for assertive action—to stop harm, to establish solid boundaries, and to help prevent harm in the future—rather than focusing on blaming and punishing. To help you think about compassionate alternatives to angry thinking, consider the event that triggered your anger and, again, ask ourselves some questions:

- How might you see this situation if you weren't stressed or angry?

- If there were a neutral, caring person around, how might this person see this event and help you think it through? (It can be useful here to bring your ideal compassionate image to mind.)

- How would you prefer to look at this if you were calm and collected?

- How will you see this in three months? Will you even remember it?

- From the perspective of your compassionate self, what might you say to a friend who had experienced this? How would you help your friend feel supported?

Let's look at this using some examples drawn from Sheila's situation.

Angry Thoughts	Compassionate Thoughts
Joshua is lazy with no concern for his future.	I'm frustrated with the choices he's making because I want him to have a good life. Maybe I could express my concerns as a caring parent rather than as an angry one. Maybe I could ask him what his plan is.
He takes all my help for granted. He doesn't appreciate anything I've done for him.	I feel like he disregards my advice because he makes choices that I don't agree with. Parents often want their children to do the things they think are best, but sometimes children just need to find their own way in the world. Maybe this is more about that. I could explore this with him. Just because he doesn't do everything I ask doesn't mean that he doesn't appreciate what I've done for him.

My colleagues must think that I'm a terrible parent. I've failed at the most important task of my life.	*There is no evidence that I have failed. My son is a kind person— a decent human being—even if he does sometimes struggle in terms of knowing what he wants to do.* *My colleagues brag about their own kids because they are proud of them. That doesn't mean they're looking down on Josh and me. It's hard to watch Josh make different choices than I would like, but they are his choices to make. I can't control him, and I want him to be his own man. Things could be a lot worse.*
First he jumps from degree to degree, and now he settles on art. He'll never have a good job, and he'll probably be dependent on me his entire life. My parents would have cut me off a long time ago!	*I care about Josh, and I'm worried about him being able to support himself as an artist. In some ways, though, I admire his courage in choosing to pursue something that makes him happy rather than just rushing through school like my parents pushed me to. I've made a good living, but I often hate my job. I may actually be jealous of Josh! Maybe I should worry less about him and focus more on my own life.*

As we see above, compassionate thinking doesn't offer easy solutions to life's difficulties. Many aspects of our lives simply don't have easy answers, even though anger (and the cultural messages we get from advertising, for example) may try to convince us otherwise. However, taking a compassionate perspective can help us become aware of the various parts of situations that cause us to feel threatened, cope with the discomfort this can cause, and work with life's difficulties in ways that are thoughtful and consistent with our values.

THE COMPASSIONATE-THINKING FLASH CARD

It's helpful to think about what our typical triggers are for anger when we're *not* angry. Consider these triggers and the kinds of thoughts you have when you're angry. Try to be honest. See how anger can often take your thinking to extremes. Now, think carefully about what alternative thoughts would help you avoid getting carried away in the anger stream, the sort of things you might say to a dear friend—or that your ideal compassionate image might say to you. If you were at your most compassionate—wise, confident, calm, and motivated to help—what sort of thoughts would you come up with? How would your compassionate self think and behave in that situation? Consider making a compassionate-thinking flash card,[9] a small card that you can carry around with you, maybe with a picture or phrase you find comforting or inspiring on the flip side. At the top of the card, write down one or two of your typical angry thoughts. Then write down some compassionate alternatives, thoughts that would help you keep your cool. When you've written those thoughts down, go through them slowly and read them with as much kindness, support, and encouragement as you can. Imagine the kind, wise, authoritative voice of your compassionate self talking to you as you read through your alternatives. It can be very helpful to carry this card with you and to read it from time to time. This habit will help you revisit your commitment to becoming the compassionate self—reminding yourself of how your compassionate self thinks and the kinds of things it would say. When you begin to get angry, take a moment to look at your card.

"WHAT WOULD MY COMPASSIONATE SELF DO?"

While we've focused a good deal on working with the mental experience of anger, we should also look at the real-life situations that trigger it. Many of the exercises we've done are designed to help us shift from a threatened state of mind that judges situations from an angry perspective to one that understands them from a compassionate point of view. By doing so, we can return to the situation and work with it skillfully. Sometimes there will be things we can do to change the situations that trigger our anger; at other times, we'll be faced with situations that we don't like but can do little or nothing to change. These different types of situations demand different sorts of responses, including action, acceptance, and combinations of the two.

It's useful to recognize that your motivation and the process of compassion-focused problem solving help you to not simply get your way but to *find the best possible response* to the situation. These sorts of responses minimize harm to yourself and others and are consistent with your values. This process is different from the "win at any cost" mentality that flows forth from the threat and drive systems—a mentality that can easily lead to anger. If we look at things from a compassionate perspective, we recognize that, despite our best efforts, things often will not go the way we want them to. However, we will also be able to understand that even if we haven't been able to achieve what we desired in the short term, by behaving compassionately we're more likely to attain happiness in the long term. A wise, compassionate perspective helps us recognize that we don't want to compromise our long-term priorities (your emotional health, good relationships, living in ways that are consistent with the sort of person you want to be) in the service of minor, short-term goals.

So let's look at the steps involved in compassionate problem solving. Begin with thirty seconds or so of soothing-rhythm breathing to access your compassionate mind and consider the qualities of kindness, calm authority, and wisdom. Then bring to mind the situation or difficulty that has triggered your anger:

1. Start by bringing compassion to the situation and to everyone in it.

   - We'll be working with this much more in the following chapters. For now, start by considering that each person in this situation (including yourself) ultimately just wants to be happy and free from suffering.

   - We all have tricky brains with sensitive threat systems and the problems that come with them. This is not your fault or anyone else's.

   - If another person in the situation is irritating or frustrating you, see if you can cultivate some empathy for that person:

     - Have you ever behaved as that person is behaving? How were you feeling at the time? What may be driving that person's behavior?

- What thoughts, fears, and desires might be contributing to this person's actions?

- Consider that this person, like you, may be having lots of automatic reactions to the situation based on how the human brain works and how we can be affected by our previous experiences.

- If that person is being hostile and acting in anger, remember that this is a form of suffering and that it isn't fun for him or her, either. This person is doing it because, like you, she or he feels threatened.

- If this person's threat system is activated, be aware that his or her attention is likely to be narrowed and that she or he is thinking less flexibly.

2. Break big problems down into manageable bites.

- Often, the problems and situations we are faced with can feel overwhelming, as if they are just too big to do anything about.

- Before we can address them, we need to break them down into smaller, more manageable bites, just as we would approach any large task—like writing this book, for instance. I can't write a book in a day, but I can write a few pages. Sheila might not be able to heal her relationship with Josh in a day, but she can plan to have a friendly and compassionate conversation with him.

- Ask yourself, *What is a reasonably sized piece of this problem that I could actually address?* You may want to take fifteen minutes or so to draw up a plan of action.

- List the problems or tasks from easiest to most difficult, and start with the easiest one. This helps you begin making progress toward your goals and gain confidence as you see yourself beginning to have success.

3. Consider the problem and generate compassionate responses.

- What are some of your possible responses to the situation? Generate as many ideas as you can. They don't have to be realistic.

- Shift into the perspective of your compassionate self when you're thinking of these possible responses. What would your compassionate self say and do? Responses can involve both action (working with the situation) and acceptance (accepting the situation, working with your response to it).

4. Consider the consequences of the various responses you've generated.

- From the perspective of your compassionate self, consider the short-term and long-term consequences of your various responses. How do they fit with both your desired outcomes and your values?

A bit more needs to be said about how to choose possible responses, so allow me to take a small break from our list for the moment. We'll get to the fifth step shortly.

If the situation you're considering involves other people (as most anger-producing situations do), there are various factors and priorities you can consider when choosing the best response:

The *objective* or outcome you want to occur

Your *relationship* with the other people involved

The most helpful *expression* of your feelings[10]

These factors often compete with one another. For example, if someone were doing something that irritated me, I might be able to get that person to stop doing so very quickly (the *objective*) by yelling at him or by threatening him ("Shut up or I'll smack you a good one!" which also allows the *expression* of my frustration). However, this response is likely to damage our *relationship*. We saw this with Sheila, who expressed her frustration with Joshua in ways that created distance between them and which, in turn, actually got in the way of her objective (helping him sort out his degree and job situation). This isn't uncommon. Often, we may damage important relationships (with spouses or children, for instance) in the service of objectives that may or may not be that important, or by expressing our emotions in hostile ways. We can choose to accept certain situations that we might not prefer in order to maintain good relationships. This isn't the same as passively just "taking it." I'm talking about making *active choices* to prioritize relationships over certain objectives. This distinction is important: we're not martyring ourselves, *we're taking responsibility* and *choosing the priorities that matter most to us*. Alternatively, some objectives are worth prioritizing over relationships. For example, if someone is harming us, another person, or herself, acting to prevent harm may in some cases create problems in our relationship with her—but we act anyway.

With this in mind, let's continue with step 5:

5. Select a response.

    - From the perspective of your compassionate self, select the solution that seems likely to work the best for you and for others.

    - Choose an option that you have the skills to carry out. Keep in mind that one option may involve your asking for help.

6. Consider what you need in order to implement the response.

    - Think about the things you may need to put your response into action. Do you need anyone's help or advice?

    - Would talking things over with someone you trust help you to look at the situation from a more helpful perspective?

    - Part of being competent means knowing when to seek help when we're overwhelmed or overmatched.

7. Plan and implement the solution.

    - Before putting your response into action, use your imagination to walk through how it will go. Imagine yourself responding as you've planned, trying to anticipate obstacles that might come up and how you can deal with them compassionately. This will help you practice, or rehearse, dealing with difficult situations and prepare you for the real thing.

    - Implement your solution, doing what you've practiced. As you carry out your response, try to mindfully observe the process as it plays out. Try to see it as an experiment in trying something new. This can help keep you from getting caught up in little details, particularly if things don't go exactly as you practiced. It can also keep you from giving up if things don't turn out the way you hoped, as will sometimes be the case.

8. Evaluate the solution.

    •   Consider your response to the situation: how did it turn out?

    •   What worked or seemed to be helpful?

    •   What didn't work so well?

    •   Consider these things when you plan how to respond to similar situations in the future.

There are lots of things that will have an impact on the way any given situation will turn out, many of which are out of your control. The key is to try to see your efforts as a series of experiments occurring over the time frame of your life. Like scientists, we take what we learn from each situation or experiment—what helped, what didn't—and use this information to increase the likelihood of success when we approach the next situation. We're patiently honing our skills, trying to get a little better each time and to develop a toolbox of approaches and behaviors that will reflect our values rather than automatic, knee-jerk responses to threats.

CONCLUSION

In this chapter you've learned more about how to work compassionately with your experience of anger and with situations that trigger it. Acting from the perspective of your compassionate self can help transform threatening situations into opportunities for growth, improving your ability to deal with stress and enhancing relationships with others and your own happiness. Because so many of the situations that trigger anger involve other people, it's important to specifically consider your interactions with them. In chapter 10 we'll focus on how we can relate compassionately and effectively with others, particularly in difficult situations.

10

Compassionate Behavior: Relating Compassionately with Others

Interacting compassionately with others isn't about just being nice and giving in to people all of the time. Some of the most compassionate things people have ever said to me have taken the form of direct critical feedback, kindly but assertively advising me to change tactics when I was doing something that was causing problems for me. When we see someone stepping in front of a speeding car, the most compassionate thing we can do is prevent that person from being run over! Compassion certainly doesn't mean letting people take advantage of us. It means communicating genuinely and assertively—acting in ways that respect both other people and ourselves, seeking benefit for everyone and harm for no one.

In chapter 2 we examined the three circles model and learned about three emotion-regulation systems: the threat system, the drive and resource acquisition system, and the safeness system. It's helpful to have an awareness of these systems as we interact compassionately with other people—so helpful, in fact, that I use this model to help train graduate psychology students in learning to work with clients and to help myself interact with other people in my own life. The idea is to recognize that we are triggers for other people's emotion-regulation systems—we can activate each or any combination of their three circles—and to ask ourselves the question, *What do I want to trigger in them?*

We activate other peoples' threat systems when we insult, threaten, or speak rudely to them. This interaction is reflected in the phrase "pushing his/her buttons." When we flirt, seduce, or sell, we are attempting to stimulate others' drive and resource acquisition systems. And when we comfort, validate, and empathize, we are attempting to activate their safeness systems.

So here's the thing: *things work better when people feel safe.* When our safeness systems are active and we feel comfortable, neither trapped in a state of threat nor caught up in the pursuit of some strong desire, we can bring our minds fully to the task at hand. As we've seen, at these times our attention can broaden to include many possibilities and we're able to think clearly and flexibly. Freed from the burden of feeling as if we need to protect ourselves, we can move toward our highest potential.

Unfortunately, we all sometimes have conflicts, disagreements, and stressful interactions with others—just the sort of situations that trigger our sensitive threat systems. In this chapter we'll explore some useful skills for bringing compassion to how we relate to others, focusing on behaviors that can help us solve problems while helping everyone in the situation feel safe so that our interactions aren't dictated by our threat systems.

ASSERTIVENESS

Anger can disrupt our communication with others by motivating us to interact with them in ways that are aggressive (insulting, attacking); passive (biting our tongues, stewing); or passive-aggressive (refusing to interact, sarcasm). Unfortunately, none of these approaches works very well. Why? Well, let's consider them in terms of the three factors we saw in the problem-solving section of chapter 9:

- They often lead to the situation turning out poorly for ourselves and/or others (*objective*).

- They often damage our *relationships* with other people.

- · They do not allow us to *express* our emotions in ways that can be received and understood by the other people involved.

In contrast, assertiveness is a way of interacting with others that allows us to control the emotions and clarify the message. It involves respecting ourselves—standing up for ourselves—and respecting the people we're dealing with.

When we respond to people with aggression, their minds become focused on defending themselves from our hostility. This can make it almost impossible for them to listen to what we're trying to say, to grasp the point we are trying to get across. And if your own threat system is in charge, even *you* might not be clear about what message you want to convey and why. Assertiveness allows us to express ourselves in challenging situations while minimizing how much we and other people feel threatened, so that we are not pouring fuel on the fire.

So what is assertiveness? Psychologist Willem Arrindell[1] and his colleagues describe four abilities that characterize *assertiveness*:

- **Display of negative feelings**. This is the ability to be able to express annoyance or refusal, to ask others to change behavior that bothers us, and to stand up for ourselves as we pursue what we want.

- **Expressing and dealing with personal limitations**. This means being able to face and admit to our own limitations, uncertainty, or lack of knowledge. Assertiveness helps us admit mistakes and accept appropriate criticism without being ashamed of what we don't know. It also involves asking others for help when we need it.

- **Initiating assertiveness**. This is the ability to deal with differences of opinion—being able to express opinions that may differ from others and to accept that other people may have opinions that are different from ours, though no less valid.

- **Positive assertion**. This is the ability to appreciate and express admiration for the strengths, talents, and achievements of others and to accept praise for ourselves.

Let's now discuss how to use assertiveness in a few different situations.

EXPRESSING EMOTIONS AND DESIRES

It can be very difficult to express feelings like embarrassment, disappointment, frustration, anxiety, or sadness. Faced with such emotions, it can seem almost impossible to simply tell the other person how we feel. When we pause to think, it makes sense that this might be difficult. Acknowledging our feelings and sharing them with others can make us feel vulnerable, and when we feel vulnerable, our default threat response is often a defensive one: *Cover it up! Hide it! Get angry instead!* However, our wise, compassionate selves can recognize that we all have these emotions and that assertively communicating our feelings in a way that *doesn't attack others* can help us find solutions to difficult problems. This works much better than trying to work around or against these emotions, or attacking the people we think are causing them.

On the wall of almost every child and adolescent treatment center where I've worked is a poster featuring this sentence:

"When _____, I feel _____,
and I would like _____."

Although it is straightforward and easy to understand, this classic example of assertive communication isn't just for children. To use it, we briefly *describe the situation, how we feel about it,* and *what we would like to see happen:*

- "When you call me that, I don't like it, and I would prefer that you call me by my actual name."

- "When you let us out of the meeting (or class) late, I feel rushed and anxious about getting where I need to be, and I'd like to keep to the schedule in the future."

At first, people sometimes feel a little silly when they use this format—it can seem unnatural if we aren't used to it. The idea is to begin expressing our feelings in nonaggressive ways. By "nonaggressive," I mean not including any extras that insult the other person, such as, "When you call me by that name, I don't like it, and I'd like you to *stop being such an ass.*" That's aggressive! You'll see in the next exercise that the focus of assertive communication isn't just to get your way; it's also important to help the other person understand where you're coming from—to get your perspective across.

Exercise 10.1: Assertive Expression of Emotion

As with all the exercises, begin by slowing down your breathing for thirty seconds or so by using soothing-rhythm breathing and by accessing the kind, wise, confident perspective of your compassionate mind.

In his book, *Overcoming Depression*,[2] Paul Gilbert describes four steps involved in expressing angry emotions (which work well with other sorts of emotions as well):

1. Acknowledge your anger (or whatever emotion you're feeling).

2. Recognize in what way you feel hurt or frustrated (and try to discover if you might be exaggerating the harm done).

3. Focus on where this hurt comes from and your wish that the other person could understand your feelings and your point of view.

4. Don't insist that the other person must agree with you.

Once you've gone through these steps, try to create an assertive statement that communicates your experience to the other person *without attacking that person*. Focus on the specific issue or behavior. Here are some examples:

- "When you interrupt me, I feel hurt because I think that you don't value what I'm saying."

- "I like it much better when you (describe the behavior you'd prefer to see)."

- "I understand that you feel like _____, but my point of view is _____."

You'll notice that the examples of assertive communication use the word "I" in relationship to our emotions, and for this reason these are sometimes called *I-statements*. With I-statements, we state our emotions or desires directly, communicate ownership of them, and don't add unnecessary information that could be insulting to others. By "ownership," I mean not giving other people control of your emotions, for example, by saying, "You make me feel _____." Instead, simply state how you feel, as in, "I'm very angry right now, and I think I need to take a break before we talk about this further." I-statements make it clear that this is *your perspective*, versus "the way it *is*." Just because I happen to like something (or not) doesn't make it intrinsically good or bad:

- "I've never really liked baseball (or hockey). I like football." (assertive)

- "Baseball sucks. Real men play football." (aggressive)

Let's consider how you might apply this assertive approach to a recent conflict.

Exercise 10.2: Considering Conflict

Think back to a time within the last few weeks when you had a conflict with another person. Think about what was actually said. As always, start with thirty seconds of soothing-rhythm breathing; engage with your wise, kind, and confident compassionate self; and spend a moment or two thinking about the argument from that compassionate point of view:

- Replay the argument in your mind and imagine how it would go if you communicated assertively.

- You might even want to write down how you could handle the conflict in a different way, using the skills described in exercise 10.1.

- Note what mental blocks come up. For example, is there a part of you that thinks, *Well it's okay in theory, but I don't think the person I had the argument with would take any notice*? You might be right about that—assertiveness works better if we behave this way consistently over time. If other people are used to our aggression rather than our assertiveness, it may seem strange to them when we do things a little differently, and they may not respond as we'd like them to. However, if we consistently behave assertively, people learn that we mean what we say, and they will respond to it. Don't assume that things will change with one interaction. As with all of the skills in this book, practice really helps.

WORKING WITH YOUR LIMITATIONS

Our threat systems have evolved to be very sensitive to messages that we aren't good enough and that relate to how other people view us—what they think of us and feel about us. Additionally, we live in a world that is constantly bombarding us with messages about how we're supposed to be, telling us how we're supposed to look, feel, and behave. It's easy to internalize these messages about how we should be and to feel all sorts of difficult emotions when it seems we don't measure up.

If we look at this through the wise eyes of the compassionate self, however, we can gain some perspective and realize that even if we aren't perfect, it doesn't mean that there is anything wrong with us. Our compassionate selves know that *no one* is perfect, and that the way we've developed is due to many factors that we didn't choose or control. The key is that we exist right here, right now; and while we can't change the things that led us to this point, we have a great ability to influence how things go from now on. We can all find ways to act assertively even in situations that feel intimidating. We also need to be able to honestly admit when we aren't up to a task and to get help.

Here are a few ways to begin working with our personal limitations.

Check It Out

First, try to decide whether the issue really is a limitation or if it's simply a negative judgment on your part. One of my clients, Robert, strongly believed that he was a bad father (largely based on the harsh criticism he received from his emotionally abusive father-in-law). However, when we looked closely at how he interacted with his children and his ability to give them what they needed to thrive (and sought feedback about this from his wife), Robert discovered that he actually did a good job as a parent. When he was feeling low or depressed, he was particularly likely to question his ability to be a good parent. And just like Robert, you may also feel as if you have all sorts of weaknesses or limitations that simply aren't there, particularly when you're feeling low. As Robert did, one way to check this out is to ask for the opinion of people you value and care about—compassionate people who have your best interests at heart. You can ask them something like, "I think this is a

limitation of mine," or "I think that I struggle with _____.
What do you think?"

Acceptance

Imagine that your compassionate self is your coach. How would your compassionate self help you to accept your limitations and focus on your strengths? Just as you may use your self-critical inner voice to convince yourself that you can never be happy while you have this limitation, you can use the voice of your compassionate self to comfort yourself, and remind yourself that *we all* have limitations and that this is okay.

A good example of this is Paul, whom I met during a course I was teaching on mindfulness. Paul had been an athletic student but became paralyzed from the neck down as a result of an accident. During the course, he courageously discussed with the class what it was like to learn to define himself in a completely new way. He powerfully described how accepting the way things were for him now, including the limitations caused by his paralysis, was the first step in rebuilding his life. He refused to allow his paralysis to hamper his ability to be happy and to pursue his educational goals. But in doing this, he had to work with the way his life really was (versus the way he might wish for it to be).

Exercise 10.3: Accepting Limitations

Cast your mind back to a time when you had to accept a limitation. Once again, begin with thirty seconds of soothing-rhythm breathing and engage with the kind, wise, and confident qualities of your compassionate self:

1. **Validate your disappointment.** No one likes to have limitations: *It makes sense that I would be bothered by this limitation. This feels important to me.*

2. **Focus on the process of kind acceptance.** Allow yourself to accept this limitation without blaming or shaming. Notice how it feels when you don't fight with it and just let it be a part of you: *This is the way it is for me. Everyone has limitations, and this is one of mine. I don't have to be perfect, and although I don't like it, this limitation doesn't mean that I can't be happy.*

If self-critical voices come up, repeat from step 1.

Problem Solve

You can also use your compassionate self to help you figure out ways to be successful and happy despite your limitations. Rick, an Iraq veteran who had been disabled during the war, was deeply upset that he could no longer play soccer, which he'd enjoyed all his life. Ultimately, he was able to accept that he could no longer play, and instead he chose to coach a children's soccer team. While he missed aspects of playing, his disappointment was more than compensated for by the joy he got from teaching the kids about his favorite game.

Do It Anyway

If your limitation is related to a lack of skill, then you can pursue train-ing and advice to help you improve. On the other hand, you can also learn to take yourself a bit less seriously and choose to attempt (and enjoy) activi-ties even if you aren't very good at them. Suppose that you would love to dance but think you have two left feet. How could you learn to face up to that feeling of inadequacy and just do it—feel the fear and do it anyway? One way could be to note your critical thoughts, be mindful of the bodily feelings of anxiety or embarrassment, engage your compassionate self, and then just *dance*. The more you do it, the less self-conscious you'll be likely to feel. You could also choose to take dance lessons. In my life, I've found that one secret to happiness is to enjoy doing things that I'm not particularly good at. Some of these things (like guitar playing) I choose to improve by taking lessons, and some (like mountain biking) I just keep doing, poorly but enjoyably. Once again, the key is to shift your focus from a self-critical mind-set to a compassionate, helpful mind-set by accessing your compas-sionate self.

Let It Go

Sometimes understanding your limitations is extremely important because it stops you from obsessively trying to achieve things that are just not going to happen. For example, imagine that your heart is set on becom-ing a doctor but unfortunately you don't have the grades and examination scores to get into medical school. This can be a painful realization, but if you can find a way to accept this, it's likely that you may be able to find something else that may be equally fulfilling, such as nursing or working for a medical charity. Clinging to unrealistic goals can prevent us from pursuing others that would make us just as happy. Accepting our limitations means that we need to be honest with ourselves about what we *can* do, what we *might* be able to do, and what we'll *never* be able to do.

At the same time, you don't want to give up on your dreams too quickly. There are many challenging pursuits in life that you can succeed at if you're willing to keep at it. I've heard it said that one secret of success is the *willingness to fail*. When we're children we don't think so much about it—when we're learning to walk, we fall over loads of times before we become steady on our feet. But you don't see many toddlers falling over and just lying there for the next fifty years or so! They fall over and then get back up again. As we get older, however, we start judging ourselves, and that can make us fearful of failing, which can lead us to give up or not try at all. Developing compassionate assertiveness within ourselves allows us to face failure—to dust ourselves off and get up again—without getting caught up in the inertia of self-criticism. Working with anger is like this; if you've struggled with anger for years, you won't be able to completely change overnight. You'll slip up again and again. But if you can bring compassion to the struggle, encouraging yourself to keep at it over time, you will change.

EXPRESSING DISAGREEMENT

All relationships involve differences of opinion, but these differences don't have to produce angry conflicts. A compassionate perspective allows us to disagree in ways that express our position while also communicating respect for others. It's okay to disagree, and we can do so openly and appropriately:

- **Other person's statement**: "Jim is a jerk!"

- **Disagreement**: "I disagree. He's always been nice to me, and I've seen him treat others kindly as well. Did you have a bad experience with him?"

The key is to express your perspective respectfully without stating or implying that the other person's opinion is stupid, naïve, or misguided.

Exercise 10.4: Expressing Disagreement

Begin by slowing down your breathing a bit by using thirty seconds of soothing-rhythm breathing. Access the kind, wise, and confident qualities of your compassionate self. Consider a situation when you have disagreed with another person and would have liked them to know how you felt. Imagine the result of the disagreement turning out differently as you approach it from a compassionate, assertive perspective:

- State your perspective. It's okay to say very directly, "I disagree..."

- Refrain from criticizing others or their perspectives or implying that they are stupid or shortsighted for not agreeing with you. It's easy to attack someone without meaning to when you feel strongly about something, but doing this almost *guarantees* a poor result. Other people are just as entitled to their opinions as you are, and attacking them sets them up to attack you back, or at least to dig in and oppose you.

- Show respect for others by expressing interest in their perspectives and asking questions to help you understand why they feel the way they do. This sets up a positive interaction by helping them to feel safe and valued, and it communicates that you're willing to hear what they have to say. This step also helps you better understand where they are coming from.

- Practice the interaction in your mind so that you're less likely to be thrown off guard in the actual situation when it occurs next. Assertively expressing disagreement is a skill, and we get better by practicing. You can also role-play by using two chairs (sitting in one, imagining the other person in the other) or by asking someone you trust to play the part of the other person (your friend can give you feedback on how he she experiences what you're saying).

When disagreement occurs, it can help to pay close attention to the emotions and experiences that emerge. For example, the angry little flush that begins to go through your body can be a cue to slow your breathing and engage with the wise, calm authority of your compassionate self, who desires to find the best solution for both parties. Deliberately recognizing the need to slow down (and then slowing down) can help prevent your threat response from rushing you along in an increasing whirl of angry thoughts and impulses.

The ability to deal with conflict is a skill—something to work toward. Relationships are pretty easy to manage when everyone agrees and everything goes well, but the true test comes when things get rocky. Assertiveness isn't about trying to keep everything quiet, avoiding disagreements, or blowing up at the first sign of conflict; it's the ability to work your way through difficulties while maintaining control of your feelings. This ability comes with *practice*. Remember that if you feel that your emotions have taken control of you, it may mean that it's time to break off contact for a bit and give yourself some space from the situation that's triggering your anger. If we find ourselves driving on ice, it's probably a good idea to slow down so we don't begin to slip and slide all over the road. And once you've calmed down and shifted into the perspective of the compassionate self, it becomes easier to work with the conflict in a way that isn't driven by your threat system. Taking a break to center yourself isn't running away—it's good emotion management.

When you're in the heat of anger, you'll likely have a hard time seeing the other person's perspective as you are captured by your own threat system's narrow point of view. Disagreements are easier to handle when you actually *understand* what the other person is saying (we'll investigate this even more in the next chapter). It's helpful to learn about what the other person is thinking and feeling by asking questions to clarify their point of view:

- "Could you tell me a bit more about that? I want to understand where you're coming from."

- "I can see this is really important to you. Could you explain that to me?"

- "What's the most upsetting/important thing to you about this?"

The tone of voice you use is important—asking clarifying questions doesn't work when your tone and body language are aggressive or contemptuous. When people feel we're making genuine efforts to see their point of view rather than forcing our own perspectives on them, they're much more likely to work with us (though not always, of course). It can be very useful to actually practice this. When you have a moment, consider a conflict, shift into your compassionate self, and feel the sense of slowing that comes with it. Imagine the situation and practice asking these questions while seeing yourself as a thoughtful, inquiring person who wants to resolve this conflict. By doing this, you are shifting focus and control away from your anger's desire to overcome the other person, and moving into a compassionate desire to work out the conflict. Once again, the key is to *practice being the self you want to become.*

RECONCILIATION

Since all relationships will involve disagreement and occasional hurt feelings, it's important to learn how to reconcile—to come back together and mend relationships when they've been split by conflict or disagreements. One of the reasons people can struggle with being assertive or expressing anger is that they're frightened they will damage their relationships beyond repair. This sometimes develops from a childhood experience of parents or caretakers who were very quick to punish or to withdraw affection from a child if he or she showed anger or was disobedient. If we've had that sort of background, we may learn to be very careful about expressing our emotions. For example, Tim was a marital therapy client of mine who sometimes felt quite angry with his wife. He was very frightened to express this anger because when he did, he felt that at any moment she might say, "That's enough of you," and walk out. Another client, Gary, had a similar fear, which played out in an aggressive way: "Fuck you...I don't need you anyway!" In fact, both men love their wives, but they didn't know how to deal with conflict without becoming either sulky and submissive or nasty and aggressive. Parts of their struggles were based on not knowing how to reconcile after having conflicts or disagreements. Both felt that the angry self was unlovable and that expressing their feelings could lead to a split in the relationship that couldn't be overcome. We can feel that reconciliation is difficult or impossible, or that it feels like submission—like having to try to win parental approval again. The good news is that when both people are committed to a relationship, reconciliation is usually possible. There are some things we can do that can help with this.

Plan Ahead

Discuss beforehand how you will work with conflicts and reconcile when they're over. For example, "Chances are that we'll have some heated disagreements at some point. How would you like to work things out when that happens? What things can we do to help us come back together again?" For example, you can agree to take time-outs when one or both of you need to cool down. This break will give each of you space (so that you don't continue to argue), and you can return to the discussion when both are able to communicate calmly.

Work Together to Help One Another Feel Safe

To prepare for the conflicts that will inevitably arise in any relationship, you may try opening with a statement like, "Conflicts are part of life. How can we make our relationship feel safe enough so that we know that any blocks are temporary and that we can reconcile?" This will establish room and the opportunity to work together to ensure a feeling of safety. For example, couples can write "in case we are fighting" letters to each other from the perspective of their compassionate selves. These are letters that each can read (either to themselves or aloud to each other) when things feel distant. They'll remind each partner of the other's caring and commitment to work through the difficulties and come together again. For instance, "Richard, if you're reading this, it's probably because we're fighting. Although I may be upset with you right now, I want you to know that I love you very much and that I'm committed to working with you to solve whatever problems might come up in our relationship…" The idea is to find a way to get our safeness systems going, and to remind ourselves that we're on the same team when our threat systems try to make us relate to one another as enemies.

Help Your Partner Feel Safe and Valued during Reconciliation

"What's the best way for me to approach you when we've had a conflict and I'm ready to make up?" One of my clients often tried to reconcile by bringing his fiancée flowers or small gifts, and he was surprised to find that these efforts actually made her feel distant and irritated—"because she felt like I was trying to 'buy her off,' like I thought the flowers made it okay for me to be rude to her." It turned out that she much preferred an honest apology or expression of caring, like, "I know we had a disagreement, but I want you to know that I still love you and that I value our relationship very much. I'd like to make up when you're ready."

Interrupt Rumination

It's easy to get caught up in repetitive thoughts about disagreements or conflicts, even when they're about minor issues. You can shift your state of mind by remembering the good times you've had with this person and the reasons you've chosen to be in a relationship with them. People who struggle to express their hurt feelings may hold on to them, building resentment that then seeps out and causes more trouble. This is why we often talk about arguments "clearing the air." You can use disagreements as opportunities to remove stumbling blocks in your relationships by focusing on the issues without personalizing the disagreement. Just because people disagree with you doesn't mean that they don't respect you, care about you, or want to have a relationship with you. If these things were true, they probably wouldn't even bother talking with you at all.

Move from Shame to Regret

Those of us who struggle with anger may experience a great deal of shame, which can get in the way of reconciling with others. As we've seen, shame happens when we observe that we've behaved in certain ways that run contrary to our values, and we then conclude that we're somehow bad or flawed, or that what we've done is unforgivable. The problem with shame is that it keeps us stuck in the past and focused on ourselves. We can find that we avoid confronting the problems we've created because doing so brings up painful self-evaluations.[3] This shame can also lead us to avoid people we feel that we've harmed, which prevents reconciliation. As we learn to reconcile and commit to working with anger in ways that are more effective, we must learn to let our shame go. As we've seen, this can be hard to do because it may feel as if you're letting yourself off the hook. Don't worry, you're not— but you *are* learning to recognize that shame doesn't help, to mindfully relate to shameful thoughts as mental events, and to redirect your attention to other thoughts that actually *can* help. As an alternative to shame, consider regret.[4] Regret allows us to acknowledge that we've done something that has caused harm to others, yet instead of getting us caught up in self-criticism or negative emotions that paralyze us, regret focuses on *not repeating* the act, *repairing the relationship*, and *doing better* in the future. It keeps our focus on improving.

APOLOGIZING

All of us sometimes do things, purposefully or not, that are hurtful to others. When we become aware that we've hurt others, it may bother us (this is good—a sign of compassion). However, as we know, embarrassment or shame over our actions can get our threat systems moving and lead us to respond in ways that aren't helpful:

- We may justify or rationalize our responses: *He deserved it because…*

- We may shame ourselves: *I'm a terrible person!*

- We may push it out of our minds, avoid thinking about it, pretend it never happened, or even forget about it.

- We may minimize its importance.

These are all ways that we use to avoid dealing with the fact that we've caused harm to another person, and they prevent us from doing anything about it. None of these responses helps mend the damage that was caused by our behavior, and they often magnify it. Apologizing does not erase the harm we've done or excuse us for it. However, acknowledging our fault and committing to do better (and *meaning* it) can create movement toward healing. It also reinforces the compassionate habit of taking responsibility for our actions.

The ability to apologize requires us to tolerate guilt and regret—to allow ourselves to feel sadness or remorse when we've harmed someone. Angry people often struggle with allowing themselves to experience regret, perhaps feeling that they would be overwhelmed by vulnerable emotions such as sadness and remorse. It takes courage to open yourself to these feelings. The truth is that, mostly, we don't intend to be so hurtful—what we want is to be recognized, respected, loved, valued, and wanted. Much of our anger flows from these desires being blocked or frustrated. Behind our anger is often a lot of emotional pain that we would prefer to avoid. If we are courageous enough to face these emotions and experience them as they are, we won't need to avoid them by hiding behind anger.

A good apology involves directly acknowledging the harm we've done, expressing regret, and expressing the intention not to repeat it. A good apology *does not* include elaborating in ways that let us off the hook ("I'm sorry, but...") or that imply that the other person is at fault ("I'm sorry that *you felt* like my comment was insulting"). Consider these examples of apologies:

- "I'm sorry I lost my temper. I was feeling overwhelmed, and it wasn't your fault at all. I would really appreciate an opportunity to talk about this when you feel okay with doing that."

- "I want to apologize for calling you names. I know that this must have been very hurtful for you. I was angry about the situation, and I took it out on you. I'm working on handling my anger better, and I'm going to treat you better in the future, starting with no more name-calling."

- "I'm sorry I used the last of the _____ and didn't replace it. It didn't occur to me that it would inconvenience you, and I'll try to be more thoughtful in the future."

- "I apologize for criticizing you in front of your friends. I can imagine that this was very embarrassing for you. It was very inconsiderate, and I won't do it again."

Once again, consider your tone of voice and body language when you apologize. Try not to be overly submissive and childlike, or aggressive and dismissive. Instead, speak from the perspective of your compassionate self. The key here is that you're *claiming responsibility* for your actions (not blaming them on others), doing your best to make the situation right, cultivating and *communicating an intention to do better* in the future, and then *following through* with it. This last point is a very important one. It's not enough to simply intend not to harm the other person again and then forget your commitment as soon as the interaction is over. Apologizing and then repeating the behavior teaches the other person that your apology means nothing. Committing to change may mean getting help (such as going to couple's therapy, for example). Again, we see that the path of compassion isn't always an easy one—it means acknowledging problems directly and facing them head-on.

Exercise 10.5: Apologizing

Begin with thirty seconds of soothing-rhythm breathing and access your kind, wise, and confident compassionate self. Bring to mind what you want to apologize for. Develop an apology that includes the following kinds of statements:

- A direct statement of apology and remorse: "I am very sorry that I...," "I apologize for..."

- An empathic statement of the hurt you may have caused: "I can imagine that this was very hurtful to you."

- A commitment not to repeat the action in the future: "I'm committed to not doing this again."

Follow through. If you say that you're committed to not harming this person again, take appropriate steps to make sure that you don't.

FORGIVENESS

If you're reading this book, chances are that some of the people you have felt angry toward have harmed you or hurt your feelings in some way. Learning to *forgive*—to let go of the negative emotions that you feel toward those who have harmed or angered you—can be an important step in freeing yourself from the grip of chronic anger. Forgiveness doesn't mean thinking that what they did to you was okay, giving them permission to harm you again, or trusting them. In fact, you may no longer want to see them or have any kind of relationship with them. Forgiveness certainly doesn't mean that your relationship with them will just go back to the way it was before.

The ability to have conflicts and then to reconcile and forgive can actually strengthen and bring about positive changes in our relationships. It can help to think about the things that help us to forgive and the things that can get in the way. If somebody is unkind to you in the heat of her anger but then apologizes, what would help you to forgive her? What might make it hard for you to forgive her? What would make you continue to hold on to your resentment?

Forgiveness means choosing to let go of the anger and suffering that you've experienced as a result of clinging to your experience of being harmed. It means accepting that you have been hurt and *making the decision* to let go of the bad feelings that you hold toward the other person. I've intended the following exercise to be done privately. Whether or not you choose to communicate your forgiveness to the other person is up to you. In making this decision, consider whether or not communicating it would be helpful—first to you, and second to the other person.

Exercise 10.6: Forgiveness

Begin with thirty seconds of soothing-rhythm breathing and access the kind, confident, wise qualities of your compassionate self.

When beginning the work of forgiveness, it's good to start by forgiving little things, moving on to larger harms once you've got the hang of it:

- Bring to mind someone who has embarrassed, upset, or harmed you in ways that you've struggled to let go of. Consider the ways that holding on to the hurt, resentment, and anger has caused suffering in your life—how it has made the harm that you received seem to last longer.

- Consider how it would feel if you no longer had to carry the burden of this harm, if you were released from the burden of these negative emotions.

- Next, imagine that the person who harmed you arrived into the world as a baby, just like you. Just like you, this person didn't ask to be here or to have the genes or the brain that he was given or the life experiences that have shaped him. Just like you, he sometimes struggles and does things that aren't helpful. Feel a sense of the common humanity between you.

- Commit yourself to letting go of the ill will that you experience toward this person, to free yourself from the suffering of clinging to it. Picture the person in your mind and say to yourself, *I forgive you.*

- Notice the blocks that occur when you do this. If you find yourself struggling, imagine how you would feel if you *could* do it—what it would feel like if you no longer had this grudging feeling inside of you? Would that feel good, or would you feel that you've lost something? Are you frightened of letting the person off the hook or letting him get away with it? Consider how your compassionate self would work with this thought, understanding that it's your anger that is the issue here, not the other person.

- Direct compassion toward yourself. Imagine being free of this suffering.

- If your "angry self" resists the effort to forgive, see if you (from the perspective of your compassionate self) can extend compassion to your angry self, recognizing the hurt that has caused you these feelings and wishing yourself to be free of it.

WHEN THINGS DON'T GO THE WAY YOU'D LIKE

Keep in mind that the goal of assertiveness is to communicate clearly and to express ourselves in appropriate ways that are consistent with our values. Over time, some of our interactions and behavior will produce the outcomes we hope for, and some won't. As we've seen, there are lots of situations in life (such as other people's reactions) that we simply can't control, and often things won't turn out the way we want them to, despite our best efforts. When this happens, it can be tempting to become disillusioned and think, *Well, that didn't work…but I tried, so now I can feel free to go back to my same old angry habits.* Don't fall into this trap! Your compassionate strategies may not always achieve your short-term objectives, but I'd encourage you to try them over time and see if they don't work more often than your angry threat responses have. You may find that, although specific situations here and there may not be resolved in the way you'd like, other priorities (such as your happiness and relationships) may still benefit. For example, Sheila was unable to control Joshua's choices about his university degree. But when she worked with her own emotions and became able to communicate her concerns assertively with him, she gained things that were even more valuable: she was able to see that the high-pressure way she had been raised wasn't the only way to pursue a career, she learned to respect Josh as an adult who was thoughtfully considering his future, and she was able to strengthen her relationship with him by discussing things with a level of honesty she'd never reached before.

Even when the situation doesn't work out the way we want, we can still behave in ways that are respectful to ourselves and to others, that minimize harm to our lives and those of others, and that reflect the sort of people we want to be. Remember, we're trying to create changes in our minds and brains that will shape our lives in the future. Even when we can't control a situation, we can control our own behavior, and we can work with our difficult threat systems to have better relationships and happier lives. We may lose some battles, but we can win the war.

POSITIVE INTERACTIONS: THE BUILDING BLOCKS OF GOOD RELATIONSHIPS

In their book *We Can Work It Out*,[5] Clifford Notarius and Howard Markman describe the "Relationship Bank Account" as a way of understanding the importance of positive interactions in human relationships. The idea is simple but profound: imagine that every positive interaction you have with another person is a "deposit" into the relationship bank account and that every negative interaction is a "withdrawal." The idea is that if we have lots of positive interactions, the occasional conflicts are easier to bear because they occur within a relationship that is defined overall by kindness and positive experiences. Imagine getting an eighty-dollar traffic ticket when you've got twenty thousand dollars in your bank account. It's not fun, but you can handle it without too much difficulty. If, on the other hand, you've only got fifty dollars in your bank account, that eighty-dollar ticket will feel a lot worse. When we're having lots of negative interactions and only a few positive ones (or even equal amounts, as negative interactions seem to be more powerful than positive ones), small conflicts can become a really big deal—the straw that broke the camel's back. Let's look at some ways to build up a healthy balance in your relationship bank account.

Minimize "Zingers"

One way to create a surplus in your relationship bank account is to decrease negative interactions. The ways we speak to one another can cause terrible hurt, even if we aren't doing things like yelling or name-calling. *Zingers* are the little verbal "pokes" we give one another—little jokes, insults, or comments containing toxic bits of criticism.[5] Regardless of whether or not your intentions are good, zingers hurt and can erode a relationship at breathtaking speed. Better to just bite your tongue and remember that the relationship is more important than the expression of that bit of irritation. If you really want to address an issue with the other person, use the assertive communication skills described previously.

Don't Sulk or Stonewall

Stonewalling means refusing to interact or to engage helpfully with the other person.[5] Pulling back from other people and punishing them by being passively hostile or simply refusing to interact with them is similar to saying, "I'm going to punish you until you do what I need you to do to make me feel better." Such tactics are coercive and tend to make it *less likely* that others will give you what you need. This is because this behavior serves to create distance in relationships. When these tactics *do* get you what you want, they do so in a fashion akin to bullying or blackmail. It may tend to irritate the other person so much that she won't want to work with you, even if she knows what it is you need from her (and she may not, since you aren't telling her). If you look at the situation from a compassionate point of view, you can recognize the urge to sulk or stonewall as an expression of your hurt; but you can also recognize that this behavior will keep you stuck. By using assertiveness instead, you can communicate what you need, help yourself feel more powerful, and actually address the situation that has made you so upset.

Plan Positive Interactions

Find ways to have fun together, whether it's taking your teenage son or daughter out for a movie in the afternoon or having a brief conversation about a television sitcom at the watercooler at work. Intentionally create situations in which you can enjoy one another's company. Be creative! Coming up with positive interactions can seem like a lot of effort at first, but once you've established the habit, fun opportunities will begin to present themselves as you begin to notice, *He would really enjoy this.* A good way to plan positive interactions is to *ask the other person* what he might enjoy and suggest doing it, even if it's something you wouldn't normally care to do. It's not about the activity, it's about having a positive interaction. Even activities that you might not expect to enjoy (like cleaning the garage, for example) can sometimes be great opportunities for positive interactions—particularly if you can bring some humor to the situation.

Be Polite

Cliché it may seem, but "please" and "thank you" communicate respect when spoken sincerely. Let people know when you appreciate them and their efforts. We hate to be taken for granted, and so do other people! Politely expressing our sincere gratitude to others acknowledges that they've treated us well, and can improve our relationship with them and help us to feel better.

Offer Kind Greetings and Farewells

Your best interactions will stimulate the safety systems of both you and the other person. A kind greeting that communicates, "I'm glad to see you," or a farewell that says, "I enjoyed my time with you," helps us to feel valued, appreciated, and liked. Kind greetings set the stage for positive interactions, and good partings leave the person with positive feelings about the relationship, possibly even helping to keep her safeness system activated as she moves out into the rest of her day. This is a gift that costs you nothing to give, but one that can have really positive effects on other people's lives (and your own).

Give Sincere Compliments

I'm not encouraging flattery, which is insincere and can be insulting. Good compliments simply involve communicating what we appreciate about others. I think the best compliments acknowledge and reinforce positive things that other people *do* rather than the quality of their appearance, for example. "I really appreciated what you said about _____." You can also get in the habit of acknowledging others' success and attempting to genuinely feel happy for them because of it (which Buddhists call *empathic joy*). This can be challenging, because your sensitive threat system may respond to others' success by generating thoughts related to feeling overshadowed (because *they* did it and you *didn't*). Over time, however, making a point of practicing empathic joy can help undermine tendencies to be self-focused and resentful, and to see yourself as being in competition with others—tendencies that can get in the way of having good relationships. Alternatively, showing genuine happiness for others' success will help them feel closer to you. Besides, if you can learn to be happy for others' successes as well as your own, you'll have a lot more things to be happy about!

CONCLUSION

In this chapter, we explored how you can use compassionate behavior to interact with others in ways that help everyone involved feel safe rather than threatened. Acting from the perspective of your compassionate self, you can work with difficult situations in ways that show respect to others and to yourself, and communicate in ways that are genuine, respectful, and assertive. You can attend to your relationships when you're not in a state of conflict and cultivate a wealth of positive interactions so that the inevitable difficulties don't seem quite so impossible to handle. In chapter 11, we'll explore how to bring compassion to our experience of others and how to develop compassionate attributes such as empathy.

11

Bringing Compassion to Your Experience of Others

In chapter 10 we focused on developing compassionate behavior that will help you interact effectively with others, even in times of conflict. These skills can be used even more effectively if you learn to *feel* more compassionately toward others, to develop the habit of experiencing others through the eyes of your compassionate self. Indeed, this approach can help to reduce the tendency to get angry in the first place, because you're developing aspects of yourself that are resistant to anger. But this development takes practice. Several times, I've heard the Dalai Lama point out that developing compassion for others is helpful even if we're operating from a purely selfish standpoint. This is because developing compassion for others creates changes in our own minds—helping to undermine the anger and other threat-based emotions that can cause us so much discomfort. It also will help us have better relationships.

In this chapter, we'll focus on our experience of other people—how we perceive them and assign meaning to them. One of the most troublesome things about anger and other threat-based emotions is that they rob other people (and ourselves) of our common humanity. As our threat systems try to defend us, they simplify our experience of reality. The nuances and shades of gray disappear as our world is condensed into "right/good" and "wrong/bad." Of course, we usually see ourselves as good (or at least, as the ones who are right, who need protecting or avenging) and those that trigger our threat systems as being bad (or at least, as the attackers or the ones who are in the wrong).

When we're in the grip of anger, the scope of our attention and thinking narrows and focuses our minds on the aspects of the situation (and the other person) that threaten us. In chapter 1, we noted that anger is typically linked to the frustration of our goals, feeling as if we can't do what we want, experiencing a sense of injustice and unfairness, or sometimes perceiving ourselves as powerless, shameful, or inadequate. Our minds then take these perceptions and translate them into emotional experiences of not being cared about, of feeling disrespected, or of being attacked or rejected in some way—of *not feeling safe*. It's rare for us to feel angry if we feel that people really are trying their best to be caring and respectful toward us.

We tend to attach these negative emotional experiences to the people who trigger them. We often find ourselves reacting as if these people exist only to anger us, as if other people are *deliberately* not caring about us. Every other quality they have, every other aspect of their lives and personalities seems to disappear as we mentally reduce them to "the ones who are annoying me."

We see the tragedy in this when the roles are reversed. For example, the men I work with in our prison groups are somewhat distinguished by the fact that their entire lives—how they spend their days, how others relate to them, the assumptions people make about their characters—are dictated by the worst things they've ever done. Imagine what that would be like, if the *only thing* someone knew about you was the worst thing you'd ever done.

Actually, you may very well know how this feels. Many of us who struggle with anger may finally seek help because we observe that others relate to us as a problem—that, to them, we have become "that angry person" or simply, "that ass." Their threat systems reduce us to one-dimensional characters in their minds the same way that our anger reduces others in our own minds. To our anger, other people aren't human beings, with complex lives and a wide range of hopes, dreams, motivations, and emotions. When our threat systems are in charge, other people are obstacles to be feared or overcome. This isn't our fault or theirs—it's just how our tricky brains work. Once that threat label is attached to someone, we shift into a defensive mode that leaves little room for new information to sink in. When this happens, it can become almost impossible for others to *not* activate our threat systems, because we tend to interpret their behavior in ways that fit with the ideas we've formed about them. By learning to consider others through the lens of compassion, we can work to change how they are held in our minds and, likewise, how we are held in theirs.

COMPASSIONATE RECOGNITION OF OUR COMMON HUMANITY

The first half of this book discussed various factors that can cause our lives to be difficult, many of which we did not choose or design. The realization that some of these factors are not our fault can help us begin to let go of our self-criticism and to develop compassion for ourselves and for other people. *Just like us*, everyone else found themselves here, born into the flow of life, with brains they didn't design, in environments they didn't choose. Just like us, they *didn't get to choose* whether or not their young brains got what they needed to be able to cope well with difficult emotions. Just like us, they want to be happy and to be free from suffering. Just like us, they are doing the best they can with the skills, knowledge, and resources they have. And just like us, they sometimes fall short.

Despite what our anger sometimes tells us, pretty much no one gets up in the morning and thinks, *Today, I'm going to mess up my kids so that they have difficult, miserable lives* or *Today, I'm going to create a hostile work environment for my colleague.* And how miserable must their lives be if they *do* think this way. Cultivating this awareness of others can be a gateway to compassion—we acknowledge that life is hard and that we're all dealing with it in the best way we can. We can begin to recognize that we are truly all in this together.

Both parts of the exercise that follows are designed to help you connect with a deeper realization and understanding of the lives of others. The idea is to strengthen the habit of realizing that everyone else struggles with the same basic emotions and challenges that we do, of recognizing that their life stories run just as deep as ours do. When this realization first hit me, it was very moving. But while I've found that having the occasional compassionate epiphany (the "oh my gosh" moment) can be very powerful, it's all too easy to forget these moments when I'm again faced with day-to-day irritations. By purposefully bringing this awareness into your daily life *again and again*, you'll make it more likely that you won't be completely overwhelmed when your threat system begins to kick in. Here are some tips to help do this:

- Carry a small stone or special coin in your pocket as a reminder. Every time you feel it, access the kind, confident, wise qualities of your compassionate self. Then look to the first person you see. Hold that person in your mind and briefly practice connecting with the awareness of him or her as a human being, just like you.

- Start with people you like or those you don't know (rather than with people who trigger your anger or irritation).

- The next time you stop at a red light while driving or riding public transportation, observe someone in a vehicle around you. Remind yourself that this person's story runs as deep as yours, that just like you, she or he just wants to be happy and free from suffering.

- Similarly, go on a "compassion walk." As you stroll, silently recognize everyone you come across as a human being who just wants to be happy and has suffering and struggles, hopes and dreams, just like you. Extend compassion to them and wish them well.

- Focus on the feelings that come up as you practice these activities. Or, if this is difficult, imagine how your compassionate self might feel while doing them.

With practice, you can do these exercises very quickly. Gradually they will become quick but powerful reminders rather than exercises that take lots of time to complete. The idea is simply to quickly connect with the awareness of others as people whose lives run much deeper than the brief slice that we're exposed to, and to quickly bring up a kind feeling of compassion for them. With practice, this awareness can occur in seconds. I've also found that it makes the experience of life much more interesting to really consider the experiences and perspectives of other people—how they are different from me, and how they are the same.

Exercise 11.1: Compassionate Understanding of Others

For each of these practices, begin with thirty seconds of soothing-rhythm breathing and by accessing the kind, confident, and wise authority of your compassionate self:

1. Bring to mind another person, perhaps someone you don't know that well. Consider what you've learned in this book and how it applies to that person:

    -   Consider that this person was born into a situation that he didn't choose.

    -   Consider that, like you, he has a threat system that has evolved to organize his mind around powerful emotions such as anger and fear, and that narrows his attention and his ability to think flexibly.

    -   Consider that, just like you, he wants to be happy and to be free from suffering. He wants to be accepted, cared for, and success-ful, just like you.

    -   Consider that, just like you, this person may have learned to pursue happiness in ways that don't work for him, ways that sometimes cause him even more difficulties.

    -   See if you can feel compassion for this person, recognizing the difficulties we all share and wishing him well as he works with the challenges that life presents him.

2. Bring to mind another person and imagine her progression through life. For each of the realizations I offered in the first step of this exercise, imagine how it may play out in her life:

    -   Imagine her being born and emerging into a world she doesn't understand.

    -   Imagine her moving through her first years, learning to speak, crawl, and walk. Imagine her falling and crying, laughing and being nurtured.

    -   Imagine her as a child, happily playing with friends. Imagine her experiencing the pain of rejection. Imagine her attending school, struggling and succeeding, struggling and failing.

- Imagine her in adolescence, struggling to define herself as she moves toward adulthood. Imagine her coping with insecurity, discovering love, experiencing the pain of loss.

- Imagine her as an adult—perhaps working, marrying, and having children (or not)—getting jobs and losing them, having success and heartbreak. Imagine her struggling with her emotions and her expectations of herself and who she wants to become, the disappointment of falling short sometimes.

- Imagine her aging, perhaps looking at her children and grandchildren, or perhaps not. Perhaps she's surrounded by loved ones, or perhaps she is alone. Imagine her as she observes her body aging, her appearance changing, her physical strength fading and wisdom growing.

- Imagine her on her deathbed, reflecting on her life. Imagine how she might feel, approaching death. Imagine her closing her eyes.

CULTIVATING EMPATHY

The narrow, defensive focus of our threat systems centers our attention on *our* experience and tends to blind us to what others may be feeling. As a result, we're robbed of information that could help us understand many difficult situations in ways that are less threatening. Compassion, on the other hand, involves empathy: seeking to understand the emotional experience of others, finding out what the other person is feeling, and how it makes sense that he is feeling that way. This understanding can help shift us out of the "us versus them" reasoning that drives our anger so that we can find solutions that work for us *and* them. Empathy also helps reduce our anger and ill will toward others because when we seek to understand the feelings of another person, we humanize him. We begin to recognize that there is much more to this person than whatever happens to be irritating us in the moment. Getting in touch with empathy is difficult to do when we're feeling threatened, so the best way of preparing to do this is to practice when we're not feeling threatened—to get in the habit of trying to understand the feelings of those around us.

Exercise 11.2: Developing the Habit of Empathy

I designed this practice to help you stretch the "mental muscles" of empathy, so that you can become better able to understand the emotions of others and more likely to make the attempt to do so. As with the other exercises, take thirty seconds to slow down your body and mind with soothing-rhythm breathing, and bring to mind the qualities of your compassionate self: a kind motivation to help, calm confidence, and the wisdom to draw upon your life experience.

Start by practicing with people you aren't angry with. Consider another person and attempt to understand what he is feeling and how it might make sense that he's feeling and behaving this way. You can even practice this when you're watching television. Observe a character and think about how she might be feeling. Try to practice this whenever it occurs to you, as often as possible. It doesn't have to take a long time.

When you develop an empathic understanding of how someone else is feeling, you can draw upon a number of different sources of information:

- His behavior. What do his actions say about what he might be feeling? Have you ever behaved similarly? How were you feeling when that happened?

- His facial expression and posture. How does his nonverbal behavior express his emotions?

- Your emotional reaction to his experience. How do you feel as you witness his experience?

- Your knowledge of your own emotional reactions. How have you felt when you've been in similar situations in the past?

- Your knowledge of his personality, background, and how he differs from you. You might feel a certain way if you were in his situation, but you can't assume he feels the same way. Using what you know of him, how might *he* experience this situation (potentially in ways that are very different from how you might)?

- Consider how it makes sense that he would feel this way.

- If you really want to know how someone is feeling, ask him, and listen to what he says. When faced with a question like, "I was wondering how you were feeling about all of this?" people will often tell us—we just have to be ready to listen. The key is to listen from the perspective of the compassionate self and refrain from judging or evaluating the appropriateness of the other person's reactions.

DEEPENING EMPATHY WITH MENTALIZATION

Once we have an idea of what another person is feeling, we can deepen this experience by considering *why* they might be feeling and behaving this way. In the first three chapters of this book, we looked at how our emotion systems have evolved and the different ways anger can organize our minds. We also discussed various factors (attachment history, learning, implicit memory) that have an impact on how we express our emotions and our ability to regulate them. Considering that we've had very little choice in so many of these factors, I suggested to you that much of the experience we have of our emotions is not our fault. We didn't *choose* to have difficulties with anger.

It turns out that all of these factors affect everyone else, too. And *it isn't their fault, either*. Recognizing this doesn't mean that we won't be inconvenienced, frustrated, or angered by their behavior, and it doesn't mean we won't address it. However, if we think about why others are feeling and behaving the way they do, we may find ourselves feeling less angry toward them and more sympathetic.

To do this, we compassionately consider that, just like us, other people simply want to be happy and to be free from suffering, and that pretty much all of their behavior is somehow directed toward achieving these broad goals. We then draw upon the mentalizing skills that we examined in chapter 9 and we ask ourselves certain questions. Go ahead and try this next brief exercise to see how this can work.

Exercise 11.3: Using Mentalization to Deepen Empathy for Others

Once again, take thirty seconds or so to slow yourself down with soothing-rhythm breathing and access the kindness, confidence, and wisdom of your compassionate self. Bring to mind a recent situation in which you experienced irritation with another person—perhaps someone whose behavior inconvenienced you, for example:

- Consider how the other person is behaving and ask yourself, *What thoughts and feelings might be leading this person to behave in this way?*

- What needs is this person attempting to meet? Safety? Social connection? Status? Material needs?

- What desires, concerns, or fears might be motivating this person's behavior?

- Consider this person's life story. What struggles might she (or he) be facing that you might not know about? Maybe she's struggling with money. Perhaps she has health problems. She may have problems with children or sick relatives. Maybe her marriage is ending. Could the combination of her genes and early life experiences make it difficult for her to experience empathy for others? When we experience others as being difficult, there are often many factors affecting their emotions and behavior that we won't be aware of. Considering this, we still may not agree with their actions, but we may be able to understand, sympathize, or keep from judging them.

- Think of the different reactions you might have to this person and how your reactions could make this person's life easier or more difficult. Consider what impact or effect you want to have on her. How does your compassionate self want to affect this person's life?

Considering why other people do certain things and act in certain ways can be a powerful antidote to our anger. For example, if we look again at Sheila and Josh, whom we got to know in chapters 8 and 9, we see that Sheila's anger decreased a great deal when she was able to see that Josh was taking a long time to graduate from college not because of laziness, but because of a desire to find a career that would lead to a fulfilling life. Trying to understand the reasons behind the other person's behavior, and how it *makes sense* that he might be feeling or acting in this way, can help us shift out of the limited perspective of our angry minds and into our thoughtful, compassionate selves.

I've been very impressed with how the men in our anger groups have taken to this practice. It's hardest to have empathy for people who are treating us badly, and in prison there are lots of people who act rudely, angrily, and aggressively. A fair amount of discussion in our group is spent on working out ways of understanding and responding to these sorts of interactions so that violence is not the end result. Violence in prison has lots of grim consequences, such as being placed in solitary confinement, having time added to your sentence, and, of course, the likelihood of physical harm for everyone involved. When we've discussed such situations, group members have done a great job of exploring, "Why might he be acting like that?" In most cases, they've been able to consider and understand even the most aggressive behavior of other inmates as being motivated by feelings like insecurity or the desire for status or respect. Even in prison, we've found that there are many possible responses apart from aggression or passivity (which can make you a target for further victimization, the consequences of which can be quite dangerous). And when we understand why someone else is doing something, it's a lot easier to come up with skillful ways to respond.

A number of our group members have become masters at bringing compassion to their understanding of what motivates other people's behavior. I've lost count of how many times I've heard comments like, "He must have had a pretty terrible life if that's the only way he knows how to get respect," "He must be feeling pretty bad about himself to treat other people that way," or "She's not always like that. I'd bet she was having a pretty terrible day." These comments reflect a recognition that disrespectful, harmful, or cruel behavior is often rooted in suffering or misguided attempts to meet our own needs. Bringing this understanding to others doesn't mean that we aren't holding them responsible for what they do. What it means is that we attempt to *understand* their behavior in terms of why it's occurring rather than just pass judgment, take it personally, and respond to them out of anger. This isn't easy, but I've seen men serving hundred-year prison sentences for violent offenses do exactly this. If they can do it, we can, too.

SYMPATHY

While empathy is about understanding what others are feeling, sympathy involves allowing ourselves to be moved by their suffering—to be touched or feel some sadness when we see others in pain. Sympathy is an important part of compassion because it provides us with an emotional experience that resonates with others' suffering and motivates us to try to lessen it. Emotions have evolved to activate us, and sympathy is an emotion that can activate us to help. It works best when we combine the motivation of our sympathy with empathic understanding. Our empathy allows us to better know what other people need so that we can skillfully help them. This again relates to the qualities of the compassionate mind—the kind *motivation* to help, the *wisdom* to gain an understanding of what would be most helpful, and the *confidence* to put this into action.

The development of sympathy for others is particularly important for dealing with anger. If we really allow ourselves to connect with the suffering others experience as a result of our angry behavior, we can find that we have no choice but to work with our anger, to learn to manage it more effectively. Our sympathy for their suffering can create a situation within us that makes it impossible to bear the thought of harming them anymore. The key here is to use this emotion as fuel to motivate our improvement—as a motivation to keep working with situations and other people in more helpful and more compassionate ways. When our past behaviors have caused great pain to others, opening to sympathy and empathy can sometimes cause us to feel pain ourselves. This can seem overwhelming. Some of us may have avoided allowing ourselves to sympathize in this way because doing so causes us so much pain or shame. As we saw in the last chapter, when we experience shame, it can be tempting to retreat into callousness, anger, indifference, or denial. Remember, shame focuses our attention on us and how "bad" we are—which doesn't help anyone. Alternatively, sympathetic regret opens us to the pain that others feel and helps us commit to helping them (or at the least, to not harming them further). By choosing to shift our focus to a compassionate motivation to help others, we can find the courage to work with both our shame and the angry behavior that led to it.

BRINGING EMPATHY TO YOUR ANGRY INTERACTIONS

We struggle with empathy when we're angry and may have great difficulty seeing things from another person's point of view. But understanding things from a different perspective isn't just for the benefit of other people: without empathy, it's easy to be confused about why others are behaving the way they are. This makes it hard to understand the impact we (and our angry words and behaviors) are having on others, which in turn makes it easy for us to harm others without even knowing that we're doing it. We may think we're just expressing ourselves.

Let's consider someone who had been abused as a child and, as an adult, experienced rapid, extreme mood swings. (I'll call her Jessica.) She was quick to feel rejected and alone and had been diagnosed with borderline personality disorder. Jessica tended to take things very personally and would become very angry with her children if she felt they had disobeyed her. She took their behavior as a sign that they didn't respect her and didn't care about her. At times, she would blow up in anger and would yell at them, calling them names and then storming out of the house to leave them terrified and alone. It wasn't until Jessica connected with how she had felt when her own mother had acted in the same way that she began to consider and understand how her behavior affected her own children. At this point, Jessica began to let go of the self-justifying thoughts that she had used to support her angry behavior, and committed to working with her emotions compassionately. Once Jessica understood the distress that her actions caused her children (and the regretful feeling of heartbreak that this created in her), she couldn't continue allowing herself to act this way. She began taking parenting classes to learn new, more effective ways to deal with her children's defiant behaviors (which occurred far less frequently as Jessica's own behavior changed).

Allowing ourselves to connect with others' experience of our anger allows us to see it, and ourselves, in a new light. Again, the key is to use these perceptions as fuel for change—as motivation to develop our compassionate selves.

Exercise 11.4: Becoming the Other

This exercise, developed by Paul Gilbert, is designed to help you consider, in a safe and semiplayful way, what others might feel in response to your anger:

- Set up two chairs facing each other. Sit in one of the chairs (we'll call this the "angry chair") and imagine that the person you've been angry with is sitting in the chair opposite.

- Direct your anger toward this person, and say the sorts of things to him (or her) that you said during your interaction (or if you're planning the interaction, the things you plan to say to him). Express your anger to him.

- Now, take a breath, get up, and sit in the other chair. Imagine that you are the person on the receiving end of your anger and accusations. Notice how you might be feeling, how you might want to react. Imagine the facial expression of the angry self. Allow yourself to experience what you might feel as this anger is directed at you. Consider the thoughts and feelings that come up for you.

This exercise can give you the opportunity to think about what you sound like and look like, and the impact you have on the other person when you're angry. The exercise can also be used to practice different ways of dealing with difficult interactions. For example, in chapter 10 I offered a number of ways to communicate assertively. The exercise above can allow you to try out different ways of approaching a situation. Using role-play first in one chair and then the other, you'll have an opportunity to imagine how the other person might feel, think, and respond to your efforts at communication. This exercise is nice because it gives you the chance to practice your assertiveness and empathy skills all at one time.

COMPASSIONATE IMAGERY: BRINGING COMPASSION TO A CHALLENGING OTHER

In exercise 7.2 you tried an imagery exercise that involved extending compassion to someone you care about, and in exercise 7.3 you directed this compassion toward yourself. In the exercise that follows, you'll stretch your compassion muscles a bit further, extending this exercise to send compassionate wishes to someone you've struggled with, had conflict with, or even just dislike. This practice is obviously more challenging than the others, but bear in mind that you are *training your mind*. Just as with physical training (for example, if you're training to run a marathon), sometimes you have to push yourself. It can seem difficult, but I'll bet that you've done lots of difficult things in your life as you pursued things that were important to you.

You'll start by first accessing the kind, wise, and confident authority of your compassionate self and reconnecting with the "Deepening Compassion" exercise (7.2). In this one, you'll visualize someone you care about, bring up the compassionate feeling of wanting to help this person, and send compassionate wishes out to them. Once you've done this, you will then bring to mind the image of a "challenging other": someone you've been having difficulty with. You'll then go through the practice again, this time generating compassionate feelings for this person and wishing for her (or him) to have happiness and freedom from suffering, and that she flourish and find peace. You could also start by doing exercises 11.1, 11.2, and 11.3 in this chapter but, this time, holding your challenging other in mind. The purpose of this exercise isn't to make you *like* the other person—you may never like her and may decide that your life is better if you keep away from her. The point is to try to shift your mind's orientation from being angry to being compassionate toward her. In this way, this exercise is similar to forgiveness.

If you find yourself losing the sense of compassion as you practice this exercise, return to the image of the person or animal that you started with— the one you care about, for whom compassion flows naturally. Once you've reconnected with those compassionate feelings, try to extend them again to your challenging other. This is an advanced practice, particularly for those of us who have been harboring anger for a long time. So don't worry if you aren't able to feel it. Just try to imagine what it would feel like *if you could* feel and express compassion and kind wishes toward this person. Also, when you begin to extend compassion to those you dislike or have conflict with, it's best to start small—perhaps with someone who causes you relatively minor irritation rather than someone you feel great anger towards or who has caused you intense pain. It isn't easy, but with practice you can find that you're able to feel compassion even for the people who push your buttons most regularly.

Exercise 11.5: Directing Compassion to a Challenging Other

Begin by moving through "Cultivating the Compassionate Self" (exercise 7.1) and "Deepening Compassion" (exercise 7.2) and by taking a few minutes to assume the qualities of the compassionate self. Connect with compassionate wishes that you extend to someone you care about. Focus on your compassionate feelings and the sense of kindness, calm confidence, and wisdom of your compassionate self. Connect with the deep wish for this person to be happy.

When you feel connected with feelings of kindness and compassion for the person or animal you care about, shift your focus to someone with whom you've struggled—perhaps someone with whom you've had repeated conflicts. Imagine this person as fully as you can, and begin to focus your compassion on him. Imagine him as a fellow human being who has arrived in this world, who just wants to be happy and to avoid suffering, and who is doing the best he can as he is faced with difficult feelings and life circumstances. Remind yourself that even his difficult or hurtful actions were done in the attempt to be happy and to be free from suffering. Keep your compassionate, friendly expression and a sense of your warm voice, *name the person*, and imagine directing the following phrases toward him:

- *May you be* free of suffering. (Pause for ten to thirty seconds.)

- *May you be* happy. (Pause for ten to thirty seconds.)

- *May you* flourish. (Pause for ten to thirty seconds.)

- *May you* find peace. (Pause for ten to thirty seconds.)

Next, for a minute or so, continue to repeat these phrases (out loud or in your head) as you visualize this person in your mind. With each phrase, focus on the wish you are directing. Attempt to *feel* the wish that this person be free of suffering, happy, and able to flourish and find peace. If he has harmed you or others, imagine him being free of the suffering and confusion that lead him to commit this harm.

If you find yourself resisting—for example, feeling as if you *don't* want this person to be happy or free from suffering—mindfully notice these thoughts and feelings as normal ways that your threat system is seeking to protect you.

Gently bring your focus back to your kind, confident, wise compassionate self and reconnect with the phrases. Notice what feelings arise as you direct these kind wishes toward this other person and how it feels in your body as you begin to let go of the ill will you hold toward him.

CONCLUSION

As you work to deal with your anger more effectively, you can broaden your experience of other people. As our experience and understanding expands, our view of others is no longer driven by threat systems that narrow our attention and bias our reasoning. Your compassionate self understands that we are all complex beings who only want to be happy and to be free from suffering, creatures whose behavior reflects a variety of motivations, emotions, and thought processes. When we practice compassion for others and establish the habit of having empathy, sympathy, and the compassionate motivation to be helpful, we begin to remove the fuel that drives our anger and strengthen the mental muscles of our compassionate minds. In chapter 12, we'll bring our compassionate focus back to where we started—to ourselves.

12

Full Circle: Bringing Compassion and Kindness to Yourself

Throughout this book you've worked hard to use compassion to help you work with anger and to improve your relationships. This has required you to direct a lot of attention toward problems—how to work with things when they're difficult and what to do when things go wrong. In this chapter we'll approach things a bit differently. In chapter 10, I introduced Notarius and Markman's Relationship Bank Account,[1] which helps us to understand how difficulties and arguments in relationships are a lot easier to handle if the relationship contains many more positive interactions than negative ones—if the relationship is otherwise strong. Similarly, things that go wrong in our own lives are a lot easier to bear if they occur in the context of an otherwise happy life. We're a lot less likely to fly off the handle in the face of minor difficulties if our lives are otherwise filled with lots of positive experiences for which we are grateful. Alternatively, if we're stressed out, unhealthy, and stretched to the limit...well, this creates the perfect setting for our threat systems to make mountains out of molehills.

So while the topic of how to have a happy life goes way beyond the scope of this book, I wanted to include this brief chapter to introduce a few potent ways to bring positive emotional experiences into your life. The idea is to build up your personal resources so that you're better able to handle things when the difficulties, annoyances, and crises hit. Then, you'll be less likely to buy into your highly reactive threat system when it tries to convince you that everything is falling apart.

COMPASSIONATE BEHAVIOR: SELF-CARE

Bringing compassion into our own lives means taking care of ourselves and giving our bodies, brains, and minds the support and resources they need to function at their best. All too often we eat unhealthily, get little sleep, budget no time for leisure, recreation, or positive interactions with others, and then wonder why we feel stressed out and irritable. Just as thinking in certain ways can help create the causes and conditions for more positive states of mind, there are also some basic things we can do to help ourselves cope well with stress and difficult situations, and to have increased happiness as well. When you work to bring compassion to yourself, I'd strongly encourage you to try the following:

- **Get sufficient sleep.** For most people, it's good to aim for seven to eight hours per night.

- **Eat a reasonable diet.** Limit your intake of highly processed foods containing lots of sugar, fats, and processed carbohydrates that are high in calories and low in nutrition. Make sure to include plenty of fresh fruits and vegetables in your diet, and keep portion sizes reasonable. Buying a set of moderately sized dishes helps with this. We tend to fill our plates and then eat until the food is gone.[2] If you feel that you overeat, I'd suggest trying to use smaller plates for a week or so—you may find that you're satisfied even though the portion size is smaller than what you may normally consume.

- **Avoid drugs, and if you consume alcohol, do so moderately.** Lots of harmful behaviors associated with anger occur while we are under the influence of drugs or alcohol. If you're alcoholic (you crave alcohol, make excuses to drink, and find that the amount you drink has increased gradually over time) or have had problems related to alcohol intoxication, it's probably better to refrain altogether. Working with substance issues can be almost impossible to do on your own, and I would encourage you to get help, which is an act of compassion toward yourself.

- **Get some exercise.** Find fun ways to get your body moving. Exercise has all sorts of positive benefits in our lives, including reducing stress and improving our physical and mental health.

- **Learn to manage your time.** There are lots of ways to do this, but a good start would be to use a day planner to keep track of your time, hour by hour, for a week. You may find lots of hidden pockets of time that you could use in ways that are more productive or more fun!

- **Identify major life stressors and find resources to help you address them.** If there are things in your life that cause you a great deal of stress, don't just ignore them and hope they'll go away. Often there may be helpful, low-cost resources available (for example, free local classes on managing finances), and the Internet has made it easier to find them.

- **Learn to manage your spending.** Spending ourselves into huge amounts of debt creates lots of stress and can keep our threat systems on high alert. This is beyond the scope of this book, but there are plenty of other resources to help you learn how to manage money. Reducing impulsive spending can be a lot like working with angry behavior, although impulsive spending is driven by the drive and resource acquisition system.

- **Identify sources of social support and connect with them.** Identify people in your life whom you enjoy spending time with and who accept you as you are. Find ways to spend more time with them. Remember, our safeness systems naturally respond to kind, supportive interactions with others.

- **Seek out new sources of social support.** Find other people who share your values and spend some time with them. Consider developing a hobby that will allow you to connect with people who have similar interests.

- **Find ways to help others.** Look for opportunities to help other people or animals. There are often little things we can do to improve the lives of others that require relatively little time or effort on our part. Doing so helps them and helps us feel better (and better about ourselves) as well. Volunteering directly will help you develop your sense of compassion and is a great way to meet and develop friendships with other like-minded and compassionate people.

- **Build in time for fun.** Create opportunities for positive emotional experiences in your life. Make time for doing things that you enjoy, and then follow through and do them! Give yourself permission to take it easy and have fun sometimes. Try finding and introducing a variety of brief, pleasurable activities (like pausing for a pleasant cup of tea or coffee) throughout the day.

- **Get help when you need it.** Sometimes we just aren't able to solve our problems on our own, even with the help of books like this one. In this case, pursue the services of a qualified therapist (or other health professional). Stubbornly refusing to admit when you can't handle something on your own just compounds misery. When your car is giving you problems despite your best efforts to fix it, you take it to a mechanic. Why shouldn't you treat yourself at least as well?

These suggestions aren't rocket-science treatment methods; they're just the kind of things that happy, healthy people tend to do. You can try these methods or create some of your own. The idea is to maximize the enjoyable, healthy, rewarding, and nurturing things in life; to avoid unnecessary stressors; and to accept and work patiently with those difficulties that are inevitable. We want to build up internal and external resources that we can draw upon in times of need. Living compassionately is about taking care of ourselves *and* others, and we need a balance between these two in order to do both well.

BROADENING YOUR PERSPECTIVE

As we've seen, when we're angry or irritable, our thoughts tend to ignore the positives and focus on the negative aspects of the situations we find ourselves in (and of our lives in general). We then tend to ruminate over these things—turning them over and over in our minds. The brief exercises in this chapter are designed to counter this habit of the angry, irritable mind and to help you begin to establish the habit of seeking out and recognizing the *positive* aspects of life. When we look closely, we often find that despite our struggles and challenges, there are often many aspects of our lives that are going well—things that we can be grateful for.

Positive Emotions: Broadening and Building

In this chapter, I present a number of exercises designed to facilitate positive emotional states, many of which involve paying attention to good things in your life and things that you can be grateful for. While this may at first seem like "just think happy thoughts" therapy, there are reasons to believe that using such methods can be beneficial. As we've learned, threat emotions like anger and fear *narrow* our attention and restrict our ability to think flexibly. When we're in danger, this can help us think and respond quickly to threats. However, it can also create problems in modern life when we're faced with difficulties that require thoughtfulness rather than rapid action. Recent research has shown that positive emotions *broaden* our attention and allow us to think more flexibly[3] (which can be helpful when we're figuring out how to deal with difficult situations).[4, 5]

Over time, negative or positive life experiences can produce "negative spirals" or "positive spirals," affecting our brains so that the more negative emotional experiences we have now, the more likely we are to have such negative experiences in the future. The same applies to positive emotional experiences. The take-home message here is that by focusing your attention and thoughts in certain ways, you can create the sorts of emotional experiences that can get these spirals moving in the direction of having a happier life, better relationships, and the ability to cope more smoothly with life's difficulties. One way to create these positive emotions is to practice meditation that directs kindness and compassion toward yourself and others,[6] just as we've done in many exercises in this book.

Attending to the Good Things: The Gratitude Journal

In *Buddha's Brain: The Practical Neuroscience of Happiness, Love, and Wisdom*,[7] neuropsychologist Rick Hanson and his coauthor, neurologist J. Richard Mendius, discuss how bringing our attention to the positive aspects of our lives can have beneficial effects for our brains. The good news is that we can learn to intentionally work with our tendency to focus thought and attention on the aspects of our lives that feel most threatening. We can instead choose to bring our attention to the many positive aspects of our lives. This doesn't mean that we ignore or avoid the difficulties in our lives—we've spent lots of time exploring how to work with them. However, when we aren't directly working with these difficulties, ruminating on them only serves to fuel our threatened states of mind. The key is to *get in the habit* of noticing the positive things in your life, such as a good meal or hearing a piece of music you enjoy. If you can shape the habit of noticing and allowing yourself to experience the things that go well, your experience of life will be lighter and more positive.

Gratitude can be defined as a feeling of thankful appreciation for favors or benefits that we've received from others.[8] Increasingly, research suggests that experiencing and expressing gratitude can increase our ability to feel positive emotions, improve well-being, and contribute to better relationships.[9] Research has also shown that people who have written down things they were grateful for showed an increase in positive emotions, a reduction in negative emotions, improved sleep, and increased satisfaction with their lives.[10] Grateful people are also more likely to help others with personal problems or to offer emotional support to others—in other words, to act with compassion. Focusing on the kindnesses we've received from others seems to help trigger our own tendency to connect with our kind, wise, and compassionate minds.

This next exercise will help you begin to get into the habit of noticing positive things to be grateful for, even if they seem small, generalized, or otherwise inconsequential. For example, today I'm aware that I can be grateful that my computer is working properly; that it's a nice, sunny day; that I've got a tasty cup of coffee to drink as I write; and that I have a family who cares about me. Even when things go wrong (like last week when I fried one of my favorite guitar amplifiers by mindlessly plugging it into the wrong speaker cabinet and turning it on), there are often things that we can be thankful for (like the fact that I have someone in town who is great at fixing guitar amplifiers!).

Exercise 12.1: The Gratitude Journal

First, take thirty seconds or so for soothing-rhythm breathing. As you slow your breath, bring to mind the characteristics of your compassionate self: *kindness, confidence,* and *wisdom.*

- There are many things in our lives, both large and small, that we might be grateful for. Think back over the past week and write down up to five things in your life that you're grateful for.

- As you write them down, allow yourself to be appreciative of these good things you've received in your life.

Interdependence, Gratitude, and a Wealth of Unintended Kindness

Buddhism has had thousands of years to develop mind-training techniques that can help us focus our minds on compassion rather than on anger, and in CFT we draw upon a number of these techniques. When we're feeling threatened or angry, we can feel as if it's us against the world and that we receive little kindness or support from others. When we go through life feeling this way, the world can seem a very lonely, threatening place.

However, we can counter these feelings by recognizing our interconnectedness and interdependence—the idea that we all live in dependence upon one another. The idea is that our lives are supported and made possible by the actions of other people, and as we go about our own lives, we support them in turn. For example, when I purchase a pair of tennis shoes, I support the lifestyles of those who work to produce shoes, even as their efforts make it possible for me to have them. If we consider this idea of interdependence a bit further, we can discover that we are truly and deeply connected with one another.

His Holiness the Dalai Lama frequently mentions a mind-training technique for developing this understanding, which we can call "considering the unintended kindness of others."[11] Instead of focusing your attention on the harms, insults, or inconveniences that we may feel others have brought us, we can choose instead to focus on the many aspects of our lives that exist only because of the efforts of other people (and beings) on this planet. This allows us to become aware of two things: first, we notice that rather than being alone, our lives are completely interdependent and intertwined with those of other people. Second (and related) is the awareness that almost everything that makes our ways of life possible is *a direct result of the efforts— the "unintended kindnesses"—of other people.*

Consider something you may take for granted, such as the clothes you're wearing. How many hundreds or thousands of other people worked so that you might be able to wear these clothes? The shirt I'm wearing exists only because of the farmer who grew the cotton, the person who transported the cotton to where it was processed into cloth, the people who processed the cloth, the people who cut and sewed the material into a shirt, and the countless people involved in packaging, transporting, stocking, and finally selling it to me so that I might wear it. At every stage in this process, the efforts of *those* people were only made possible by the efforts of *many more* people who designed machines and tools, built factories, laid roads, and so on. When I really think about it, this shirt that I almost always take for granted represents the hard labor, the unintended kindness, of thousands upon thousands of people. If we place the moments of our lives under examination, we find that almost every aspect of our lives is like this—the food we eat, the transportation we count on, the computers we type on—all possible only because of the hard work of countless other people, most of whom we will never be able to meet or thank.

Once we begin to think about such things, we can begin to realize how much we have to be grateful for. And just because we don't get to express our gratitude to all of these people and other beings doesn't mean we can't acknowledge it to ourselves. Doing so can transform our minds and allow us to see how interdependent and interconnected we all are. This realization can be a gateway to compassion. Nevertheless, we may experience resistance and think perhaps, *Well, those people didn't do these things to benefit me—they did it to earn a living. They didn't intend it as kindness.* But even if this were true, does it mean that they don't deserve our gratitude? Regardless of their intentions, don't we still benefit? From this perspective, we can see that our current lives are made *possible* because of their hard work. This is why the Dalai Lama calls these things unintended kindnesses, because although unintended, the fact that we benefit from them makes them acts of kindness. When we look at life in this way, we can see ourselves surrounded by the kindness of others, living a life that is only possible because of them. We are anything but alone.

Exercise 12.2: Contemplating the Unintended Kindnesses of Others

First, as with all exercises in this book, begin with thirty seconds or so of soothing-rhythm breathing to access your compassionate mind and its various characteristics, including kindness, calm confidence, and wisdom. Imagine what it would be like to have these characteristics and then draw upon them as you do this exercise:

- Choose a specific aspect of your life: something that benefits you, makes your way of life possible, or is simply something you enjoy. It could be the road you use to get to work, the food you eat, the clothes you wear, and so on.

- Consider what it took for this aspect of your life to come into being: the number of people and other beings whose efforts made this aspect of your life possible. Consider that without them and beings like them, these aspects of your life *would not be possible*—they could not exist.

- Allow yourself to view their efforts as acts of kindness that benefit you. Allow yourself to experience gratitude toward them.

- Observe how you feel as you consider these things. Notice the sensations that arise in your body.

Bringing It Together: Compassionate Letter Writing

In this chapter I've presented a number of ways to bring kindness and compassion to yourself. One way to bring many of these approaches together with the other compassionate practices we've covered is through *compassionate letter writing*,[12] which involves writing a letter to yourself from the perspective of your compassionate self. In this letter, you provide yourself with encouragement, kindness, validation, and advice. You can reread the letter when you're having difficulties, to comfort and motivate yourself to stay on track—dealing with your anger in ways that are more effective. You can write the letter to remind yourself of things that can help in difficult situations:

- Your ability to feel concern and to genuinely care for others.

- Your compassionate self and its sensitivity to your distress and needs.

- Your ability to tolerate distress and face your feelings, even when they may be painful.

- Your ability to become more understanding of your feelings and the reasons you behave in certain ways.

- A nonjudgmental and noncondemning point of view.

- A genuine sense of warmth, understanding, and caring.

- The behavior you may need to adopt in order to get better.

- The need to broaden your perspective and recognize good things, including your strengths and the things to be grateful for.

- The reasons you're making efforts to improve.

Here's an example:

Dear Jim,

This has been a difficult week for you, and it makes sense that you're having a number of strong feelings. You have been trying very hard to work with your anger, and it's easy to feel disappointed and upset with yourself when you see yourself acting in ways that you're not proud of. Remember that your anger is a part of a threat system that you didn't choose, and that it's not your fault that you experience it. Habits run deep, and they are hard to change. The key is to keep trying. You have been very courageous in taking responsibility for your anger and learning to work with it, and you deserve compassion too. Learning to direct your mind in new ways is difficult, and you won't always get it exactly right. It's okay to feel the way you do right now. The fact that you're feeling bad means that you care *about doing better, and it's a sign that your hard work is paying off (even when it may not seem that way). You've made a lot of progress, and other people are noticing this and encouraging you. Think of how you are now compared to how you were when you started.*

Maybe there are some skills you've learned along the way that might help you now. You've always liked the safe-place exercise. Or maybe you could talk with Robert about how you're feeling—he always listens to you and tries to understand. Try to give yourself a break, and remember that you are doing this to set a good example for your son and daughter. They deserve your love and compassion, and so do you. Most importantly, keep going. Keep working to be the man you want to be. You can do it.

Sincerely,

Jim

CONCLUSION

In this chapter we've explored a number of ways that you can use your compassionate mind to take better care of yourself and to cultivate positive emotional experiences in your life. By using compassionate behavior to take good care of yourself, you create the opportunity to be at your best as you face the challenges that life has to offer. Learning to focus your thoughts on the positive aspects of your life and connecting with gratitude, interdependence, and kindness can help counter the feelings of isolation and resentment that so often fuel anger. Finally, you can use compassionate letter writing to draw upon and remind yourself of the skills you've covered in this book and to kindly give yourself encouragement when you need help.

13

Moving Forward: Approaching Anger and Life with Compassion

In this book, I've attempted to present you with a new, compassionate way of understanding your anger, and I've tried to help you work with anger effectively by developing the qualities of your compassionate self. We've looked at our emotion-regulation systems and the tricky ways our brains work, and how this can sometimes create difficulty for us. We've learned practices for working with our emotions, thoughts, and behaviors in order to prevent our lives from being hijacked by our threat systems. We've covered a lot of ground, so in this final chapter, I'd like to wrap up by attempting to give you a way to organize all of this and apply it in your life.

ORGANIZING OUR APPROACH TO ANGER: THE RAGE MODEL

Compassion focused therapy helps us develop many different skills for working with anger in more effective ways. We've examined a variety of these skills and tools in the second half of this book. The RAGE model is my attempt to organize these skills so that you can use them when you notice yourself becoming angry.[1] RAGE stands for *recognizing* anger arising; *accessing* your compassionate mind, *accepting* your experience, and *activating* your safeness system; *generating* a compassionate perspective and compassionate alternatives to anger; and *enacting* compassionate responses that move you toward your long-term goals. Let's look at these processes in more detail. You may notice some overlap between the steps, but that's by design—the idea is for each step to support the others.

Now let's take a closer look at each element of RAGE. We'll start with "R," which includes a reminder to recognize, reduce, and refrain:

Recognize Anger as a Threat Response

The first step in managing angry behavior is to recognize the signs of anger as they arise. Learning mindful attention (chapter 6) can help you notice the shifts in your mind and body that signal coming anger, and compassionate thinking (chapter 9) helps you identify, anticipate, and plan for situations that tend to trigger your anger so that you can be ready for them. You can also recognize that the anger you're feeling is your threat system working to protect you. This can help you mentally "step out" of the anger and the situation that provoked it, and begin to see things in a broader context. In doing so, you can use compassionate thinking to become aware of what might be causing you to feel this way. Using mentalizing skills (chapter 9), ask yourself, *What is the threat that my brain is reacting to?* You can examine the different emotional reactions you may be having (like embarrassment or shame) that might be fueling your anger. This will help you know what you're dealing with so that you can work with it, instead of having your behavior controlled by anger.

Reduce Angry Arousal

Your angry state of mind is fueled by arousal in your body, which can make it very hard for you to think clearly, and can keep you stuck in an angry state. Once you've recognized angry arousal in your body, you can work to reduce it by using compassionate attention skills like soothing-rhythm breathing (chapter 5) and the compassionate imagery practices (chapter 6).

Refrain from Anger-Driven Behavior and Habits That Amplify Anger

Many problems with anger are related to habitual behavior—either acting out or suppressing your anger. The first step in changing these habits is *refraining from doing them* once you're aware that you're getting angry. The skills you learned in chapter 8 can help you tolerate the experience of your anger without acting on it. Additionally, anger tends to organize our minds in ways that can lead us to ruminate about what happened and to justify our angry responses. These factors amplify our anger and keep it going. Learning to mindfully identify these processes and step back from them using the skills we've covered gives you the opportunity to shift away from the perspective of your threat-driven mind.

Now we'll move to the "A" in RAGE. It stands for accessing, accepting, and activating:

Access Your Compassionate Self

The ultimate goal of the CFT approach is the development of your compassionate self (chapter 4). In chapters 7 and beyond, we went into more detail about how you can cultivate this state of mind. The goal is to develop the habit of accessing your compassionate perspective as early in the progression of your anger as possible, bringing forth compassionate qualities like kindness, wisdom, confidence, empathy, and so on.

Accept and Endure Anger-Related Discomfort

As we saw in the first two chapters, anger and other threat-related emotions carry with them a strong urge to act. You can experience this urge and the anger itself as discomfort, like an itch that you desperately want to scratch. To work with your anger, use your compassionate understanding to accept that this is just the nature of anger—it's how our threat responses work. It's uncomfortable, but it won't kill us, and in order to work with anger more effectively, we need to accept this discomfort for what it is and learn to endure it. You can even see this discomfort as a signal that tells you that *right now* you have an opportunity to actively work with your anger and practice the skills you've learned. To help, you can use the strategies in chapter 8, which are specifically designed to assist you in tolerating the discomfort associated with anger. Likewise, you can use mindfulness to refocus your attention so that you can observe and work with this discomfort rather than act out (or give up) in response to it. One of the best strategies you can use is outlined in the final "A."

Activate Your Safeness System

Now that you've recognized your threat response for what it is, you can work to balance it by stimulating your safeness system. We covered a number of exercises for doing this in the compassionate imagery chapter (chapter 7), and you can also use compassionate letter writing (chapter 12). Using your compassionate mind to activate your safeness system helps bring your emotions back into balance, setting the stage for you to work more effectively with the situation and your emotions.

Now let's consider the "G" in RAGE, which reminds you to generate and give:

Generate Compassionate Alternatives to Habitual Anger Behavior

Once you've stepped out of the cycle of your habitual anger response, you can use your compassionate mind to come up with new responses to help in the situation. The chapters in the second half of the book, particularly those on compassionate thinking (chapter 9) and compassionate behavior (chapter 10) outline several skills for doing this.

Give Yourself Permission to Experience Whatever You're Experiencing

Developing a compassionate mind doesn't mean that you'll never feel angry or think hurtful thoughts. If you notice that you're having such thoughts or emotions, try not to beat yourself up or shame yourself for it. Instead, you can use compassionate thinking and acceptance to recognize these experiences as mental events that are normal products of your threat response. Then you can generate different thoughts and emotions. The key is to keep from attacking yourself for the mental experiences you're having, and instead to patiently work with your mind to create the experiences you *want* to have. The mindfulness exercises in chapter 6 can help you accept your experiences, and the compassionate imagery practices in chapter 7 and the compassionate letter writing exercise in chapter 12 give you opportunities to practice extending compassion to yourself. Finally, the compassionate thinking exercises in chapter 9 offer you compassionate ways to work with unhelpful thinking.

Moving on to the "E," you're reminded to enact, evaluate, establish, and experience:

Enact Compassionate Alternatives

Now that your compassionate mind has come up with better ways of addressing the situation, it's up to you to select the ones you'll use. It's time to start building new habits that better reflect the person you want to be, and this takes *practice*. In this stage, you put what you've come up with into action.

Evaluate Compassionate Alternatives

Here you take a look at the compassionate alternatives you've used and ask, *How did they work?* As we know, many situations won't turn out the way we'd prefer, no matter what we do. That's just how life is. You can't base your success on factors that you can't control. *The goal is for your behavior to reflect your values, so that you can be happy with how you respond no matter how the situation turns out.* As you do this, you'll begin to discover some options that tend to work better than others, and you'll start to build up a toolbox of compassionate strategies to use in difficult situations. This will help you approach difficulties with confidence because you will begin to understand that the way you respond can be under your control. This sense of control naturally tends to calm your threat system, helping you stop your anger before it really gets rolling.

Establish New Patterns in Your Brain

Every time you act from a compassionate motivation or choose a compassionate alternative instead of engaging in habitual anger behavior, you're helping to *establish new patterns in your brain* that will shape how you respond in the future. It's important to keep in mind that it isn't just about one particular situation—you're working to develop abilities that will help you cope with the struggles you'll face throughout the rest of your life one small step at a time. You're building a new set of life skills and working to establish them as your typical response. It's inspiring when you start to see your compassionate alternatives begin to appear as new habits.

Experience Yourself as a Compassionate Person

As you observe yourself acting from the perspective of your compassionate self rather than that of your threatened mind, you can begin to relate to yourself in a new way—as a compassionate person. You'll never be perfect, and you don't have to be. The idea is that you are acting out of a compassionate motivation to reduce your own suffering and that of others, and to help everyone in the situation. You'll fail, as we all do, but you'll get back up and try again. This is a lifelong effort, but it gets easier (and more fun) as you go. Resources to support the practices in this book, including copies of the forms and MP3 versions of guided meditations, can be found in the "Working with Anger" section of www.compassionatemind.net.

CONCLUSION

As we conclude our compassionate journey together, I'd like to offer you a hearty word of congratulations. You've reached the end of the book, and hopefully you've learned about how your brain works and ways to begin managing your anger and other difficult emotions, and perhaps have begun to experience compassion toward yourself and others. Now the work really begins! Take heart, and remember to take it one step at a time, to take the things you've learned and continue to apply them in the individual moments of your life—to *bring them into the here and now*. This present moment is where it all happens. By simply choosing to shift into your compassionate self, to think and act from that perspective, you begin to cultivate and establish new habits and brain patterns. With practice, these new habits and patterns can last for the rest of your life. This may sound difficult, but here's a secret: once these new patterns are well established, they will tend to continue—and they can replace the old, angry habits. You're wearing in new pathways and letting the old ones slowly erode.

You may be wondering when you'll see the effects of your efforts. People often think that change happens suddenly, like the sun shining down through a sky that was cloudy just a moment before. In my experience, the process of real change is more like watching the minute hand on a clock or trying to watch a child grow—while we're watching, we can't see any movement or growth at all. We never really *see* anything change. However, after a time we notice that although we may not remember changing, our lives have become different than they were, like when you look back up at the clock and notice that the minute hand has moved on. Similarly, one day you'll look at your life and notice that it has been days or weeks since you last yelled, that you can't remember the last time you spoke unkindly to your spouse or child, that you've been having many more positive and meaningful interactions with others and have more friends, or that things just seem to be going better in general. You may even notice that you're happier.

Keep going, keep practicing, one small step at a time. There will be setbacks and problems, but the secret is to keep yourself pointed in the direction you want to go. When you fall down, get up, dust yourself off, and take another step. You *will* fall down, which is one reason having compassion for yourself is so important. It isn't easy, but most important things in life aren't—you've known this for years. You are worth this effort, and *you can do this.*

—rk

Appendix

USEFUL BOOKS AND CDS FOR WORKING WITH ANGER

H. Kassinove and R. C. Tafrate, *Anger Management* (Atascadero, California: Impact, 2002).

W. R. Nay, *Overcoming Anger in Your Relationship: How to Break the Cycle of Arguments, Put-downs, and Stony Silences* (New York: The Guilford Press, 2010).

R. C. Tafrate and H. Kassinove, *Anger Management for Everyone* (Atascadero, California: Impact, 2009)

Buddhist Approaches to Working with Anger

T. Chodron, *Working with Anger* (New York: Snow Lion, 2001).

Thich Nhat Hahn, *Anger* (New York: Riverhead, 2001).

Self-Compassion

C. K. Germer, *The Mindful Path to Self-Compassion: Freeing Yourself from Destructive Thoughts and Emotions* (New York: The Guilford Press, 2009).

K. D. Neff, *Self-Compassion: Stop Beating Yourself Up and Leave Insecurity Behind* (New York: William Morrow, 2011).

The Compassionate-Mind Model and Compassion Focused Therapy

P. Gilbert, *Compassion Focused Therapy: Distinctive Features* (London: Routledge, 2010).

———, *The Compassionate Mind* (London: Constable and Robinson, 2009).

The Mind, the Brain, and How They Interact to Form Who We Are

S. Begley, *The Plastic Mind: New Science Reveals Our Extraordinary Potential to Transform Ourselves* (London: Constable and Robinson, 2009).

R. Hanson and R. Mendius, *Buddha's Brain: The Practical Neuroscience of Happiness, Love, and Wisdom* (Oakland, California: New Harbinger Publications, 2009).

D. J. Siegel, *The Developing Mind* (New York: The Guilford Press, 1999).

———, *The Neurobiology of "We": How Relationships, the Mind, and the Brain Interact to Shape Who We Are* (Boulder, Colorado: Sounds True, 2008).

D. J. Siegel and M. Hartzell, *Parenting from the Inside Out* (New York: Tarcher/Penguin, 2003).

Western Applications of Mindfulness and Acceptance

T. Brach, *Radical Acceptance: Embracing Your Life with the Heart of a Buddha* (New York: Bantam, 2004).

J. Kabat-Zinn, *Coming to Our Senses: Healing Ourselves and the World through Mindfulness* (New York: Piatkus, 2005).

———, *Full Catastrophe Living* (New York: Delta Publishing, 1990).

———, *Mindfulness for Beginners* (Boulder, Colorado: Sounds True, 2006).

———, *Wherever You Go, There You Are: Mindfulness Meditation in Everyday Life* (New York: Hyperion, 1994).

D. J. Siegel, *The Mindful Brain* (New York: Norton, 2007).

Buddhist Psychology

J. Kornfield, *The Wise Heart: A Guide to the Universal Teachings of Buddhist Psychology* (New York: Bantam, 2008).

Y. M. Rinpoche, *The Joy of Living: Unlocking the Secret and Science of Happiness* (New York: Harmony Books, 2008).

Marriage/Relationships

J. Gottman, *The Relationship Cure: A 5-Step Guide to Strengthening Your Marriage, Family, and Friendships* (New York: Three Rivers Press, 2002).

———, *Why Marriages Succeed or Fail: And How You Can Make Yours Last* (New York: Simon and Schuster, 1995).

C. Notarius and H. Markman, *We Can Work It Out: How to Solve Conflicts, Save Your Marriage, and Strengthen Your Love for Each Other* (New York: Perigree, 1993).

USEFUL WEBSITES

Resources (forms, guided audio exercises) to support this book can be found in the "Working with Anger" section of my website: compassionatemind. net. This is the website for the Inland Northwest Compassionate Mind Center, located in Spokane, Washington. We provide training, consultation, and some clinical services based in the CFT approach. This website also links to and is affiliated with that of the Compassionate Mind Foundation: www.compassionatemind.co.uk.

See also:

American Psychological Association: www.apa.org

Association for Behavioral and Cognitive Therapies: www.abct.org

For Compassion-Focused Work

Compassionate Mind Foundation: www.compassionatemind.co.uk. A non-profit organization set up by Professor Paul Gilbert, the Compassionate Mind Foundation's website contains information on CFT, resources for individuals using CFT to work with life difficulties, research supporting CFT interventions, and links to other compassion-focused websites.

The Center for Compassion and Altruism Research and Education: ccare .stanford.edu. This site has lots of information, media clips, and training opportunities on the evolving science of compassion and ways that compassion is being cultivated in the modern world.

Mind and Life Institute: www.mindandlife.org. This is the website for the collaboration between the Dalai Lama and Western scientists.

Self-Compassion: self-compassion.org. This is Dr. Kristin Neff's website. Dr. Neff is one of the earliest and most influential researchers on self-compassion.

Mindful Self-Compassion: www.mindfulselfcompassion.org. This is the website for Dr. Chris Germer, author of *The Mindful Path to Self-Compassion*. It contains lots of guided meditations and handouts.

Anger Monitoring Form

The purpose of this form is to help you become familiar with the situations that tend to provoke your anger and the ways you tend to respond. It aims to help you generate compassionate alternatives. Pick one time during the week when you experienced anger, rage, or irritation.

Situation/Trigger:

Emotions:

Thoughts:

Behaviors (What did you do?)

What does your compassionate self say?

What would your compassionate self do?

Outcome?

Notes

INTRODUCTION

1 For more information, I would suggest reading the following:

K. D. Neff, *Self-Compassion: Stop Beating Yourself Up and Leave Insecurity Behind* (New York: William Morrow, 2011).

C. K. Germer, *The Mindful Path to Self-Compassion: Freeing Yourself from Destructive Thoughts and Emotions* (New York: The Guilford Press, 2009).

P. Gilbert, *The Compassionate Mind* (London: Constable and Robinson, 2009).

————, *Compassion-Focused Therapy: Distinctive Features* (London: Routledge, 2010).

CHAPTER 1: ANGER—INTRODUCTION AND OVERVIEW

1   The following resources by Ray DiGuiseppe, Howard Kassinove, and Raymond Chip Tafrate provide a more detailed discussion of the various forms that anger can take (and lots of other excellent information on anger and its treatment). These authors have done much excellent work on anger, and their works were very useful in the preparation of this chapter.

R. DiGuiseppe and R. C. Tafrate, *Understanding Anger Disorder* (New York: Oxford University Press, 2007).

H. Kassinove and R. C. Tafrate, *Anger Management* (Atascadero, California: Impact, 2002).

2   While unpublished, this manuscript from University of California psychiatrist Martin Paulus and colleagues provides an excellent overview of anger and its health consequences. Kassinove and Tafrate's *Anger Management* also presents a nice overview of the health consequences of anger.

M. P. Paulus, J. Fedler, S. G. Leckband, and A. Quinlan, "Anger: Definition, Health Consequences, and Treatment Approaches" (Unpublished manuscript, 1–45. Retrieved from koso.ucsd.edu/~martin /AngerReview.pdf).

H. Kassinove and R. C. Tafrate, *Anger Management* (Atascadero, California: Impact, 2002).

3.   P. Ekman, "An Argument for Basic Emotions," *Cognition and Emotion* 6 (1992): 169–200.

4.   J. P. Tangney, P. Wagner, C. Fletcher, R. Gramzow, "Shame into Anger? The Relation of Shame and Guilt to Anger and Self-Reported Aggression," *Journal of Personality and Social Psychology* 62 (1992): 669–75.

J. P. Tangney, P. Wagner, D. Hill-Barlow, C. Fletcher, D. E. Marschall, R. Gramzow, "Relation of Shame and Guilt to Constructive versus Destructive Responses to Anger Across the Lifespan," *Journal of Personality and Social Psychology* 70 (1996): 797–809.

5. D. J. Siegel, *The Developing Mind* (New York: The Guilford Press, 1999).

6. P. Gilbert, *The Compassionate Mind* (London: Constable and Robinson, 2009).

7. For more information on Buddhist approaches to working with anger, I recommend reading Venerable Chodron's excellent book, *Working with Anger*, as well as His Holiness the 14th Dalai Lama's *Healing Anger*, based on teachings from Shantideva's *A Guide to the Bodhisattva's Way of Life*:

    T. Chodron, *Working with Anger* (New York: Snow Lion, 2001).

    Dalai Lama, *Healing Anger* (New York: Snow Lion, 1997).

8. E. Harmon-Jones, K. Vaughn-Scott, S. Mohr, J. Sigelman, and C. Harmon Jones, "The Effect of Manipulated Sympathy and Anger on Left and Right Frontal Cortical Activity," *Emotion* 4 (2004): 95–101.

9. The literature on how anger can impact our judgment and decision making is nicely summarized in the following chapter:

    P. M. Litvak, J. S. Lerner, L. Z. Tiedens, and K. Shonk, "Fuel in the Fire: How Anger Impacts Judgment and Decision Making," in *International Handbook of Anger*, eds. M. Potegal, G. Stemmler, and C. Spielberger (New York: Springer, 2010): 287–310.

10. L. Z. Tiedens and S. Linton, "Judgment under Emotional Certainty and Uncertainty: The Effects of Specific Emotions on Information Processing," *Journal of Personality and Social Psychology* 81 (2001): 973–88.

11. G. V. Bodenhausen, L. A. Sheppard, and G. P. Kramer, "Negative Affect and Social Judgment: The Differential Impact of Anger and Sadness," *European Journal of Social Psychology* 24 (1994): 45–62.

12. C. S. Carver and E. Harmon-Jones, "Anger Is an Approach-Related Affect: Evidence and Implications," *Psychological Bulletin* 2 (2009): 183–204.

CHAPTER 2: THE COMPASSIONATE-MIND APPROACH TO UNDERSTANDING ANGER

1. One of the most exciting developments in modern psychology is the discovery of the dramatic ways that our experiences impact our developing brains in ways that continue to reverberate throughout our lives. Dr. Dan Siegel is a pioneer in this area, and a good place to start is with his seminal text, *The Developing Mind*. I've listed a few other references below as well, which provide a few more texts to read through for those wishing to explore this exciting area of psychological science. Dr. Siegel's audio-CD set, *The Neurobiology of "We,"* provides a particularly accessible entry point into this area of study.

    L. Cozolino, *The Neuroscience of Human Relationships: Attachment and the Developing Social Brain* (New York: Norton, 2006).

    J. LeDoux, *The Emotional Brain* (London: Weidenfeld and Nicolson, 1998).

    A. Schore, *Affect Regulation and the Origin of the Self* (New York: Taylor and Francis, 1994).

    D. J. Siegel, *The Developing Mind* (New York: The Guilford Press, 2001).

    D. J. Siegel and M. Hartzell, *Parenting from the Inside Out* (New York: Tarcher/Penguin, 2003).

    D. J. Siegel, *The Neurobiology of "We": How Relationships, the Mind, and the Brain Interact to Shape Who We Are* (Boulder, Colorado: Sounds True, 2008).

2. P. Gilbert, *The Compassionate Mind* (London: Constable and Robinson, 2009).

3. This model is based on the work of neuroscientists such as Richard Depue, Jack Panksepp, and Joseph Ledoux.

    R. A. Depue and J. V. Morrone-Strupinsky, "A Neurobehavioral Model of Affiliative Bonding," *Behavioral and Brain Sciences* 28 (2005): 313–95.

    J. LeDoux, *The Emotional Brain* (London: Weidenfeld and Nicolson, 1998).

J. Panksepp, *Affective Neuroscience* (New York: Oxford University Press, 1998).

4. W. G. Moons, N. I. Eisenberger and S. E. Taylor, "Anger and Fear Responses to Stress Have Different Biological Profiles," *Brain, Behavior, and Immunity* 24 (2010): 215–19.

5. J. Gould, C. Trapasso, and R. Schapiro, "Worker Dies at Long Island Wal-Mart after Being Trampled in Black Friday Stampede," *New York Daily News*. Retrieved December 4, 2010, from http://www.nydailynews.com/ny_local/2008/11/28/2008-11-28_worker_dies_at_long_island_walmart_after.html.

6. K. Stansbury and M. R. Gunnar, "Adrenocortical Activity and Emotion Regulation," in *The Development of Emotion Regulation: Biological and Behavioral Considerations: Monographs of the Society for Research in Child Development,* 59 (2–3, Serial No. 240), (1994): 108–34, ed. N. A. Fox.

7. L. Cozzolino, *The Neuroscience of Human Relationships: Attachment and the Developing Social Brain* (New York: Norton, 2006).

8. P. Gilbert, *Compassion-Focused Therapy: Distinctive Features* (London: Routledge, 2010).

9. J. A. Coan, H. S. Schaefer, and R. J. Davidson, "Lending a Hand: Social Regulation of the Neural Response to Threat," *Psychological Science* 17 (2006): 1032–39.

10. C. S. Carter, "Neuroendocrine Perspectives on Social Attachment and Love," *Psychoneuroendocrinology* 23 (1998): 779–818.

11. L. J. Seltzer, T. E. Ziegler, and S. D. Pollak, "Social Vocalizations Can Release Oxytocin in Humans," *Proceedings of the Royal Society B: Biological Sciences* 277, no. 1694 (September, 2010): 2661–66.

12. D. J. Siegel, *The Developing Mind* (New York: The Guilford Press, 1999).

CHAPTER 3: WHEN THINGS BECOME UNBALANCED

1. J. M. Twenge, B. Gentile, N. C. DeWall, D. Ma, K. Lacefield, and D. R. Schurtz, "Birth Cohort Increases in Psychopathology among Young Americans, 1938–2007: A Cross-Temporal Meta-Analysis of the MMPI," *Clinical Psychology Review* 30 (2010): 145–54.

2. J. M. Twenge and W. K. Campbell, *The Narcissism Epidemic: Living in the Age of Entitlement* (New York: Free Press, 2009).

3. R. Eckersley, "Is Modern Western Culture a Health Hazard?," *International Journal of Epidemiology* 35 (2006): 252–58.

   R. Eckersley, "Cultural Fraud: The Role of Culture in Drug Abuse," *Drug and Alcohol Review* 24 (2005): 157–63.

4. P. Gilbert, *The Compassionate Mind* (London: Constable and Robinson, 2009).

5. S. D. Calkins, "Origins and Outcomes of Individual Differences in Emotion Regulation" in *The Development of Emotion Regulation: Biological and Behavioral Considerations: Monographs of the Society for Research in Child Development*, 59 (2–3, Serial No. 240), (1994): 53–72, ed. N. A. Fox.

6. There is a wealth of research in the area of attachment that explores the importance of these sorts of relationships for infants and across the life span. For an excellent review of this literature that will point you to many other valuable sources of information about attachment, please see:

   M. J. Dykas and J. Cassidy, "Attachment and the Processing of Social Information across the Life Span: Theory and Evidence," *Psychological Bulletin* 137 (2011): 19–46.

7. D. J. Siegel, *The Developing Mind* (New York: The Guilford Press, 1999).

8. A. Schore, *Affect Regulation and the Origin of the Self* (Hillsdale, NJ: Erlbaum, 1994).

9. S. Gerhardt, *Why Love Matters* (London: Routledge, 2004).

D. J. Siegel, *The Mindful Brain* (New York: Norton, 2007).

10. D. Siegel and M. Hartzell, *Parenting from the Inside Out* (New York: Tarcher/Penguin, 2003).

11. This was first described by the psychologist Dr. Albert Bandura:

A. Bandura, *Social Learning Theory* (Englewood Cliffs, New Jersey: Prentice Hall, 1976).

12. C. B. Ferster, "A Functional Analysis of Depression," *American Psychologist* 28 (1973): 857–70.

13. P. Gilbert, *The Compassionate Mind* (London: Constable and Robinson, 2009).

14. Although there are many sources that do an excellent job of describing implicit and explicit memory, for our purposes, I recommend the work of Dan Siegel, particularly for his description of the ways implicit memory can shape our experience of the present:

D. J. Siegel, *The Developing Mind* (New York: The Guilford Press, 1999).

————, *The Neurobiology of "We": How Relationships, the Mind, and the Brain Interact to Shape Who We Are* (Boulder, Colorado: Sounds True, 2008).

CHAPTER 4: THE CASE FOR COMPASSION

1. Dalai Lama, "Understanding our Fundamental Nature" in *Visions of Compassion: Western Scientists and Tibetan Buddhists Examine Human Nature*, eds. R. J. Davidson and A. Harrington (New York: Oxford University Press, 2002).

2. Compassion, in *Webster's New World Dictionary*, 3rd college edition, ed. V. Neufeldt (New York: Webster's New World, 1988).

3. C. Schwartz, J. B. Meisenhelder, Y. Ma, and G. Reed, "Altruistic Social Interest Behaviors Are Associated with Better Mental Health," *Psychosomatic Medicine* 65 (2003): 778–85.

4. P. Gilbert, *The Compassionate Mind* (London: Constable and Robinson, 2009).

5.   P. Gilbert, *Compassion-Focused Therapy: Distinctive Features* (London: Routledge, 2010).

6.   T. Brach, *Radical Acceptance: Embracing Your Life with the Heart of a Buddha* (New York: Bantam, 2004).

CHAPTER 5: FIRST STEPS

1.   P. Gilbert, *The Compassionate Mind* (London: Constable and Robinson, 2009).

2.   Therapies such as acceptance and commitment therapy (ACT) have highlighted the power of reconnecting with our core values as a powerful motivator for change.

S. C. Hayes, K. D. Strosahl, and K. G. Wilson, *Acceptance and Commitment Therapy: An Experiential Approach to Behavior Change* (New York: Guilford Press, 1999).

3.   Soothing-rhythm breathing and many of the other exercises in this book were developed by Professor Paul Gilbert in collaboration with the other members and affiliates of the Compassionate Mind Foundation. We've worked to continuously refine these techniques to make them as useful as possible, and I've attempted to adapt them where appropriate to apply specifically to working with anger. In addition to my website, a number of resources and audio exercises like soothing-rhythm breathing can be found on the website for the Compassionate Mind Foundation: compassionate mind.co.uk.

4.   D. R. Carney, A. J. C. Cuddy, and A. J. Yap, "Power Posing: Brief Nonverbal Displays Affect Neuroendocrine Levels and Risk Tolerance," *Psychological Science* (2010): 363–68.

5.   S. F. Davis, and J. J. Palladino, *Psychology*, 3rd ed. (Upper Saddle River, New Jersey: Prentice-Hall, 2000).

CHAPTER 6: THE CULTIVATION OF MINDFULNESS

1. S. G. Hofmann, A. T. Sawyer, A. A. Witt, and D. Oh, "The Effect of Mindfulness-Based Therapy on Anxiety and Depression: A Meta-Analytic Review," *Journal of Consulting and Clinical Psychology* 78 (2010): 169–83.

2. In his book *The Mindful Brain*, Dan Siegel describes mindfulness as having certain qualities, including curiosity, openness, and acceptance.

    D. J. Siegel, *The Mindful Brain* (New York: Norton, 2007).

3. J. Kabat-Zinn, *Wherever You go, There You Are: Mindfulness Meditation in Everyday Life* (New York: Hyperion, 1994).

4. Tara Brach provides an excellent and moving exploration of mindful acceptance in working with life difficulties.

    T. Brach, *Radical Acceptance: Embracing Your Life with the Heart of a Buddha* (New York: Bantam, 2004).

5. J. Kornfield, *The Wise Heart: A Guide to the Universal Teachings of Buddhist Psychology* (New York: Bantam, 2008).

6. B. K. Holzel, J. Carmody, M. Vangel, C. Congleton, S. M. Yerramsetti, T. Gard, and S. W. Lazar, "Mindfulness Practice Leads to Increases in Regional Brain Gray Matter Density," *Psychiatry Research: Neuroimaging* 191 (2011): 36–43.

7. The MBSR program is described in detail, along with the mindfulness practices it entails, in this book by Jon Kabat-Zinn.

    J. Kabat-Zinn, *Full Catastrophe Living* (New York: Delta Publishing, 2009).

8. Y. M. Rinpoche, *The Joy of Living: Unlocking the Secret and Science of Happiness* (New York: Harmony Books, 2008).

CHAPTER 7: COMPASSIONATE IMAGERY— DEVELOPING THE COMPASSIONATE SELF

1. The exercises included in this chapter are direct adaptations of those developed by Paul Gilbert and other members of the Compassionate Mind Foundation and CFT community.

    P. Gilbert, *Audio Exercises for Compassionate Mind Training: Instruction, Soothing-Rhythm Breathing, Compassionate Self, and Compassionate Image* www.compassionatemind.co.uk.

2. Kind thanks to Dr. Miriam Berkman for providing me with this excellent technique a number of years ago.

3. P. Gilbert, *The Compassionate Mind* (London: Constable and Robinson, 2009).

4. Of particular note are psychologists Kristen Neff, developer of the Self-Compassion Scale, and Christopher Germer, author of *The Mindful Path to Self-Compassion.*

    K. D. Neff, "The Development and Validation of a Scale to Measure Self-Compassion," *Self and Identity* 2 (2003): 223–50.

5. K. D. Neff, *Self Compassion: Stop Beating Yourself Up and Leave Insecurity Behind* (New York: William Morrow, 2011).

6. C. K. Germer, *The Mindful Path to Self-Compassion: Freeing Yourself from Destructive Thoughts and Emotions* (New York: The Guilford Press, 2009).

7. D. M. Wegner, D. J. Schneider, S. R. Carter, and T. L. White, "Paradoxical Effects of Thought Suppression," *Journal of Personality and Social Psychology* 53 (1987): 5–13.

8. Psychologist Deborah Lee initially developed this exercise to help trauma survivors who suffer from post-traumatic stress disorder (PTSD).

    D. A. Lee, "The Perfect Nurturer: A Model to Develop a Compassionate Mind within the Context of Cognitive Therapy," in *Compassion: Conceptualisations, Research, and Use in Psychotherapy*, ed. P. Gilbert (London: Routledge, 2005).

CHAPTER 8: WORKING COMPASSIONATELY WITH ANGER— VALIDATION, DISTRESS TOLERANCE, AND EXPLORING OUR EMOTIONAL SELVES

1. K. Goss, *The Compassionate Mind Approach to Beating Overeating using Compassion-Focused Therapy* (London: Constable and Robinson, 2011).

2. R. D. Ray, F. H. Wilhelm, and J. J. Gross, "All in the Mind's Eye? Anger Rumination and Reappraisal," *Journal of Personality and Social Psychology* 94 (2008): 133–45.

3. F. Perls, *The Gestalt Approach and Eye Witness to Therapy* (Ben Lomand, California: Science and Behavior Books, 1973).

CHAPTER 9: WORKING COMPASSIONATELY WITH ANGER— MENTALIZING, COMPASSIONATE THINKING, AND PROBLEM SOLVING

1. P. Fonagy and P. Luyten, "A Developmental, Mentalization-Based Approach to the Understanding and Treatment of Borderline Personality Disorder," *Development and Psychopathology* 21 (2009): 1355–81.

   P. Fonagy, G. Gergely, E. Jurist, and M. Target, *Affect Regulation, Mentalization, and the Development of the Self* (New York: Other Press, 2005).

2. P. H. Lysaker, A. Gumley, and G. Dimaggio, "Metacognitive Disturbances in Persons with Severe Mental Illness: Theory, Correlates with Psychopathology and Models of Psychotherapy," *Psychology and Psychotherapy: Theory, Research, and Practice* 84 (2011): 1–8.

3. G. Liotti, and P. Gilbert, "Mentalizing, Motivation, and Social Mentalities: Theoretical Considerations and Implications for Psychotherapy,"

Psychology and Psychotherapy: Theory, Research, and Practice 84 (2011): 9–25.

4. A. T. Beck, *Depression: Clinical, Experimental, and Theoretical Aspects* (New York: Harper and Row, 1967).

———, *Cognitive Therapy and the Emotional Disorders* (New York: International Universities Press, 1976).

5. S. C. Hayes, M. L. Villatte, and M. Hildebrandt, "Open, Aware, and Active: Contextual Approaches as an Emerging Trend in the Behavioral and Cognitive Therapies," *Annual Review of Clinical Psychology* 7 (2011): 141–68.

6. Z. V. Segal, J. M. G. Williams, and J. D. Teasdale, *Mindfulness-Based Cognitive Therapy for Depression: A New Approach to Preventing Relapse* (New York: The Guilford Press, 2002).

7. M. M. Linehan, *Cognitive-Behavioral Treatment of Borderline Personality Disorder* (New York: The Guilford Press, 1993).

8. S. C. Hayes, K. D. Strosahl, and K. G. Wilson, *Acceptance and Commitment Therapy: An Experiential Approach to Behavior Change* (New York: The Guilford Press, 1999).

9. As with many of the exercises covered in this book, the Compassionate-Thinking Flash Card was suggested by Paul Gilbert.

10. This method of considering objectives, relationship, and emotional expression priorities in deciding what action to take was presented to me by a teacher at some point very early in my educational career, and while I have drawn upon this wisdom in my own life and with clients for decades, I have been unable to track down its original source. My dear thanks to the teacher who shared it with me and to whoever originally articulated the idea. It has benefited me greatly, and if I were able to credit you here, I would.

CHAPTER 10: COMPASSIONATE BEHAVIOR—RELATING COMPASSIONATELY WITH OTHERS

1. W. A. Arrindell, R. Sanderman, H. van der Molen, J. van der Ende, and P. P. Mersch, "The Structure of Assertiveness: A Confirmatory Approach," *Behavior Research and Therapy* 26 (1999): 337–39.

2. P. Gilbert, *Overcoming Depression* (New York: Basic Books, 2009).

   Not surprisingly, in his professional progression that ultimately led to the development of compassion focused therapy, Professor Paul Gilbert spent much time considering (and writing about) shame. The volume below is an excellent collection, which Paul and his colleague Bernice Andrews organized and edited.

3 P. Gilbert, "What is Shame? Some Core Issues and Controversies," in *Shame: Interpersonal Behavior, Psychopathology and Culture*, eds. P. Gilbert and B. Andrews (Oxford: Oxford University Press, 1998).

4. Venerable Thubten Semkye, Personal communication (March 23, 2011).

   My thoughts on shame, guilt, and regret were helped greatly by a brief conversation I had with Ven. Thubten Semkye, a Tibetan Buddhist nun, during a retreat I attended in late March 2011 at Sravasti Abbey. I was expressing to her that I saw shame as being very problematic but guilt as being more helpful, as it involved feeling bad about what someone had done without the negative self-labeling. Ven. Semkye communicated that in her tradition, they used "regret" instead, as it tended to put the focus more on making things right than on locking us into focusing on the self (usually in a "feeling bad about me" sort of way). I completely agree.

5. Based on research conducted by the authors (both clinical psychologists), along with their adviser (the famed marriage researcher John Gottman), this book is an excellent resource for couples or for anyone who wants to have good relationships and the ability to negotiate conflict within them.

C. Notarius and H. Markman, *We Can Work It Out: How to Solve Conflicts, Save Your Marriage, and Strengthen Your Love for Each Other* (New York: Perigree, 1993).

CHAPTER 12: FULL CIRCLE—BRINGING COMPASSION AND KINDNESS TO YOURSELF

1. C. Notarius and H. Markman, *We Can Work It Out: How to Solve Conflicts, Save Your Marriage, and Strengthen Your Love for Each Other* (New York: Perigree, 1993).

2. In his book *59 Seconds*, British psychologist Richard Wiseman has culled the scientific literature for helpful advice and brief exercises for having a happy, healthy, and effective life. This book presents a wealth of such information, touching on healthy eating habits for weight management and many other life areas.

    R. Wiseman, *59 Seconds: Think a Little, Change a Lot* (London: MacMillan, 2009).

3. B. L. Frederickson, and C. Branigan, "Positive Emotions Broaden the Scope of Attention and Thought-Action Repertoires," *Cognition and Emotion* 19 (2005): 313–32.

4. B. L. Frederickson, "The Role of Positive Emotions in Positive Psychology: The Broaden-and-Build Theory of Positive Emotions," *American Psychologist* 56 (2001): 218–26.

5. E. L. Garland, B. Frederickson, A. M. Kring, D. P. Johnson, S. M. Piper, and D. L. Penn, "Upward Spirals of Positive Emotions Counter Downward Spirals of Negativity: Insights from the Broaden-and-Build Theory and Affective Neuroscience on the Treatment of Emotion Dysfunctions and Deficits in Psychopathology," *Clinical Psychology Review* 30 (2010): 849–64.

6. B. L. Frederickson and M. A. Cohn, "Open Hearts Build Lives: Positive Emotions, Induced through Loving-Kindness Meditation, Build

Consequential Personal Resources," *Journal of Personality and Social Psychology* 5 (2008): 1045–62.

7. Rick Hanson and J. Richard Mendius developed the "Focusing on the Good" exercise. Their book is a warmhearted, accessible reference for those who want to understand how working with our minds can help us to change our brains.

R. Hanson and R. Mendius, *Buddha's Brain: The Practical Neuroscience of Happiness, Love, and Wisdom* (Oakland, California: New Harbinger Publications, 2009).

8. P. C. Watkins, K. Woodward, T. Stone, and R. L. Kolts, "Gratitude and Happiness: Development of a Measure of Gratitude and Relationships with Subjective Well-Being," *Social Behavior and Personality* 31 (2003): 431–52.

9. P. C. Watkins, M. van Gelder, and A. Frias, "Furthering the Science of Gratitude" in *The Oxford Handbook of Positive Psychology*, 2nd edition, eds. C. R. Snyder and S. Lopez (New York: Oxford University Press, 2009).

10. The gratitude-journal instructions in the exercise are taken directly from "Counting Blessings versus Burdens."

R. A. Emmons and M. E. McCullough, "Counting Blessings versus Burdens: An Experimental Investigation of Gratitude and Subjective Well-Being in Daily Life," *Journal of Personality and Social Psychology* 84 (2003): 377–89.

11. If we truly want to cultivate compassion, there is perhaps no better place to start than with the writings and public addresses given by Tenzin Gyatso, the 14th Dalai Lama of Tibet. He combines a mastery of 2,500 years worth of mind-training techniques for generating compassion with an ability to speak directly to the hearts of modern listeners. He's written many books on the subject. Here are some of the ones I've found most helpful.

Dalai Lama, *Ethics for the New Millennium* (New York: Riverhead Trade/ Penguin, 2001).

———, *An Open Heart* (Boston: Little, Brown and Co, 2001).

Dalai Lama, *Transforming the Mind* (London: Thorsons/HarperCollins, 2000).

12. P. Gilbert, *The Compassionate Mind* (London: Constable and Robinson, 2009).

CHAPTER 13: MOVING FORWARD— APPROACHING ANGER AND LIFE WITH COMPASSION

1. R. Kolts, "Making Peace: A Compassion-Focused Therapy Approach for Working with Anger," unpublished treatment manual (2010).

Russell L. Kolts, PhD, is a clinical psychologist and professor at Eastern Washington University outside of Spokane, WA, and is founder of the Inland Northwest Compassionate Mind Center. He has many years' experience treating anger problems in his work with combat veterans, sexual assault survivors, and mood-disordered clients of all ages. Kolts has pioneered the application of compassion-focused therapy (CFT) to anger, which he currently applies in private practice and prison settings.

Foreword writer Paul Gilbert, PhD, is a professor at the University of Derby in the United Kingdom, director of the mental health research unit at Derbyshire Mental Health Trust, and author of *The Compassionate Mind*.

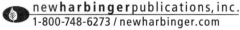